MICHIGAN AT ANTIETAM

The Wolverine State's Sacrifice on America's Bloodiest Day

JACK DEMPSEY & BRIAN JAMES EGEN
Foreword by Dave Finney

THE History PRESS

Published by The History Press
Charleston, SC 29403
www.historypress.net

Back bottom cover image of Dunker Church, taken two days after the battle. *Library of Congress.*

First published 2015

Manufactured in the United States

ISBN 978.1.62619.927.9

Library of Congress Control Number: 2015943860

Notice: The information in this book is true and complete to the best of our knowledge. It is offered without guarantee on the part of the authors or The History Press. The authors and The History Press disclaim all liability in connection with the use of this book.

To my wife, Jody, and daughter, Scarlett—
the two loves of my life.
–Brian

To those who sacrifice for love of our country.
–Jack

CONTENTS

Foreword

It is almost implausible to recognize that Michigan's role in the iconic September 1862 Antietam Campaign has never been chronicled in a book format. To fill this void, historians Jack Dempsey and Brian Egen have exhaustively researched the contributions of Michigan commanders and regiments that participated in the epic struggle in Maryland. Now, for the first time, their findings are brought together in this volume, which provides a valuable historical record of Michigan's significant participation in the Antietam Campaign. Dempsey and Egen's superior scholarship, research and analysis provide new insights and facts that will illuminate the record of Michigan Wolverines in this pivotal Civil War struggle.

Historians agree that in early September 1862, Confederate morale was at a peak, and a victory in Northern territory might well have guaranteed Southern independence. Since the spring of 1862, General Robert E. Lee's Army of Northern Virginia had achieved unprecedented success against Union forces. Lee was triumphant in the Seven Days Battles and at Cedar Mountain, Second Bull Run and Chantilly. Based on this string of stunning victories, Lee embarked on an invasion of Maryland that would culminate along the banks of Antietam Creek on September 17, 1862, in the bloodiest day in American history.

Lee's goals were to carry the war north of the Potomac River and encourage Maryland to join the Confederacy. Additionally, it was an opportunity to recruit Marylanders, replenish food supplies, obtain clothing for the army and destroy vital lines of communication by targeting railroads, canals and bridges.

It was also believed that a major victory north of the Potomac River would influence England and France to recognize the Confederacy.

Michigan regiments that participated in the Antietam Campaign included the 1st, 4th, 7th, 8th, 16th, 17th and Brady's company of sharpshooters, which was attached to the 16th Michigan infantry regiment. Captain Melvin Brewer's Company L, 1st Michigan Cavalry, served as escort for Generals Joseph Mansfield and Alpheus S. Williams during the campaign. Michiganders shed their blood in the fight at South Mountain, on the horrific blood-soaked fields of Sharpsburg and during the final action at Shepherdstown. The 17th Michigan attained fame for its bravery at South Mountain and was known as the "Stonewall" regiment for the duration of the war. The 7th Michigan suffered severely in the battle near the West Woods just north of the Dunker Church.

Following the Battle of Antietam, the character of the war changed. The battle may not have been a turning point militarily, but it certainly was politically, and it altered Lincoln's primary goal of saving the Union, modifying it to include the moral component of ending slavery. On September 22, 1862, President Lincoln issued the preliminary form of the Emancipation Proclamation.

No doubt exists regarding the fact that Michigan soldiers fought gallantly and shed their blood at South Mountain; the North, East and West Woods; in the Miller Cornfield; around the Dunker Church; in the Sunken Road; and at Burnside's Bridge. Yet no monument has been erected that reflects the sacred sacrifice of Michigan troops on the slopes of South Mountain, the undulating and rolling fields around Sharpsburg or along the banks of Antietam Creek. A monument recognizing all Michiganders who fought in this military campaign is long overdue but so appropriate regardless of timing. The authors are graciously and generously donating the royalties from this publication toward the creation of a Michigan monument at Antietam. Land adjacent to the old Hagerstown Turnpike has already been acquired and the necessary 501(c)(3) status obtained from the Internal Revenue Service. By purchasing this book, you are contributing to the creation of a Michigan monument at Antietam. I hope you agree that this is our time to honor and recognize those Michigan "boys in blue" who fought at Antietam to preserve the Union and end the institution of slavery.

DAVID D. FINNEY JR.
Teacher, Historian, Author
Historical Consultant on Antietam: A Documentary Film

Preface

Wednesday, September 17, 1862, was the single bloodiest day in our nation's history. From sunup to sundown, the Battle of Antietam cost approximately 23,110 lives either killed, wounded, missing or taken as prisoners of war—nearly 2 Americans every second during the course of the battle. The bloodletting came in only the second calendar year of the conflict, shocking all Americans and transforming their understanding of the war.

The Antietam battlefield was extensively photographed just days after the armies clashed. For the first time, the carnage of war was visually brought "to the doorsteps" of Americans through newspaper illustrations, reproduced images and gallery exhibitions. Mangled and bloated bodies, devastated farms, burned houses and ruined property brought home the incredible sacrifice and suffering of the combatants and civilian population of a rural section of Maryland. Among those graphic images was the hastily dug grave of a young lieutenant from Monroe, Michigan, where he fell on the field of battle.

According to one of the preeminent battle historians, "no battle of the Civil War—not Gettysburg, not Vicksburg, not Missionary Ridge—was in the end more meaningful than Antietam."[1]

The battle also yielded another outcome. Days after, Abraham Lincoln signed the preliminary Emancipation Proclamation. The War for the Union had also become a war for human freedom.

Because of its location in rural Maryland, the battlefield of Antietam remains intact, largely undisturbed by development. From the National

Park Service visitors' center one can survey much of the hallowed land, gaze out toward the high ground on South Mountain and conjure images of the fateful day when Americans viciously fought one another.

To aid remembrance, a number of states and others interested in patriotism have memorialized the sacrifices of the men who fought here. More than one hundred monuments are arrayed across the landscape. Signposts describe units and actions. Some landmarks of the terrible day, such as the Dunker Church, Burnside's Bridge and Bloody Lane—a dirt farm lane known to locals before the battle as the Sunken Road—have become iconic in Civil War literature and consciousness.

Despite the fact that Antietam was the single bloodiest day in American history, Michigan has no monument honoring its sacrifice. For reasons not readily apparent, no unit is commemorated by statue or stone. The sacrifice of one officer is commemorated by an inverted cannon, but his story is difficult to discover. The role that Michiganders played in this pivotal contest has, in the succeeding 150 years, receded into the fog of war. Whether because other battlefields such as Gettysburg and Chickamauga drew the attention and resources for monuments at Antietam or due to the veterans' feelings toward the carnage and savagery of this battle, we may never know the reasons.

Many survivors of the battle vowed never to return to a place where so much suffering and loss was sustained. One such veteran was Rufus Dawes of the 6th Wisconsin Infantry. The twenty-four-year-old major took command of the regiment when Lieutenant Colonel Edward Bragg was severely wounded. Leading the regiment across the David Miller farm and through the bloody Cornfield, Major Dawes witnessed the severe wrath of the fight: "Men, I can not say fell; they were knocked out of the ranks by dozens."[2]

With the acute intensity and inherent drama of mortal combat, especially in such a personal conflict of civil war, the details and particulars of what happened on the field, and the nuances of those monumental battles and the participants therein, have been the primary focus of authors and historians writing on the subject matter. The plethora of accounts and incredible acts of bravery, courage, tragedy, sacrifice and extraordinary acts under life-and-death situations are stories that are at the same time miserable and inspirational. For many, these stories have a gravitational pull of curiosity to understand our collective past and to comprehend, often viscerally, those key moments and events that have so indelibly left their marks on the ingredients of our country.

We must not forget that of the hundreds of thousands of soldiers lost on the field or in hospitals from disease, nearly all had families and friends back home—at minimum, each had a mother and father. The tidal wave of grief that reverberated across the land from the banks of Antietam Creek hit communities, both North and South, in an unimaginable shudder of emotional suffering and loss. The anxiety and anticipatory fears of those at home were a heavy and nearly unbearable burden. This work focuses on the action in the field during the Maryland Campaign of 1862 but firmly acknowledges the vast sea of resources and contributions, both physical and emotional, by those left home to shoulder all the responsibilities and circumstances that war fashions. Michiganders on the homefront rallied to the cause, providing tremendous resources and support to the embattled fighting for Union and freedom.

The stories of those who created a second battle front at home by working directly in the war effort or in support of the troops through various soldiers' aid societies, commissions and individualized actions have been overshadowed by the monumental battles that struck from living thousands in the space of days, if not moments. One such story, overlooked and literally relegated to the back pages of the newspapers, occurred on September 17, 1862—just about one hour after the major fighting at the Sunken Road subsided. At about 2:00 p.m., the main lab at the Allegheny Arsenal near Pittsburgh, Pennsylvania, blew up with two horrific explosions heard miles away. Overshadowed by the Battle of Antietam, most reporting of the accident can only be found, almost as an afterthought, buried in the countless other common stories of the day. The account of the accident in one such newspaper reads almost identically to those from the battlefield, yet these were civilians, mostly youth:

> *About one hundred and seventy-six boys and girls were employed in the building at the time of the disaster, of whom 75 or 80 were killed.... Those who could not escape in time were burned up. The scene was most appalling. Dead bodies lying in heaps as they had fallen; in some places where the heat was intense, whitened bones could be seen through the smoke and flames. In other places large masses of blackened flesh were visible.*[3]

The Battle of Antietam resulted in the cessation of General Robert E. Lee's invasion of the North and the immediate withdrawal of his Army of Northern Virginia back across the Potomac River into the Old Dominion state. Although not a decisive victory, it was the military success that President

Lincoln needed to issue a proclamation that he had been contemplating and drafting for some time. Confident that the precarious border states would stay exactly that and with Lee's invincible reputation dulled, Lincoln issued the preliminary Emancipation Proclamation on September 22, 1862, just five days after the battle. The document vowed that on January 1, 1863, he would emancipate all slaves held by states in rebellion against the Union. This single act not only put into motion a series of events that led to the freedom of all U.S. citizens today, but it also kept Europe from intervening on behalf of the Confederacy. The price tag for the Emancipation Proclamation was the Battle of Antietam.

Lincoln had many detractors who felt that he did not act swiftly enough on the slavery issue, as that was not of concern or an objective of his for the war. The powerful Republican editor of the *New York Tribune* wrote a direct and poignant editorial as if a cudgel to the president, stating that "every hour of deference to slavery is an hour of added and deepened peril to the Union."[4] Evidence of Lincoln's personal thoughts on slavery and how it should be embraced by the new Republican Party can be seen in a letter written to fellow party member Nathan Sargent on June 23, 1859.[5] The letter, housed in the Archive of American Innovation at The Henry Ford in Dearborn, Michigan, calls out Lincoln's evolving views of extending slavery to new states. Lincoln forecasted that if the party adopted a platform for the continuance of slavery to spread to new states, it would gravely affect the chances for victory in the 1860 presidential election.

Considering the turmoil, upheaval and sheer chaos when Lincoln took the oath of office on March 4, 1861, the speed in which he did officially address the slavery issue with the Emancipation Proclamation is impressive. Within sixteen months of his inauguration, in the midst of the Southern states seceding, establishing his administration, raising an army, sustaining several military defeats by the Union army and many more downturns, he was thinking and acting on the slavery issue. On July 13, 1862, Lincoln read a draft to two cabinet members; the month before, he had read it to Vice President Hannibal Hamlin. Given all that was at stake and a national crisis so severe, Lincoln accomplished the act very expeditiously—an endangered quality in today's national political leadership.

The Emancipation Proclamation did not free all the slaves and also required ultimate Union victory in the war to enforce, but it was the genesis of the movement that ultimately led to freedom for all. Testimony of the document's power, legacy and relevance for people today was fully revealed in an event that occurred 150 years after its issuance. On June 20, 2011, The

Henry Ford exhibited the original Emancipation Proclamation for thirty-six hours straight. Acknowledging that this was a rare, once-in-a-lifetime event through a special partnership with the National Archives, Henry Ford Museum waived admission, allowing as many people to see the document as possible. What happened over those next thirty-six hours was nothing short of an inspirational and transformative moment for all. More than twenty-one thousand guests, nearly as many as there were casualties at Antietam, stood in line for up to eight hours in order to spend a few moments seeing the original document in person.

As the Civil War sesquicentennial concludes, Michigan's contributions at Antietam will be forever memorialized. A monument will be erected to the brave men from the Great Lake State who served and fought and bled and died here. This book tells their story, and proceeds from its sales will enable the monument to rise at Antietam National Battlefield and enshrine their sacrifice. You, the reader, are helping to recover—to make—history.

As with any history, continued research and discovery of new data and information must be sustained in order to fully comprehend and come closer to the truth of our understanding of past events. The scale and scope of this book is merely an introduction and overview of Michigan's role and contribution to the Maryland Campaign of 1862. It is the intention of the authors that this work will inspire readers to delve deeper and explore the rich and deep history of this story, one that deserves our fullest and deepest admiration.

We encourage you to visit South Mountain, Antietam and Shepherdstown, the places where Michigan sacrificed so dearly.

Acknowledgements

Over the course of one's life and career, there are many individuals who influence, inspire and shape the person that one becomes. I am not an exception, for many people have provided me with those moments for which I am sincerely grateful. My co-author, Jack Dempsey, the tour-de-force of this work, had faith and trust in me to tackle this project together. A deep and abiding friendship has been forever forged. Our many e-mail correspondences during this project took on the distinct vernacular of the reports and orders found in the *Official Records of the Civil War*.

Given my family—from a grandmother in the Daughters of the American Revolution to another grandma's heritage tied directly to the earliest French settlers of Monroe, Michigan, to my Uncle Roy, aunts and uncles and cousins—I have been steeped in a family of deep appreciation and affinity for the past. Thanks to the adults of the family, who tolerated and supported my efforts in "producing" Civil War reenactments with cousins and neighborhood kids that started when I was twelve years old—even when I insisted my six-year-old cousin Seth eat stew and homemade hardtack instead of hamburgers and hotdogs. He has become a great friend and a fine Civil War living history person.

My parents, Barry and Betty Egen, made sure that summer vacations were always destinations of historical importance, with the driving routes plotted to maximize the cultural and heritage stops for my brother and I to experience—and they tolerated my attempts to convert my bedroom into a Civil War museum. For my eighth-grade graduation, they said they would treat me to a nice meal at any restaurant of my choice. They were dumfounded when I responded, "McDonald's." Puzzled, they reiterated that it could be a nice sit down–style restaurant. Without hesitation, I added, "the one in Gettysburg, Pennsylvania!" Making good on their offer, the family took a summer trip to the hallowed ground; after arriving, I realized that along with many modern structures on the battlefield, it needed to be torn down. With our William Frassanito books in hand, my brother, Bradley, and I became tick fodder as we ran from place to place on the battlefield seeking the photographic locations. My only brother, Bradley, and I have shared many awesome Civil War–related experiences, from the filming of *Gettysburg* to the many days at Antietam shooting the documentary film shown at the visitors' center.

Matt Switlik, antique ordnance authority, public historian and engineering genius, hired me in my first museum job and has been a mentor from an early age—thirty-one years later, I am still learning from him. David D. Finney, a superb educator of history and consummate professional historian, gave this once thirteen-year-old enthusiastic young boy his first Civil War bullets. He has been a supportive and guiding influence in my history career, and I am honored to have co-authored a book for which he has written the foreword. The late Dr. Richard Goff, an intense yet gentle intellectual powerhouse and energized inspirational historian from Eastern Michigan University, spent hours patiently shaping me in the academic world of history and assured me that it was perfectly okay that I preferred reading the endnotes of monographs more so than the prose. Regardless of my GPA, he encouraged me, saying that I had the raw and quintessential beginnings of a historian—a student I will always be! I regret that I will not have the opportunity of his profound yet nurturing critique.

A colleague and friend, Jim Johnson, who introduced and mentored me in the living history and public history field at The Henry Ford, continues to be a co-crusader in that arena. Almost as a return expression of appreciation, I introduced Jim to deeper Civil War history—he wrote a most excellent and comprehensive master's dissertation on the impact of the civilian population of Washington County during the Maryland Campaign.

I thank my many heroes of the Civil War public history field and authors from the National Park Service system. John Heiser and Scott Hartwig (retired) at Gettysburg and John Howard (superintendent, retired), historian Keith Snyder, superintendent Susan Trail and the staff at Antietam National Battlefield have been true inspirational figures. To a person, they are humble, gracious and always willing to share their knowledge and passion for the subject. John Hennessy, chief historian and chief of interpretation at

Fredericksburg and Spotsylvania National Military Park, has become a great friend and colleague—a historian I greatly admire and aspire to be like.

Brad Graham, director and producer of many Civil War documentary films, provided me the incredible opportunity to serve as a historical advisor and assistant director on *Antietam: A Documentary Film*. I count the experience and intimate moments with Antietam history during filming, often on the historic field itself, as some of my fondest and most cherished moments. Brad has recently become an author and shared his research and opinions freely.

Archivist Christine Kull at the Monroe County Historical Museum has always been an enthusiastic and positive proponent of local history. She has been an unsung hero in chronicling and sharing Monroe's history for more than thirty years. Chris assisted with locating and sharing a great deal of information for my portion of this work. Marty Bertera, author and historian of 4th Michigan Infantry history, shared research materials. Bill Ziemba provided information about the 17th Michigan Infantry. John Schildt, author and historian from Washington County, Maryland, provided insight and information. Dale R. Niesen of Michigan for his sharing of identified Michigan Civil War soldier images. Lifelong friend Kurt May has joined me on many historical adventures and research outings to local cemeteries.

Mrs. Lillian "Lil" Wilson and Roger Schlossberg deserve the deepest thanks for making the Michigan monument possible.

A most sincere and deepest thanks to my wife, Jody. As my "rock," she continues to love and support me despite my many shortcomings. She inspires me in her own career as an accomplished public historian and steward of cultural heritage. Her patience during this project, especially given our adventure as neophyte parents, has been remarkable. I look forward to a lifelong partnership and continued inspiration with the love of my life—she loves touring Civil War battlefields, too! Thank you, Jody (my "Kins").

My daughter, Scarlett, has been the truest and purest instrument of my transformation as human being. I never knew such love existed in the world until I met and held her for the very first time. She has not merely filled my heart with happiness; she has completely removed my old one and replaced it with one of pure and colossal love. It is my sincere hope and greatest wish that she can someday appreciate the magnitude of her impact in making this soul whole.

For these and the many more thanksgivings, I feel truly blessed.

BRIAN JAMES EGEN
Monroe, Michigan

Acknowledgements

My heartfelt gratitude goes to:

Tracy Evans, Monocacy National Battlefield Park, for assistance on the "Lost Order" story.

Rick Liblong, for service above and beyond in the cause of original research, especially at the Library of Congress.

Wayne Hammond, assistant librarian at the Chapin Library of Williams College, for cordial assistance on a key matter.

Ted Becker, for his article, for research and for colleagueship.

Keith Harrison, for research help.

Jessica Harden, Archives of Michigan, for images help.

The excellent folks at The History Press, without whom this book would not be in print.

Many libraries and archives across the State of Michigan; thanks be for the Michigan eLibrary, as well as particular contributors to research here such as the MSU Archives, Jackson District Library and Plymouth District Library.

Jason Masteller, for expert assistance with images and his unflagging encouragement.

Jackie Tinney, for devoting her most excellent skills and friendship on yet another writing project.

The family and friends who have stood with me during twenty-three thousand days and nights of highs and lows.

Most especially, my wife, Suzzanne, and daughter, Anna, as we continue on until that great day when we meet our dear beloved Michael again. JSMA forever.

Above all, him who, as surgeon Cyrus Bacon Jr. wrote some one hundred times in his journal, has been "nigh" the authors on this project. A lengthy chapter could be written of the research, sources and stories here that derived in ways for which neither of us can claim any credit, for to him it all belongs.

Jack Dempsey
Plymouth, Michigan

List of Maps

The maps found in this book provide a general overview of the key locations, landmarks and troop movements of the Maryland Campaign of 1862. Details of smaller unit actions, detached maneuvers, disparate commands, battle actions and events may be omitted for clarity to provide context of what is written. In several of the maps, Michigan units and soldiers are emphasized to provide time and place within the overall context of the action described.

The maps were created by Bruce Worden of Ann Arbor, Michigan.

For more information and detailed maps of troop movements during the Maryland Campaign of 1862, see Bradley M. Gottfried's *The Maps of Antietam* (El Dorado Hills, CA: Savas Beatie LLC, 2012).

Chapter 1

The Crisis

Invasion and National Peril

A candid photograph catches a military column temporarily halted along its march up East Patrick just west of Market Street in front of a dry goods store in Frederick, Maryland. It is September 10, 1862;[6] such action shots are rare in Civil War photography. Another curiosity: these are not Union soldiers—not boys from Maine, Massachusetts or Michigan. Their varied uniforms and equipage, as well as the lack of regulation headgear, are consistent with the descriptions of the Confederate soldier during the Maryland Campaign of 1862. Most of this Army of Northern Virginia had seen hard fighting since spring. Without reissued clothing and equipment, many took on a tattered appearance. Civilians commented on the sight and smell of these battle-hardened soldiers: "Many were barefooted and some had one shoe and one barefoot—they really looked 'ragged and tough.'…they have no uniforms, but are well armed and equipped."[7]

This is the victory-laden enemy, led by General Robert E. Lee, that soldiers of the Union Army of the Potomac—including Michigan men—will soon meet in battle. All are Americans, most not yet thirty years old. They have survived the first year of a bloody war.

The long gray line is in Frederick, taking the war to the North only forty-five miles from Washington, D.C. In 1861, the Maryland legislature met here to consider secession from the Union. The separation effort failed, but secessionists are back in town this late summer day. Armed defenders of the Union are nowhere in sight.

Army of Northern Virginia troops in downtown Frederick, September 1862, presumably on the march toward South Mountain before September 14. *Historical Society of Frederick County.*

The Army of the Potomac had an uninterrupted series of defeats in Virginia—during the lengthy Peninsula Campaign that began in May, at the Battle of Second Manassas in August and at Chantilly on September 1.[8] Now a cautious leader was back at its helm. Major General George B. McClellan's enormous task was to rapidly reorganize and reenergize the Federals and then turn back the Confederate invaders before they wreaked havoc in the North. The dolorous mood of the Union soldiers posed one of his most significant challenges.

McClellan had been general-in-chief of the Union army in the winter of 1861–62. After eight months of preparation, he finally launched a major campaign to end the war. With Richmond, Virginia, as target, his troops transshipped from the Washington environs down the Potomac River into Chesapeake Bay, landing on the James Peninsula just a day's ride from the Confederacy's capital. Between March 17 and May 31, McClellan carefully moved his forces toward its defenses. On the last of May, he repelled a Confederate assault and held the field, awaiting their next move. It came with a vengeance. Starting June 25, over the next seven days Lee attacked,

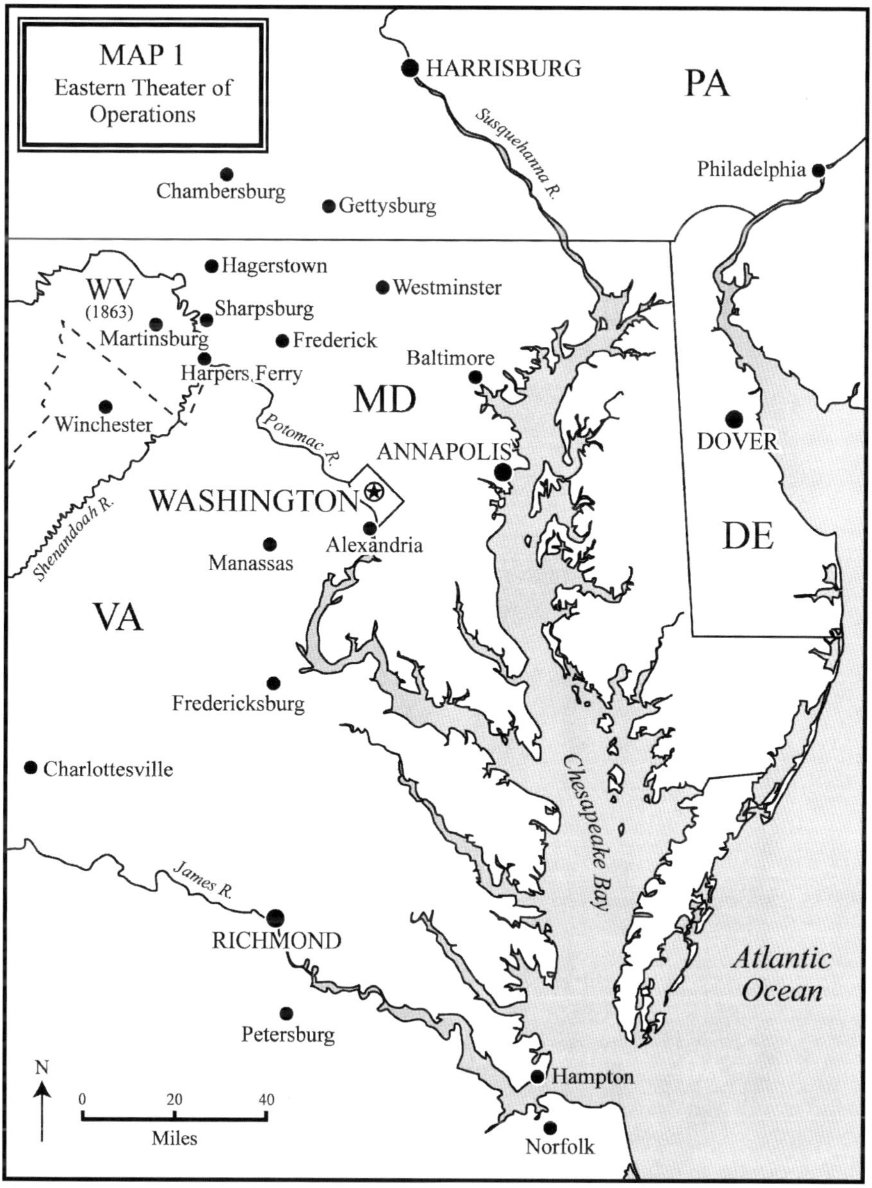

MAP 1. The stage for the Eastern Theater's primary campaigns by the Confederate Army of Northern Virginia and the Federal Army of the Potomac.

McClellan defended and the Union army retreated to the banks of the James River. The Peninsula Campaign to capture Richmond had failed. McClellan found himself out of a command.

By contrast, Lee had proven to be an audacious leader. Assuming command around Richmond on June 1, he immediately began to plan offensive operations to drive away and defeat McClellan's superior force. With the capable assistance of subordinate Generals James Longstreet, Thomas J. "Stonewall" Jackson, A.P. Hill and Jeb Stuart, Lee aggressively compelled the Army of the Potomac to retreat from Richmond. The Confederate army then turned north and marched toward Washington, precipitating the withdrawal of the Federal army to defend the national capital. A separate Union force, the Army of Virginia under General John Pope, became Lee's target before McClellan's troops arrived. In late August, the armies under Lee and Pope met near the 1861 battleground of Manassas. Lee divided his forces, lured the Union general into a trap and gained a smashing victory. The Yankees withdrew toward Washington in disarray; the further action at Chantilly left Lee in possession of that field as well. During the summer of 1862, the Confederate commander and his men had proved to be a formidable opponent. "Experience had shown" that Lee and his lieutenants "were enterprising, and that their army was extremely mobile."[9] Longstreet would recount, "When the Second Bull Run campaign closed we had the most brilliant prospects the Confederates ever had."[10] Lee's army "had acquired that magnificent morale which made them equal to twice their numbers."[11] They bore the swagger of successful combat veterans.[12]

The Confederates regarded their foes as "much weakened and demoralized."[13] The assessment had merit: reports reached President Abraham Lincoln that his main army in the Eastern Theater was poorly led[14] and the retreat from Second Bull Run plagued by disorganization:[15]

> *The capital and its environs were overrun with stragglers—officers without commands, commands without officers, bewildered individuals knocked loose from their units by the shock of battle and wandering around aimlessly in search of something to eat and somewhere to sleep. In addition, there were thousands of new recruits whose initiation into the mysteries of military life was taking place just when the army itself was in a state of high confusion.*[16]

Many Unionists were succumbing to "a sense of despair and of the inevitability of Southern independence."[17] Lee's army had developed a "habit of victory." Its opponent had a "habit of defeat" under McClellan, whose main trait seemed "want of initiative."[18] The capital city slumped—"gloom rested heavily upon the Union cause."[19]

The autumn harvest approached, and Lee held the military initiative.[20] On September 3, from headquarters on the Leesburg Pike west of the Washington defenses, he wrote to Confederate president Jefferson Davis on the many benefits of his next move. He would take the army out of the Confederacy for the first time and into Maryland. The invasion would relieve the effects of war in Lee's home state. It would secure supplies and new recruits. It would ally the people of Maryland to the Confederate cause: Lee's army would "give material aid to Maryland," afford an opportunity of liberating themselves,[21] of "throwing off the oppression" of the U.S. government. A successful campaign also might help secure foreign recognition for the Confederate States of America. Last, with only sixty days until the November Congressional elections in the North, another severe blow to flagging Union morale might foster political pressure on the Lincoln administration to negotiate with the South on independence. The "idea that decisive military triumphs could effect a revolution in Northern politics" underlay invasion, for "nothing seemed better calculated to undermine the Republican regime than Southern victories on Northern soil."[22]

Maryland held many Southern sympathizers (at war's end, Lee would be wearing a sword presented to him by a Marylander[23]). A number wore Confederate gray. Winning the state over to the Confederacy meant achieving an important Southern goal.[24] Envoys had been dispatched to invite Maryland to join its sister slave states.[25] The May 6, 1861 Confederate declaration of war applauded Maryland for refusing "to co-operate with the Government of the United States in…acts of hostilities and wanton aggression, which are plainly intended to overawe, oppress, and finally subjugate the people of the Confederate States."[26] In December, the Confederate Congress asserted that Marylanders had "suffered the same wrongs which impelled these Confederate States to withdraw from the United States"; they were "intimately associated" with their Southern brethren by geographical situation, mutual interests and similarity of institutions. Believing "that a large majority of the good people of Maryland earnestly desire to unite their State with the Confederate States," official government policy incorporated "the accession of Maryland" as "essential to the integrity and security of the Confederate Union."[27] In his February 1862 inaugural address, Davis proclaimed, "Our Confederacy has grown from six to thirteen States; and Maryland, already united to us by hallowed memories and material interests, will, I believe, when able to speak with unstifled voice, connect her destiny with the South."[28] In June,[29] Lee advocated that Stonewall Jackson's command in the Shenandoah Valley be directed to "cross Maryland into

Pennsylvania." Freeing the Old Line State would change the character of the war,[30] isolating Washington. President Lincoln worried about the loyalty of Maryland and the other border states.[31]

Lee's campaign into Maryland would be accompanied by the move north of seven other Confederate columns, including those in the Western Theater. These concurrent efforts sought "to expel the invaders from [the Confederacy's] borders."[32] Incompetent Union generalship could lead to more defeats and perhaps even threaten the national capital. Lee's main objective, though, was "the destruction of the enemy army."[33] His success could produce checkmate, win the war and secure Southern nationhood.

Upon dispatch of Lee's letter to Davis, the Confederate army began to move north.[34] On September 4, Lee sent his president another communiqué being "more fully persuaded of the benefit that will result from an expedition into Maryland" and beyond: "should the results of the expedition justify it, I propose to enter Pennsylvania."[35] Only if Davis vetoed the plan would Lee desist, and the president did not disapprove. The Confederate army crossed the Potomac River during the next few days, singing "Maryland My Maryland" as it went.[36] On Saturday, September 6, at about 9:00 a.m., two Confederate cavalrymen galloped into Frederick, to the intersection of Patrick and Market Streets, shouting praise "for Jeff Davis." Soon another one hundred soldiers appeared, announcing that "the time for your deliverance has come."[37] Lee soon issued a circular to his troops trumpeting Confederate military success in Kentucky, another slave state, pledging that "our brethren of our sister states will soon be released from tyranny, and our independence established upon a sure and abiding basis."[38]

On September 8, while headquartered near Frederick, Lee issued a circular "To the People of Maryland." It was an open call for rebellion against the U.S. government. Contending that Marylanders were "allied to the States of the South by the strongest social, political and commercial ties," the proclamation indicted the Lincoln administration for having perpetrated "wrongs and outrages" on Maryland, reducing it "to the condition of a conquered Province." The Army of Northern Virginia had arrived "to aid you in throwing off this foreign yoke, to enable you to again enjoy the inalienable rights of free men, and restore independence and sovereignty to your State." Lee's force would "assist you with the power of its arms,"[39] and that power had proved mighty. It had saved Richmond from McClellan's massively well-equipped army and defeated another Federal army in the Second Manassas Campaign. Surely Maryland was yearning for and would eagerly accept rescue.

Davis's reply to Lee approved of the invasion of Maryland and confirmed that Pennsylvania should also be an objective. Without knowing Lee had already done so, Davis directed issuance of a proclamation as an "invading army" to detail the causes for its movement. "We are," he wanted to explain, "driven to protect our own country by transferring the seat of war to that of an enemy who pursues us with a relentless and apparently aimless hostility." Confederate troops had come "to occupy the territory of their enemies and to make it a theater of hostilities." Marylanders could "put an end to this invasion" by demanding their state government secure "a separate treaty of peace which this Government will ever be ready to conclude on the most just and liberal basis."[40] Confederate soldiers felt that Maryland was being held hostage and thus spoke "very freely of their intention to treat PA very differently from MD."[41]

Other Confederate officers issued proclamations. Frederick native Bradley T. Johnson[42] addressed his fellow "people of Maryland," trumpeting that after sixteen months of oppression "the victorious Army of the South brings freedom to your doors," to those "crushed under the heel of this terrible despotism." His new nation had pledged "never to cease this war until Maryland has the opportunity to decide for herself her own fate, untrammeled by Federal bayonets." Johnson was authorized to enlist patriots in the army of the Confederacy to "strike for Liberty and right."[43] Another call to arms issued by Captain Elijah V. White, a native of nearby Poolesville, encouraged fellow Marylanders to "come at once, or make up your minds to be slaves to the Northern despotism forever."[44]

Lee was confident of success: "[T]he present position of affairs, in my opinion, places it in the power of the Government of the Confederate States to propose with propriety to that of the United States the recognition of our independence." Such an achievement was within grasp, "being made when it is in our power to inflict injury upon our adversary" in Maryland and Pennsylvania. This "proposal of peace"—or, if rejected, Confederate military success—could help very soon to elect sympathetic candidates in Northern elections to bring the war to a termination.[45]

The faith of Lee and the Confederate government in Maryland's desire to flock to the Southern cause seemed well grounded. A Michigan general feared "there is not much real loyalty in this part."[46] Both notions would prove erroneous. Like most of the Southern states, Marylanders cast their lot for Democrat John C. Breckenridge in the 1860 presidential election. The census that year listed nearly fourteen thousand slave owners and more than eighty-seven thousand enslaved people. With a Southern rights/Democrat–

controlled legislature and a proslavery but anti-secessionist governor, Maryland hung in the balance.[47] On April 19, 1861, as Federal troops from Massachusetts passed through Baltimore on their way to Washington, antiwar Democrats and pro-Southern sympathizers assaulted the Union soldiers, resulting in sixteen deaths and more than forty wounded. Frederick and Washington Counties—through which Lee's army would traverse—were home to nearly five thousand slaves. Auctions were held in the Hagerstown public square, and in the town of Sharpsburg, a slave auction block marked the corner of Main and Church Streets. Slave quarters stood outside the village on a number of farms.

Unlike other border states, Maryland was the center of dynamic and polarizing tensions between the two warring factions—oftentimes it could literally be neighbor against neighbor. The Michigan men in the coming Maryland Campaign were thrown in the thick of this fulcrum where Union and the liberty of all men rested. Not entirely sure if they were defending their own country or fighting on "foreign soil," they must have carried this uncertainty with them. For some, such as Allen Howard Zacharias of the 7th Michigan Infantry, it was even more personal: Washington and Frederick Counties were his boyhood home.

But Western Maryland was no haven for slavery or secession. The area enjoyed a significant population of free blacks, fewer slaveholders than other parts of the State, fewer slaves per capita and thus fewer in total. The region's agriculture was primarily grain growing, not tobacco or cotton. In Hagerstown, the weekly *Herald of Freedom and Torch Light* supported the Union cause. Its September 10 edition would not be published; editors had fled to Pennsylvania, fearing destruction of their antislavery presses by the invaders.[48] Pro-Southern and pro-Northern sentiment competed, with each viewpoint rising to public expression depending on which army was nearest.

Farther west arose another impediment to Confederate ambitions. Union troops at Harpers Ferry,[49] where the Shenandoah River joined the Potomac, had not evacuated after Lee crossed into Maryland. Leaving this twelve-thousand-man garrison in his army's rear caused Lee concern. His supply and communications lines running through the Shenandoah Valley would not be secure unless he controlled this town. Harpers Ferry was protected by the same mountain chain that the Confederates would cross as they moved west from Frederick. That march began on September 10. Confederate troops were halted on Patrick Street—known as the National Road outside Frederick—long enough for a photograph to be taken.

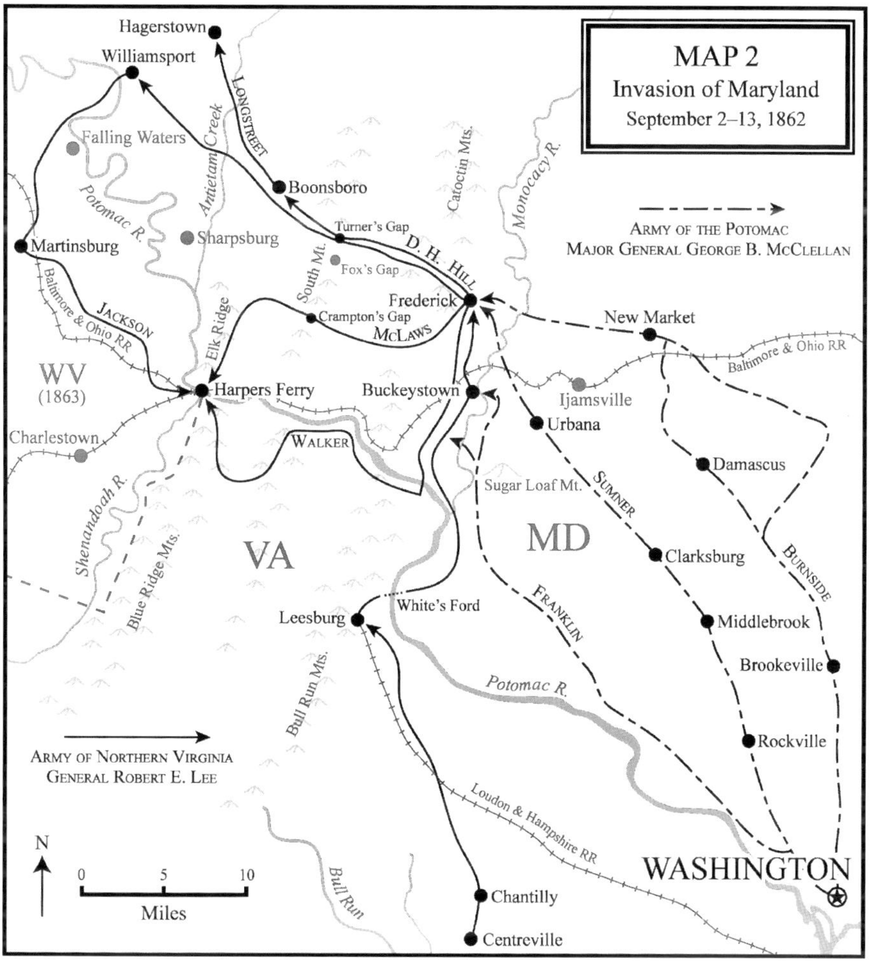

MAP 2. Invasion of Maryland, showing overall movements of the Confederate army and Union pursuit. Smaller components of each, including cavalry excursions, are not indicated.

Confidence on the Union side was also elevated. McClellan was back in command of the combined forces that had been defeated at Second Bull Run under Pope, as well as his Army of the Potomac.[50] When word spread that "Little Mac" was again in charge, the demoralizing summer setbacks were erased, and a new enthusiasm pervaded the ranks.[51] McClellan had restored *esprit* after the disaster at Bull Run in July 1861; his resumption of command did so again.

Lacking firm information but reflecting on Lee's absence from the Washington vicinity, McClellan believed that his adversary "intended to cross the Upper Potomac into Maryland."[52] Seeking confirmation, he ordered Union cavalry to Poolesville to gather intelligence. U.S. Signal Corps personnel also sought to locate the Confederates. To their small number had been detached William B. Roe of Plymouth, first lieutenant in the 16th Michigan Infantry. He had charge of the signal station on the summit of Sugar Loaf Mountain ten miles south of Frederick. From the peak, the range of vision was "unequaled." It encompassed "several prominent fords of the Potomac, the approaches to them in Virginia, and much of the country into which an army passing those fords would move."[53] McClellan "particularly desired" that this post, "which kept under observation the country upon his left, and from which the presence of the enemy could be rapidly reported, should be occupied by careful and skilled officers."[54] Information from the post proved profitable to McClellan at hazard to those who manned it; Roe narrowly escaped capture when Confederate cavalry temporarily held the station until their army left Frederick.[55]

Between September 5 and 7, the Union infantry began to move out from the Washington defenses northwest toward where the Confederate army might be. On the fifth, the II and XII Corps reached Rockville, and the I and IX Corps were near Silver Spring. The II Corps included the division of the highest-ranking officer from Michigan, Major General Israel Bush Richardson of Pontiac. Brigadier General Alpheus Starkey Williams of Detroit temporarily commanded the XII Corps. The IX Corps included the division of Brigadier General Orlando Bolivar Willcox of Detroit. On the seventh, the VII Corps arrived at Rockville, where McClellan made his headquarters.[56] Only thirty miles now separated the opposing commanders, although neither knew it. Just the day before, McClellan's cavalry had confirmed that Lee's entire army had crossed the Potomac.[57] They were not sure of the Confederate objective, though, reporting first that the aim was Washington and next that it was Baltimore.[58]

Union forces advanced carefully. On September 9, Lee learned that they were slowly moving west from Washington.[59] He remained unconcerned, writing to Davis, "I shall move in the direction I originally intended, toward Hagerstown and Chambersburg."[60] Lee planned to use the valley between the Blue Ridge Mountains (specifically South Mountain) and the Appalachian Plateau as a "highway" to penetrate into Pennsylvania. The South Mountain range now to his east, running nearly parallel to his line of march north, would provide the perfect cover for his army. Should the Northern troops leave their positions protecting Washington, Baltimore and northern Virginia in pursuit, Lee could easily defend the narrow passageways and gaps between the two ranges, allowing him the advantage of defensive fighting with an offensive campaign.

Unaware of the Confederate army's true destination and trying to balance protection of Washington and Baltimore with defending Pennsylvania,[61] McClellan was reluctant to overcommit. His goal was to turn them back to Virginia.[62] On the ninth, I and IX Corps moved just ten miles, to Brookeville, II and XII Corps the same interval northwest to Middlebrook and VI Corps to Darnestown, a short distance from the Potomac.[63] Each could then support any unit that contacted the enemy. On the tenth, the II and XII Corps marched a few miles to Damascus, while VI Corps moved to Barnesville. McClellan's headquarters remained at Rockville.[64] Reports of Confederate infantry to the west increased. The next day brought IX Corps to New Market and Richardson and the II Corps to Clarksburg; Willcox and the IX Corps reached Frederick on the twelfth. I Corps trailed by a few miles. Williams reached Ijamsville, a village on the Baltimore and Ohio Railroad, while II Corps made Urbana and VI Corps was in Licksville. On the thirteenth, I, II and XII Corps crossed the Monocacy River and were all in the Frederick vicinity. IX Corps moved out on the National Road toward Middletown that same day.[65]

Cavalry covered the Union advance but could not breach the screen by Confederate cavalry.[66] Others tried to help. McClellan received a telegram from the president on September 12: Pennsylvania governor Andrew Curtin advised that Stonewall Jackson was crossing back over the Potomac at Williamsport, suggesting that Lee intended to draw the Federals into Virginia.[67] The pursuit must kept flexible, depending on where Lee was really headed. Perhaps he did have designs on Washington. Perhaps the move at Williamsport was a feint while the rest of the army invaded Pennsylvania. Accordingly, Lincoln accepted the state's militia into Federal service for its defense.[68] Confederates were bragging to Maryland civilians that "Lee would dictate terms of peace in Independence Square, Philadelphia."[69] Perhaps McClellan should divide his army to cover all eventualities, although doing so could enable Lee to maneuver and defeat each part.

Jackson had crossed the river, as Curtin reported. Two other commands, separately, were approaching Harpers Ferry from other points of the compass to join Jackson and encircle it. Twelve thousand Federals would be trapped, the Confederate supply line opened and yet another victory achieved. Once again, Lee had boldly divided his army. It was a chancy move, but taking such risks had paid off before. The rewards this time could be immense.[70]

Chapter 2

THE LOST ORDER

Michiganders Hold the Key

To deal with the Harpers Ferry garrison, Lee issued "Special Orders No. 191" on September 9 from his Frederick headquarters. Two-thirds of the Army of Northern Virginia under command of Stonewall Jackson would divide into three columns, each taking a different route to invest the heights surrounding Harpers Ferry and its twelve-thousand-man Union force. The remainder would march northwestward to Hagerstown and wait for the separated components to return from the expedition. After securing the army's supply line, Lee could march his reunited army into Pennsylvania. He feared little from the Union forces. The Harpers Ferry contingent was too small to hold out long. The Army of the Potomac, or whatever force might be sent from Washington, must still be reeling from the latest defeats on the Peninsula and in Northern Virginia. It would require time to reinvigorate. Whether John Pope or George McClellan or any other general—either full of brash bravado or ponderously timid—the Southern forces in Virginia had bested them all.

Special Orders 191 described in detail a plan for the Harpers Ferry operation. It specified which units were to follow what routes, and it included a directive (after his mission proved successful) that Jackson "will join the main body of the army at Boonsborough or Hagerstown." The rest of the Confederate army would "resume its march tomorrow, taking the Hagerstown road." One unfamiliar with the command structure would not comprehend the troop strength involved in these orders, but some aspects were clear: a single division under General D.H. Hill formed the main rear guard on the road from Frederick to Hagerstown, preceded by the reserve artillery, ordnance and supply trains. Longstreet's men would move ahead to Hagerstown. The document was written and signed in a single hand, "By command of General R.E. Lee/R.H. Chilton, Assistant Adjutant General."[71]

On September 12, McClellan's headquarters were near Urbana, some five miles southeast of Frederick. Late that evening, he still could not ascertain his opponent's dispositions. There were indications that Jackson was advancing on Harpers Ferry.[72] McClellan ordered his cavalry to probe at daylight of the thirteenth along the roads north from Frederick. He wanted to rule out that Lee had "moved in that direction with a view of getting in our rear."[73] McClellan and his staff rode through adoring crowds in Frederick that Saturday morning and established headquarters in a farm field immediately west of town.[74] The rest of the army also moved. The XII Corps arose before dawn, crossed the Monocacy River at Crum's Ford, stacked arms and went into camp a mile from Frederick.[75]

Around 9:00 a.m. that morning, several soldiers of an Indiana regiment in the 1st (Alpheus Williams's) Division of XII Corps sat down to rest south of Frederick's city limits. The location was a wheat field by the C.E. Best farm, close by the Georgetown/Urbana Pike. It was not far from where the Confederate army had camped.[76] One soldier noticed a peculiar object on the ground under a locust tree nearby.[77] It proved to be an envelope; inside were several cigars, wrapped in a handwritten note. A quick read revealed that the paper had much greater value than the smokes. It appeared to be a Confederate army document bearing the heading "(Confidential) Hd Qrs Army of Northern Va" and designation as "Special Orders No. 191."

The sergeant on the scene carried the package to his company commander and then to the regimental commander, Colonel Silas Colgrove.[78] Seeing its strategic potential, the colonel personally conveyed the document to corps headquarters.[79]

Brigadier General Alpheus S. Williams, officially the 1st Division's commander, had been serving as temporary commander of XII Corps since the Battle of Cedar Mountain on August 9.[80] Williams held the position because of his leadership qualities; he was not a professional soldier. A Yale graduate and lawyer by training, he came to Detroit at twenty-six years of age and prospered as attorney, bank president and newspaper editor. His public roles included postmaster, probate judge and school board member. Civic-mindedness led him to join a militia company, the Brady Guards, and the men elected him first lieutenant and then captain. He was commissioned

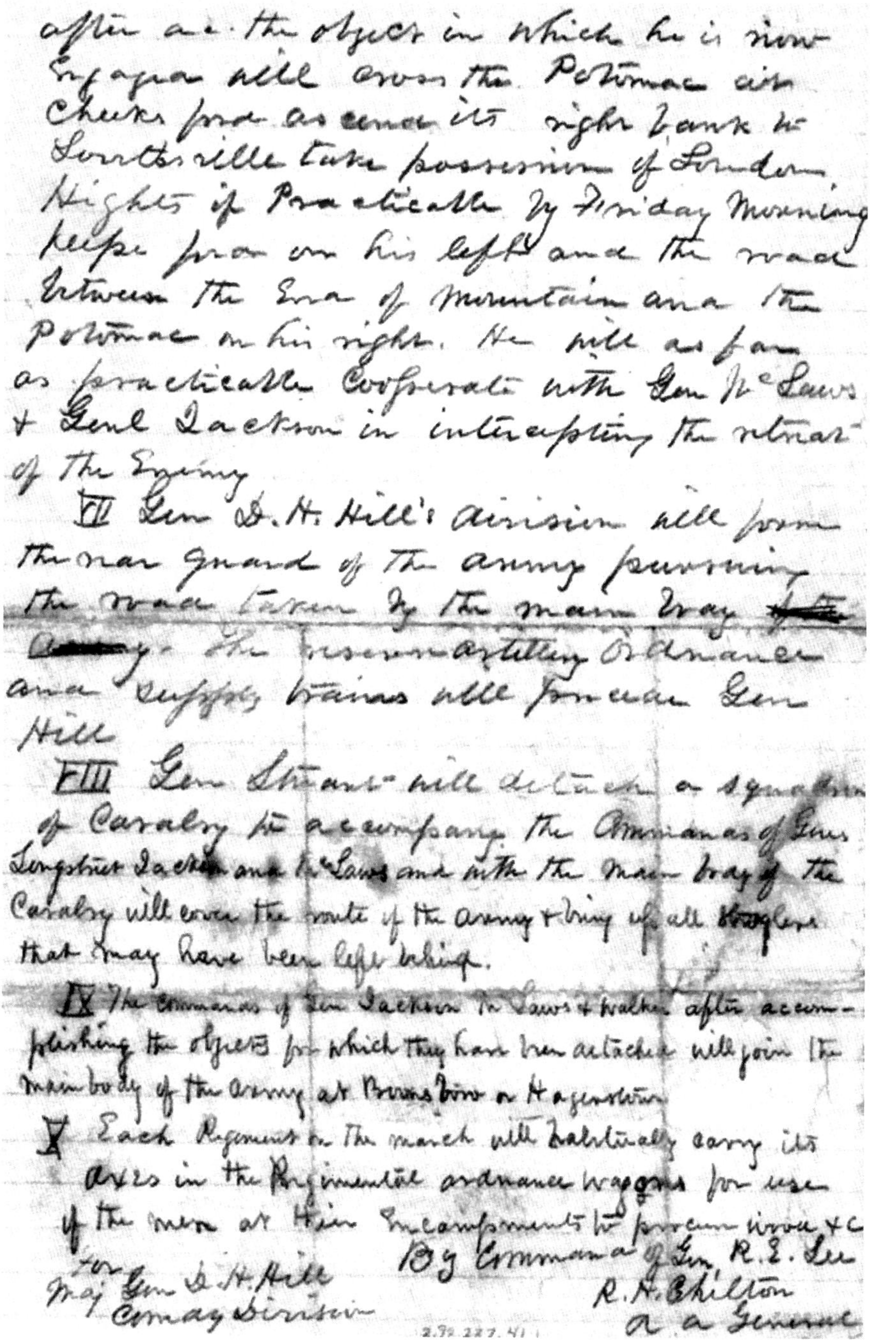

after ac the object in which he is now
engaged will cross the Potomac at
Cheeks ford ascend its right bank to
Lovettsville take possession of Loudoun
Heights if Practicable by Friday morning
Keeps ford on his left and the road
between the end of mountain and the
Potomac on his right. He will as far
as practicable cooperate with Gen McLaws
& Genl Jackson in intercepting the retreat
of the Enemy
VII Gen D. H. Hill's division will form
the rear guard of the army pursuing
the road taken by the main body
The reserve artillery ordnance
and supply trains will precede Gen
Hill
VIII Gen Stuart will detach a squadron
of Cavalry to accompany the commands of Gens
Longstreet Jackson and McLaws and with the main body of the
Cavalry will cover the route of the army & bring up all stragglers
that may have been left behind.
IX The commands of Gen Jackson McLaws & Walker after accom-
plishing the objects for which they have been detached will join the
main body of the army at Boonsboro or Hagerstown
X Each Regiment on the march will habitually carry its
axes in the Regimental ordnance wagons for use
of the men at their encampments to procure wood &c
By Command of Gen R. E. Lee
R. H. Chilton
A a General
For
Maj Gen D. H. Hill
Comdg Division

Signature page of Robert E. Lee's Special Orders 191, the famous "Lost Order." *Library of Congress.*

lieutenant colonel of Michigan's sole regiment in the Mexican-American War, which performed garrison and outpost roles. In November 1855, he became commander of the Detroit Light Guard militia unit.[81] In 1859, Governor Moses Wisner appointed him major general of the Michigan Militia. He also served on the State Military Board, where the members elected him president.[82] The first-ever state militia encampment met in August 1860 in Jackson under his direction. Williams had become "Michigan's premier citizen-soldier."[83]

After the surrender of Fort Sumter in April 1861, Williams stood among the first to volunteer to lead Michigan troops against the rebellion. His qualifications included "extensive experience in important local militia companies," wide military history reading[84] and lengthy study of "the science of war."[85] Building on this experience in setting up camps of instruction around the state, he helped train the first eight regiments from Michigan to be mustered in at Fort Wayne in Detroit.[86] He did so without remuneration.[87] Despite his Democratic Party affiliation, zeal for the Union won him appointment from Republican governor Austin Blair as "Brigadier General, Commanding the First Brigade, Michigan Infantry."[88] President Lincoln appointed Williams a brigadier general of volunteers in the U.S. Army on August 7, 1861, with rank dating from May 17.[89] He was Michigan's first Civil War general,[90] and time would prove that "in the field and in battle, few Union generals exceeded the scope of his service."[91]

Williams was "a man of medium height; stalwart build; dark, curly hair; a short, graying beard; and unmatchable mustachios." He wore gold-rimmed glasses, betraying his age; "at fifty-one he was much older than most Civil War generals,"[92] though four years younger than Robert E. Lee. Regardless, he would take only one wartime leave and none for illness.[93] Through these initial sixteen months of the war, he "displayed great skill and courage." Earlier in 1862, he held off Stonewall Jackson "in a series of brilliant engagements" and handled his division "admirably."[94] The general was idolized by his staff and the troops under his command[95] and gained the nickname "Old Pap."[96] Williams was "a keen observer"[97] and excellent judge of circumstances. His spirits waned during August: "Instead of hopeful and confident feelings we are all depressed with losses and disasters."[98] His sagacity would prove handy this fall day.

Arriving at the corps command post near the Georgetown Pike north of the Monocacy,[99] Colgrove delivered the document to Williams's adjutant general. Thirty-one-year-old Lieutenant Samuel Emlen Pittman, born in Tecumseh, Michigan, and a resident of Detroit since age seventeen, had

Brigadier General Alpheus Starkey Williams, of Detroit, acting commander of the XII Corps at Antietam. *Library of Congress.*

entered service as first lieutenant, Company B, 1st Michigan Infantry, on September 24, 1861.[100] He reported to Williams the next day for duty as aide-de-camp and had served ever since in that role. On September 13, he was also serving as acting adjutant general for XII Corps.[101] Circumstance now placed him in a position critical to the nation.

The document identified its author as "R.H. Chilton." Robert Hall Chilton was Lee's chief of staff and principal assistant adjutant general. Beginning in June, he "drafted most of Lee's general and special orders."[102] Chilton's handwriting and signature were "at once recognized by Colonel [*sic*] Pittman."[103] "I did at once pronounce the signature genuine," Pittman recounted. On what basis could he vouch for the handwriting of an enemy officer?

> *Chilton, a few years before the war, was on duty at Detroit as a Paymaster of the U.S. Army, at which time he kept his Bank account with the Michigan State Bank, and at the time I was teller of that Bank, thus paying thousands (probably) of his checks over the Bank counter that my teller's experience qualified me somewhat to judge of signatures, and that the signature on Order No. 191 was surely Chilton's.*[104]

In the face of doubts from others present, Pittman "was able to confidently assert that I was thoroughly familiar with Col. Chilton's signature and that this was genuine." After all, "a bank teller becomes more or less an expert as to signatures,"[105] especially in this era heavily dependent on such means of identification.

Of the seventy-five thousand men in blue that day, the one soldier who could personally and immediately verify the authenticity of the Confederate document had done so. One of the most important judgment calls of the Civil War rested on the experience of a Michigan soldier who felt "best qualified to confidently avouch" that the document was genuine.[106]

Taking Colgrove along, Pittman "immediately reported" to his superior, General Williams.[107] At this juncture, the general's judgment also proved critical. He had known Sam, as friends called him, since before the war[108] and in militia activities at Fort Wayne.[109] He knew his aide to be reliable and "a very faithful and useful man."[110] Williams directed his adjutant "to lose no time in placing it in Gen. McClellan's possession."[111] Pittman obeyed, sending the document off to McClellan "by a trusty courier on duty at our headquarters" and telling the orderly "to ride fast."[112] Only a moment elapsed to pen a brief note under Williams's signature:

> *General*
> *I enclose a ~~General~~ Special Order of Genl*
> *Lee Commanding Rebel forces which was found*
> *on the field where my Corps is Encamped.*
> *It is a document of interest & is no*
> *doubt genuine.*[113]

Williams's note, based on Pittman's verification, proved central to acceptance of the lost document as genuine. The matter was far from trivial—as one of Lee's most able lieutenants would comment, "ordinarily, upon getting possession of such an order, the adversary would take it as a *ruse de guerre*."[114] Two officers with Pittman when the document was presented had urged that very conclusion.[115] Four days had passed since the date of the document, and somehow it had lain fallow ever since being lost. For a cautious soldier like McClellan, the natural conclusion could have been that the Confederates were laying a trap. After leaving the security of the Washington defenses, the men of the Army of the Potomac had been "wondering all the way what the enemy meant."[116] The Michiganders gave their commander the assurance he needed—the paper was "no doubt genuine"—to spring into action.

Just over a dozen hours after believing the enemy might be in his rear, McClellan now sent a quite different order to his cavalry commander. Brigadier General Alfred Pleasonton was to verify that the "Lost Order" still governed, though four days had elapsed: "The following order of march of the enemy is dated September 9. General McClellan desires you to ascertain whether this order of march has thus far been followed by the enemy."[117] Awaiting confirmation, McClellan moved his army closer to the mountains west of Frederick. The 1st Division of IX Corps under Orlando Willcox marched from the Monocacy River to Middletown.[118]

Battlefield artist Alfred Waud's sketch of Federal troops moving through Middleton, Maryland, east of South Mountain. *Library of Congress.*

Thirty-nine-year-old Willcox had rejoined his division just five days earlier.[119] Wounded and taken prisoner at First Bull Run, he had spent six weeks in hospital and thirteen months in Southern prisons before release on August 16, 1862.[120] Arriving in Washington, he dined with President Lincoln and received a general's commission.[121] Willcox lost no more time in starting for home. He received a hero's welcome from "the good people of Detroit and some other parts of Michigan"[122] and spent precious moments reunited with his family. Mindful of the crisis facing the nation, however, he quickly returned to the army and assumed division command.[123]

Orlando Willcox rivaled Alpheus Williams for preeminence in the Michigan officer corps. He had been born in Detroit when it was a frontier town and worked as page for the territorial legislature. A graduate of the West Point class of 1847,[124] Willcox was a Mexican-American and Seminole War campaign veteran. He was a handsome soldier and sat "ramrod straight" in the saddle. His "active, intelligent mind" led him into possession "of marked literary tastes." Returning to civilian life in Detroit in 1857, he took up the practice of law. A "stirring orator," he could motivate men to service.[125] Three weeks after the fall of Fort Sumter, Willcox was commissioned colonel of the 1st Michigan Volunteers ninety-day regiment. His unit was first to arrive in Washington, D.C., from the west, first across the Potomac in the foray to Alexandria in which Colonel Elmer Ellsworth was shot down and deepest in terms of penetration of the Confederate line south of Henry Hill at First Bull Run. His men found him "the embodiment of an accomplished gentleman."[126] He had been a guest of the Confederacy at various sites of incarceration, including Libby Prison in Richmond.[127] Now he was itching to get back into action.

Action was what possession of the Lost Order justified. Would McClellan take advantage of the great opportunity that "Alpheus Williams presented him"?[128] Receiving Pleasonton's confirmation that Confederate dispositions corresponded to the document,[129] the Union general made his plans. He sent an order at 6:20 p.m. (around sunset) to the VI Corps commander, directing Major General William B. Franklin to move at daybreak to cut off or destroy the Confederate command between his position and Harpers Ferry.[130] Major General Ambrose E. Burnside's IX Corps would advance this evening and early the next morning, "followed by the corps of Sumner and Banks and Sykes division, upon Boonsborough, to carry that position." Thus, while Franklin went after the Confederates separated from their main body on the same side of the Potomac, the bulk of the Union army would pursue Lee's remnant. McClellan's plan relied on the Lost Order: "I have now full information as to movements and intentions of the enemy."[131] He sent a similar order at 8:45 p.m. to II Corps commander Major General Edwin V. Sumner, directing him to "move punctually at 7 o'clock to-morrow morning."[132]

Brigadier General Orlando Bolivar Willcox of Detroit, 1st Division commander in the IX Corps. *Monroe County Historical Museum.*

McClellan had been galvanized. He had resumed command with belief in the extreme difficulty of his mission: the troops were fatigued, his army required resupplying, many regiments were green or had little combat experience, the enemy possessed superior numbers and his counterpart, Lee, was intimidating: "I had the highest respect for his ability as a commander, and knew that he was a general not to be trifled with or carelessly afforded an opportunity of striking a fatal blow."[133] Now, just such an opportunity was McClellan's.

Later that evening, the Union commander reveled in his good fortune. To Brigadier General John Gibbon he brandished the document and exclaimed, "Here is a paper with which if I cannot whip Bobby Lee, I will be willing to go home. I will not show you the document now, but here is the signature, and it gives the movement of every division of Lee's army. Tomorrow we will pitch into his center."[134] He telegraphed General-in-Chief Henry W. Halleck at 11:00 p.m. that "an order from General R.E. Lee, addressed to General D.H. Hill, which has accidentally come into my hands this evening—the authenticity of which is unquestionable—discloses some of the plans of the enemy, and shows most conclusively that the main rebel army is now before us.... This army marches forward early tomorrow morning, and will make forced marches."[135] After a respectful interval, McClellan wrapped up the day by telegraphing the president at midnight:

> *I have the whole rebel force in front of me, but am confident, and no time shall be lost. I have a difficult task to perform, but with God's blessing will accomplish it. I think Lee has made a gross mistake, and that he will be severely punished for it. The army is in motion as rapidly as possible. I hope for a great success if the plans of the rebels remain unchanged.... I have all the plans of the rebels, and will catch them in their own trap if my men are equal to the emergency. I now feel that I can count on them as of old.... Will send you trophies. All well, and with God's blessing will accomplish it.*[136]

Although Lee did not know it, the situation had changed dramatically against him. The four-day-old Lost Order—authenticated, thanks to a Michigan man—would prove all important for Union arms during the next four days.

Chapter 3

Rookie Heroism

The Stonewall Regiment

As of September 13, Lee did not expect his enemy to march quickly. When the Confederates departed Frederick, the Union forces were moving "so slow."[137] Lee's headquarters were in Hagerstown, and he awaited news of the expedition to Harpers Ferry, now in its fourth day.[138] Once that effort succeeded, his far-flung army would reunite and march into Pennsylvania. Supplies and support had not proved abundant in Maryland, and the fertile farms of the Keystone State beckoned. Lee believed the Union army to be near Frederick, and his cavalry was posted in the valley between the Catoctin and South Mountain ranges to sound the warning should the Federal army approach. Experience had shown Lee that "McClellan never attacked, and always let him choose his own time and place for fighting."[139]

Longstreet's corps was at Hagerstown, with the division commanded by D.H. Hill near Boonsboro at the juncture of the road to the village of Sharpsburg. The rest of the army enveloped Harpers Ferry. Lee cautioned the wing nearest Frederick to be watchful lest the Union army, only twenty miles away, take that direction.[140] The distance from Harpers Ferry to Hagerstown was twenty-eight miles and between Boonsboro and Sharpsburg only six or seven miles. Lee's army was within easy reach of its components, with its adversary off a safe distance. Or so he thought.

Cavalry commander Jeb Stuart sent Lee a report late this Saturday, as did Hill. Their news was startling: the main Union force was advancing and rapidly so.[141] At 10:00 p.m., Lee directed the expediting of the Harpers Ferry operation since McClellan appeared to be on the move to save the garrison.[142] Reducing Harpers Ferry had to be achieved for the invasion to continue. Not anticipating McClellan's swiftness, Lee was caught off-guard. Unexpectedly, he needed to create delay by defending the passes over South Mountain with only part of his army.

To block the Federals, Lee directed Longstreet to move to Boonsboro within supporting range of Hill and Stuart as they took up posts at the South Mountain gaps.[143] A division commander in the Union IX Corps described two of the passes as the Army of the Potomac marched toward Boonsboro from Frederick:

> *The National road, as it goes north-westward, crosses South Mountain at a depression called Turner's Gap. The old Sharpsburg road leaves the turnpike a little west of Middletown, turns to the left, and crosses the mountain at Fox's Gap, about a mile from Turner's. The mountain crests are about 1300 feet above the Catoctin valley, and the "gaps" are from 200 to 300 feet lower than the summits near them. These summits are like scattered and somewhat irregular hills upon the high rounded surface of the mountain-top. They are wooded, but along the south-easterly slopes, quite near the top of the mountain, are small farms with meadows and cultivated fields.*[144]

Many stone fences marked Fox's Gap, affording protection to troops defending the position.[145]

The suddenly accelerated movement of the Army of the Potomac inspired its soldiers, including fighting generals like Williams. He anticipated "there will be a great battle or a great skedaddle on the part of the Rebels. I have great confidence that we shall smash them terribly if they stand, more confidence than I have ever had in any moment of the war….when we do strike I think it will be a heavy blow."[146]

September 14 was a partly sunny day with little wind and the temperature in the low seventies.[147] As the men marched toward the Confederate positions in the mountain passes this Sunday morning, "the bells of the churches in Frederick reminded them of home and loved ones."[148] Federal infantry neared the passes around noon. At Fox's Gap, the lead elements were two divisions of IX Corps, with Willcox's division next in line.[149] A plan unfolded to take this passage and use it to flank the Confederates out of Turner's Gap to the north, opening up that main route toward Hagerstown. The IX Corps infantry left the National Road and moved up the Old Sharpsburg Road. The lead division went into action, initially capturing the area on the south of the pass and then fighting to maintain control when counterattacked.[150]

Willcox and his division had an early breakfast, broke camp just beyond Middletown and were marching west on the National Road by 8:00 a.m.[151] At first, his orders were to move against the Confederate left near Turner's Gap.[152] He was then directed to cross over to the Old Sharpsburg Road and proceed toward Fox's Gap.[153] "It was two o'clock when Willcox came up." He found the Union forces on the left of the road near the summit skirmishing with the Confederates.[154] Deploying two of his regiments, he placed the 8th Michigan Infantry on the left.[155]

This veteran regiment had been recruited primarily from the central part of the state. Its ten companies were from Alma, Flint, Grand Rapids, Greenville, Hastings, Jackson, Lansing, Owosso and St. Johns. The units initially rendezvoused at Grand Rapids, arrived at Fort Wayne in Detroit on September 16, 1861, and mustered in on the twenty-third. The regiment left Detroit four days later for Washington.[156] It initially served in an expedition to the Carolinas until ordered back to Virginia in July 1862. It fought sturdily at Second Manassas and Chantilly.[157]

The 8th was commanded by Lieutenant Colonel Frank Graves of Niles. Born in 1836, Graves had been admitted to West Point in 1853.[158] He had enlisted on August 19, 1861.[159] The son of one-time Democratic secretary of state William Graves, his sister, Belle, was married to Henry A. Morrow, colonel of the 24th Michigan Infantry.[160] Graves was "a very fine, cultured, military gentleman, social to a degree, but a thorough disciplinarian."[161] Second in command was Captain Ralph Ely of Alma.

To protect the Union line near the summit, Willcox positioned a battery near the turn in the Old Sharpsburg Road so it could provide counter-fire to Confederate guns that had range from Turner's Gap. The move prompted a nearer Confederate battery to respond, and its canister and shell drove the Union cannoneers back down the road. Willcox feared that the enemy would seek to capture the pieces, and he ordered two regiments from his left across to the right of the Union line beyond the road.[162] One of the units was the 17th Michigan Infantry, through which the gunners had stampeded "wildly to the rear."[163]

Unlike their fellow Michiganders on South Mountain this day, the 17th had no combat experience. More than that, it had practically no military experience. Drawn "from all over Michigan,"[164] the officers came from Adrian, Coldwater, Colon, Detroit, Jackson, Kalamazoo, Manchester, Monroe and Muskegon. The regiment was mustered at the Detroit Barracks[165] in August

Officers and staff of the 17th Michigan Infantry. *Archives of Michigan.*

1862, with its initial training under the supervision of Inspector General James E. Pittman, older brother of Samuel.[166] One company was composed almost entirely of students from the Normal School in Ypsilanti (now Eastern Michigan University), with some from the University of Michigan. Ninety-three-man Company G listed sixty-five farmers on its rolls.[167] The regiment left for Washington on August 27, 1862, and after cursory training was dispatched to the Army of the Potomac in pursuit of the Confederate army under Lee.[168]

The boys from Michigan faced "men passionately in earnest, men who had developed a natural aptitude for fighting by fourteen months of sharp and usually successful campaigning. They had shown that they could fight hard and march hard—that their audacity and tenacity were alike remarkable—that they were far more likely to carry difficult positions than to be driven from them."[169] Battle-hardened veterans from Georgia and South Carolina were crouched behind the "stone fences" at Fox's Gap waiting for the Michiganders.

On their march toward South Mountain, the anticipation of the rookie soldiers grew. The day before, watching as Union cavalry probed, one had written, "We can hear the guns & see the smoke. It is on the side of the mountain some miles west of us. We may get into it yet but I am afraid not."[170] The situation transformed overnight. "We had an inkling" mysteriously obtained, one private would say, "that a mass meeting was to be held on that eminence to discuss the pros and cons of secession, and that we, the Seventeenth, had received a pressing invitation to be present." They marched "briskly, with long, swinging strides that carried them rapidly" toward battle. Their uniforms were impeccable, "dress coats buttoned to the chin," the regulation Hardee Hat with feather on their heads.[171] They heard a new sound: "the deep-toned thunder" of artillery fire "mingled with the crash of fierce and incessant musketry" as it "raged and roared and rolled along the mountain slopes."[172]

Commanding the regiment was Colonel William Herbert Withington of Jackson. In May 1861, Withington had joined the 1st Michigan Infantry as captain of Company B. In the First Battle of Bull Run on July 21, 1861, he was taken prisoner when he remained on the field with Willcox, his wounded commanding officer. Withington was exchanged on January 30, 1862. Returning to Michigan, he was commissioned colonel of the newly formed 17th Infantry on August 11, 1862, in time for the regiment to serve as honor guard during Willcox's return home.[173]

Like the rest of Willcox's division, Withington and his regiment were on the road after daybreak, passing through Middletown up the National Road until ordered toward Fox's Gap.[174] Little more than two weeks after departing Michigan, the seven hundred soldiers[175] found themselves under artillery fire, the slope of a mountain in their front and veteran infantry of the 50th and 51st Georgia shooting at them from behind stone walls at the summit. A road

Colonel William Herbert Withington, commander of the 17th Michigan Infantry, from Jackson. *Archives of Michigan.*

ran northward from the gap; on the east side was "a stone fence three feet high overlooking cleared fields on the east." Directly north of the Daniel Wise house, "across the Old Sharpsburg Road, was a partially cleared spot of about an acre."[176] This clearing could prove destructive to Union infantry who tried to cross it.

The fire from the Confederate battery came from only two hundred yards away.[177] Willcox knew that the 17th lacked experience, but he had an urgent question for Withington, his "old friend and fellow prisoner of war":

> *"Glad to see you, Colonel. But what can you do?"*
> *"We can march by a flank and load and fire, General."*
> *"All right, sir. You see that battery up in the gap? Now if you can steal up through the woods and pick off some of the cannoneers, that will help a great deal."*[178]

The regiment would do that and more.

The Confederate artillery unit was "near the Wise house in a small field partially surrounded by woods."[179] The 17th "promptly changed front under a heavy fire of shot and shell and moved out." It "lay in line of battle until nearly 4 o'clock P.M. exposed to a severe fire from Drayton's brigade of South Carolina infantry."[180] The enemy "were so close that we expected a charge." Despite their inexperience, the regiment's "coolness and firmness

Wise Farm at Fox's Gap, South Mountain, where the 17th Michigan earned its nickname the "Stonewall Regiment." *Mollus Mass Civil War Collection, United States Army Heritage and Education Center, Carlisle, Pennsylvania.*

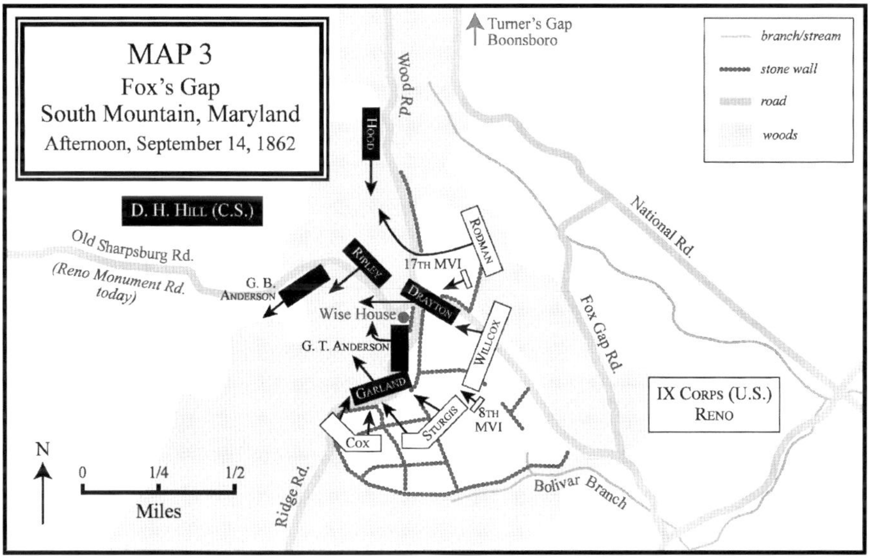

MAP 3. Fox's Gap, Willcox's Division, showing positions of the 8th and 17th Michigan. The newly recruited and raw 17th faced fire for the first time.

in changing front" under hostile fire evoked Willcox's admiration.[181] For an hour, the 17th had to remain prone while artillery "raked our position with grape and shell," inflicting many casualties.[182] The "enemy's guns continued to play on us.... We lay silent and kept concealed. Our picket officers reported the enemy in heavy force of regiments in rear of their skirmishers."[183]

New orders arrived: silence the Confederate battery at all hazards. As Willcox made his arrangements, the Confederate infantry charged out of the woods directly in his front "in a long, heavy line." Willcox gave the order: "Forward!" Withington "roared out, 'over the wall and at 'em.'" The order to charge "was received with enthusiastic cheers." The seven hundred rose up: "We rushed into them, and all the time every man shouting as loud as he could."[184] The Confederates fell back.

The far right of Willcox's command "moved rapidly forward through an open field upon the enemy's position under a storm of lead from the stone fences in front and from the batteries on the right." The Michiganders held off until within easy musket range and then, employing their Austrian rifles,[185] "opened a murderous fire upon the enemy." The left of the regiment swung around and enfiladed the Confederates behind the stone walls. The Confederates "broke in dismay," according to Captain Frederick W. Swift,[186] as the left of the 17th charged "with shouts of triumph over the walls" and pursued the remnants of Drayton's brigade over the crest and down the slope of the mountain.[187] The diminishing sunlight, now that it was past 6:00 p.m., necessitated a halt.[188]

The "boys" from Michigan had responded "in gallant style."[189] Despite their short service, the regiment's actions that afternoon resembled those of a veteran unit:

> *The Seventeenth Michigan rushed down into the hollow, faced to the left, leaped over a stone fence, and took them in flank.... after a severe contest of some minutes the enemy was repulsed, followed by our troops to the opposite slope and woods, forming their own position. Their battery in front of us was withdrawn....night came on. A large number of prisoners and the wounded were collected.*[190]

The situation had been daunting, but once the order to attack came, the Michiganders "moved steadily forward until they arrived within good range, and then opened a fire on the enemy with terrible effect." They "completely" routed the enemy, "driving him in the utmost confusion across the field into the woods, and capturing a number of prisoners."[191]

The experience of twenty-four-year-old Captain Gabriel Campbell of Ypsilanti, commanding the student-heavy Company E, exemplified the regiment's baptism of fire. At 11:30 a.m., he had checked his watch to pinpoint "his supposed time of death."[192] At the pass, the Confederate artillery shelling was fearful: "I could see the cannon balls coming bounding down" the Old Sharpsburg Road; "one came within arms length." Although "green as grass," when Willcox came "flying up on his horse, saying to me, 'Is this my Michigan? Form into line,'" Campbell obeyed. In the charge, the sound of bullets reminded him of "a hailstorm on the roof."[193]

An officer in the 8th Infantry drew notice this day. First Lieutenant Horatio Belcher of Flint, age forty-five, was helping lead Company G. The regiment "having suffered severely on the right, and being partly in confusion, he rallied about 100 men and led them up to the front." Somehow in the confusion these soldiers had become separated from their brigade. Belcher reported to a nearby division commander, requesting "a position where he might be of use until his proper place could be ascertained. He was assigned a post on the left, and...both he and his men performed their duty admirably."[194] The lieutenant had performed well before; on June 16, 1862, he was wounded in action at James Island, South Carolina, and at Chantilly had been tasked with an errand "vital to the Union cause."[195] Captain Ely of the 8th was also active, his "side so lame that I had to leave my horse, being in command all day—got very tired."[196]

The two Michigan units and their comrades held Wise's field. The day was not over, although it was now darkening. Confederate artillery continued to fire from the National Pike in order to aid infantry comrades retreating toward Sharpsburg. Two more exchanges between infantry occurred before the Confederates withdrew completely from South Mountain near midnight.[197]

To the north, where the National Road crossed the heights at Turner's Gap, Major General Joseph Hooker's I Corps had the task of dislodging the enemy. Stiff resistance by Longstreet's infantry held off attacks by two divisions. As darkness fell, Hooker prepared an all-out assault for the next morning at first light. His troops "were directed to remain in position, and Hartsuff's brigade was brought up and formed a line across the valley." The men "were directed to sleep on their arms."[198]

Brigadier General George Lucas Hartsuff, appointed to West Point from Michigan, commanded the 3rd Brigade of the I Corps' 2nd Division. *National Archives.*

Brigadier General George Lucas Hartsuff commanded the 3rd Brigade of the 2nd Division of I Corps. The thirty-two-year-old from Port Huron and Livingston County[199] was not well. Despite suffering from a stomach ailment, he had refused leave and had to be ordered to relinquish command after the Battle of Cedar Mountain on August 31.[200] He had missed the Second Manassas Campaign but returned to duty on September 7. He also bore a wound from the Seminole War in Florida, with the bullet unable to be extracted.[201] Hartsuff was an 1852 graduate of West Point, nineteenth in a class of forty-three.[202] After Florida, he served at West Point and on frontier duty at Fort Mackinac during 1859–60.[203] At the war's commencement, he participated in the U.S. Army defense of Fort Pickens at Pensacola. Hartsuff received his general's commission on April 15, 1862, based on commendations for his leadership.[204]

At dawn, as ordered, Hartsuff sent his skirmishers forward followed by the entire brigade. Only a mounted picket of the enemy remained, and it retreated as Hartsuff's Brigade advanced. Around midnight, the Confederate infantry had withdrawn, enabling Hooker's Corps to take possession of Turner's Gap on the fifteenth.[205]

Sometime that day, Willcox telegraphed his wife, Marie, "We have had a glorious victory." The 17th Michigan had "covered themselves with glory & wreaths of victory."[206] His after-action report paid the regiment high praise, first emphasizing that it "had not been organized a single month, and was composed of raw levies." The regiment "performed a feat that may vie with any recorded in the annals of war, and set an example to the oldest troops."[207] Its brigade commander echoed the praise:

> *Under any circumstances the conduct of both officers and men of this regiment was worthy of the highest commendation, but especially so when taking into consideration that they were mustered into service as late as the 21st of August, 1862, and that this was their first engagement.*[208]

The *New York Times* lauded the unit for "great bravery."[209] Several officers received commendations, besides Withington. Irish-born First Lieutenant William Vigors Richards of Ann Arbor, serving as the regiment's adjutant, received a brevet "for gallant and meritorious service."[210] John Tyler of Detroit, in Swift's Company F, would receive a brevet promotion to captain in the Regular Army.[211] Both were twenty-one years old. Soldiers in the regiment would receive eight Medals of Honor for their heroism in the war, more than any other Michigan unit.[212]

A Jackson newspaper reported a vivid account of the battle from Richards. He commended "the gallantry of Col. Withington" and the "maraculous [*sic*] coolness" of the men in the ranks.[213] Charles Salter of the 1st Michigan, recuperating in a Washington hospital since September 12, wrote home on September 20 of reading in the newspapers "that the 17th Mich regt almost annihilated" the South Carolina brigade.[214] For the actions in taking the Confederate position, the unit would be known as the "Stonewall Regiment."

The victory had its price. The Confederates incurred nearly 3,000 casualties defending South Mountain.[215] Michigan's losses were significant. In the 17th,

Lieutenant William Victor Richards of Ann Arbor, adjutant of the 17th Michigan Infantry. *Archives of Michigan.*

a total of 26 men were killed and 114 wounded.[216] Second Lieutenant George R. Galligan of Company I died of his wounds on September 24 at Middletown. From Kalamazoo, he was just twenty-five. Commissioned on June 17, his military service lasted less than three months.[217] Besides Richards, officer casualties included Captain John Goldsmith originally of Plymouth (wounded in the shoulder; enlisted at age twenty-three) and First Lieutenant Rowen Summers (in the side;[218] he was thirty-eight when commissioned), both of Company G and from Jackson. Others were Second Lieutenant George S. Newman of Detroit and Captain William W. Thayer of Company K, a Battle Creek resident who had joined at age twenty-five.[219] Lieutenant Thomas Mathews of Company E received "a severe flesh wound in the shoulder" that incapacitated him.[220] The 8th Infantry had not been part of the charge, so its participation in taking and holding the gap[221] yielded a loss of 8 wounded.[222]

Lee confronted an unexpected reality caused by McClellan's advance. The Confederate invasion was in disarray. There would be no incursion into Pennsylvania; the Union victory on South Mountain had thwarted that dream: "All the high hopes of manoeuvre [*sic*] had to be abandoned. All the air castles that had been built around Harrisburg and the Susquehanna bridge had to be vacated."[223] Lee was forced to withdraw Longstreet, Hill and

Stuart and concentrate near Sharpsburg[224] to unite with Jackson. Summing up a new plan of operations, he dictated an order at 8:00 p.m.:

> *The day has gone against us and this army will go by Sharpsburg and cross the river....Send forward officers to explore the way, ascertain the best crossing of the Potomac, and if you can find any between you and Shepherdstown leave Shepherdstown Ford for this command. Send an officer to report to me on the Sharpsburg road, where you are and what crossing you will take.*[225]

Lee's army would retreat to Northern Virginia via the Shepherdstown Road. Thanks to the Lost Order and the affair at South Mountain, it appeared that Maryland would remain in the Union. Lincoln wired an Illinois friend, "Gen. McClellan has gained a great victory over the great Rebel army in Maryland between Fredericktown and Hagerstown. He is now pursuing the flying foe."[226]

Chapter 4

Michigan Leadership

At Lansing and the Front

The foundation for the Stonewall Regiment's heroic performance along a wooded mountain in Maryland had been laid a little over two months prior. The presence of hundreds of farmers, laborers and students in arms for the Union so far from the Peninsula State was no accident.

On June 28, 1862, two important communiqués made their way toward President Lincoln's desk. One, authored at 12:20 a.m., originated from McClellan on the James Peninsula. "I have lost," the telegram confessed. Lee had gone on the attack, remained on the offensive and aggressively pushed the Army of the Potomac away from Richmond. Hopes for victory shattered, a despondent McClellan poured out his emotions: "I feel too earnestly to-night. I have seen too many dead and wounded comrades to feel otherwise than that the Government has not sustained this army. If you do not do so now the game is lost." The politicians could still retrieve Union fortunes if they would but act: "You must send me very large re-enforcements, and send them at once."[227] As if in possession of that message, politicians in the North that very day were taking such a step.

The second communiqué this date originated from Austin Blair, governor of Michigan, and seventeen other chief state executives. "The time has arrived for prompt and vigorous measures," it adjured respectfully. The president should "at once call upon the several States for such number of men as may be required…to speedily crush the rebellion."[228] "How many can you furnish?" came the Washington reply. The response: none of the

Governor Austin Blair, the "war governor." *Archives of Michigan.*

governors "proposes less than 200,000; make it 300,000 if you wish"—500,000 if bold enough.[229]

On July 1, the president accepted their offer. Lincoln directed the War Department to respond with individual state allotments and raise 300,000 fresh troops.[230] Michigan's quota was six new regiments,[231] nearly twelve thousand recruits.[232] By the end of the month, Blair could promise that "the new regiments will commence to take the field about the 1st of August, or sooner if possible, and will all be in service in the field during that month."[233] Because organization of the 17th Infantry was already underway,[234] Blair had a head start on fulfilling the requisition. By September 13, the last of the six new regiments had been mustered in.[235] An extra regiment, raised in only thirty days from authorization to muster on August 15, added to the Michigan complement.

Inspired by the surge of patriotism, Chicago composer George F. Root dashed off a tune entitled "The Battle-Cry of Freedom." First introduced at a war rally on July 24, the song soon was on the lips of millions of Northerners with lyrics that included:

We will welcome to our numbers the loyal, true and brave,
Shouting the battle cry of freedom!
And although they may be poor, not a man shall be a slave,
Shouting the battle cry of freedom![236]

The supplementary unit—the 24th Infantry—came almost exclusively from Wayne County. Most of the officers hailed from southeast Michigan as well.[237] The regiment was in position to participate in the Maryland Campaign, for on August 30–31, when Pope's army was on the run, the

Michiganders were entrained and en route. They passed through Baltimore on the final day of the month and arrived in Washington. On September 4, they were posted just south of Alexandria.[238] On the seventh, the regiment was ordered to pursue Lee, moving out for Leesburg late that Sunday night. General Williams was expecting them.[239] Rather than made party to the pursuit, however, the 24th was ordered across the Anacostia River to Fort Baker in the southeast part of the District of Columbia. As the regimental historian would recount, "by some mistake at the War Office, the Seventeenth Michigan was ordered to take our place for Leesburg.... Thus, the histories of these two regiments were interchanged." On the day of the South Mountain conflict, "the booming of guns was heard forty miles distant...and we wonder how long ere we, too, will be engaged."[240]

On the morning after the passes at South Mountain were forced—Monday, September 15—Lee paused at Keedysville. The troops who had not gone to Harpers Ferry moved on Sharpsburg, a small town only a few miles north of the Potomac. A message written the previous evening arrived from Jackson predicting imminent success at Harpers Ferry.[241] The rest of the Army of Northern Virginia now took up positions beyond the west bank of Antietam Creek, a tributary that "rises in Pennsylvania, and flows through the eastern part of the Hagerstown valley till it enters the Potomac below Sharpsburg."[242] It was a strong position, one "admirably suited for defense,"[243] with high ground east and south of town and each flank anchored near the Potomac.[244] The Confederate position featured interior lines, providing for rapid transfer of troops from one to another part.[245] Two roads converged at the east end of Sharpsburg, the Hagerstown Pike on its north–south axis and the Boonsboro Pike running northeasterly. Ridges accompanied these roads providing "commanding" vantage points.[246] Whether they would need to defend the ground remained a question. Looking back toward South Mountain, Lee noted blue columns descending Turner's Gap. The lead division was led by Israel B. Richardson.[247] Just as in the First Bull Run Campaign, he drew the point assignment.

Richardson was forty-six and a seasoned veteran. Five years at West Point culminated in graduating thirty-eighth out of fifty-two in the ill-starred class of 1841. He experienced the Seminole War in Florida from 1841 to 1842 and then served in garrison and frontier duty until the outbreak of the Mexican-American War. There, he participated in the main battles of the campaign. His leadership earned him a brevet captaincy "for gallant and meritorious conduct" at Contreras and Churubusco and brevet major for Chapultepec. On September 30, 1855, no war then raging, he

Major General Israel Bush Richardson of Pontiac, 1st Division commander in the II Corps. *Monroe County Historical Museum.*

resigned and moved to Pontiac, Michigan, to try farming. Immediately after Fort Sumter, on April 25, 1861, he accepted appointment as colonel of the 2nd Michigan Infantry, the state's first three-year regiment. His combat credentials merited promotion to brigadier general on May 17. He commanded a brigade in the First Bull Run campaign and advanced to division command on the Peninsula.

Richardson's performance in battle earned him a promotion on July 4, 1862, to major general of volunteers.[248] He was a soldier's soldier, and his men regarded him as one of their own: "Sometimes they call me General Richardson, and at other times they call me 'Greasy Dick.'"[249] They also nicknamed him "Fighting Dick," "Old War Horse" and "Old Dick," judging him "a man who understood volunteers and appreciated the difference between them and Regulars....[H]e would stay in a fight as long as any one, and looked after the comfort of his men with a fatherly solicitude."[250] His men commented on his "portly" physique; he was "a large fleshy man, generally careless in his attire," dressing "like a teamster," "the plainest general in the army" and wearing "a jacket, an old straw hat, and trousers" that "were torn down the leg." He repudiated military style in preference to a private's blouse without shoulder straps.[251]

One of his trusted associates was Assistant Adjutant General John Mason Norvell. Originally second lieutenant in Company I of the 2nd Michigan, he came from solid stock. His grandfather was a Revolutionary War veteran. His father had been a newspaper editor in Hagerstown and served in the War of 1812. He moved to Michigan Territory to become postmaster of Detroit, was a delegate to the Constitutional Convention at Detroit in 1835 and was elected to the U.S. Senate (Democrat), serving from 1837 to 1841.[252] Thirty-year-old Norvell had served as Richardson's aide since August 30, 1861, and exemplified the courageous fiber of Michigan youth in the volunteer army.[253] On August 22, the War Department confirmed his appointment to become adjutant of Richardson's Division with the rank of major.[254]

Before sunrise on the fifteenth, as expected of an aggressive officer, Richardson had his division on the move. The South Mountain pass had been cleared, and his men marched "promptly, as ordered, up the sometimes very steep and always rough and very rocky road" and "smartly"[255] down the western side. Confederate troopers engaged in delaying tactics, so he formed his command into line of battle on both sides of the National Pike and advanced in force. McClellan would commend this performance for "pressing" the enemy "with vigor" and for "following close on the heels" of Lee's army.[256] The army commander's orders were to push but not to bring on a general engagement.[257] The Confederates steadily retreated to Boonsboro, and Union cavalry joined in the pursuit. After a pitched battle through town, the Confederates withdrew toward Sharpsburg, crossing over Antietam Creek. Pleasanton's horsemen proceeded across country and linked with Richardson, who had not tarried in Boonsboro and, moving "rapidly,"[258] had marched beyond Keedysville.[259] Passing the Philip Pry house along the Pike, Richardson drew up at the creek near what locals called the Middle Bridge. He directed Norvell to throw one of the regiments out front to maintain contact with the enemy.[260] The remainder of his command deployed into line of battle and began a lively and rather long-distance exchange with the Confederates beyond the stream until dark arrived.[261]

Captain George Armstrong Custer, aide-de-camp on the staff of army commander George B. McClellan, with Virginian James B. Washington, prewar classmate and now prisoner of war. *Library of Congress.*

Richardson's degree of "combative zeal" was notable to other officers.[262] But he was not the only Wolverine to gain such notice. An aide-de-camp to McClellan—in addition to carrying orders, espying enemy positions and "galloping back with reports"[263]—would be cited for plunging into combat alongside the cavalry with "conspicuous" bravery.[264]

It would be just the latest commendation for "Captain Custer," who had made Monroe, Michigan, his home.[265] George Armstrong Custer was just twenty-two. He played a modest role at the war's onset, helping drill volunteers and assisting in the Washington defenses. During the Peninsula Campaign, he served as an aide to the topographical engineers, demonstrating

Custer wading the Chickahominy River in May 1862 scouting enemy positions. Custer's fearlessness earned him a spot on General McClellan's staff. Waud sketch. *Library of Congress.*

fearlessness in one incident by burning his hands while trying to extinguish a bridge fire. He gained mention for signal bravery and initiative.[266] On one reconnaissance, Custer "was the first to cross the stream, the first to open fire upon the enemy, and one of the last to leave the field."[267] In a May 24, 1862 message to the secretary of war, McClellan had commended "a very gallant reconnaissance" by Custer and comrade.[268] On May 28, McClellan appointed Lieutenant Custer to his personal staff.[269] The post was "a reward for an act of daring gallantry."[270]

Arriving at army headquarters in Rockville on the eighth, Custer had ridden with McClellan until ordered to report to Pleasonton for the attack on Turner's Gap.[271] They waited together for Hooker's Corps to clear the pass;[272] at daylight on the fifteenth, at Pleasanton's order, Custer joined Colonel Elon J. Farnsworth's 8th Illinois Cavalry for the venture into Boonsboro. Together they met the Confederate rear guard, "charged them repeatedly, and drove them some 2 miles beyond the town." Pleasonton was pleased with the outcome: the cavalry plus a section of Union guns caused the enemy to break and run, leaving two artillery pieces, eighty killed and wounded and several hundred prisoners.[273] Custer breathlessly reported

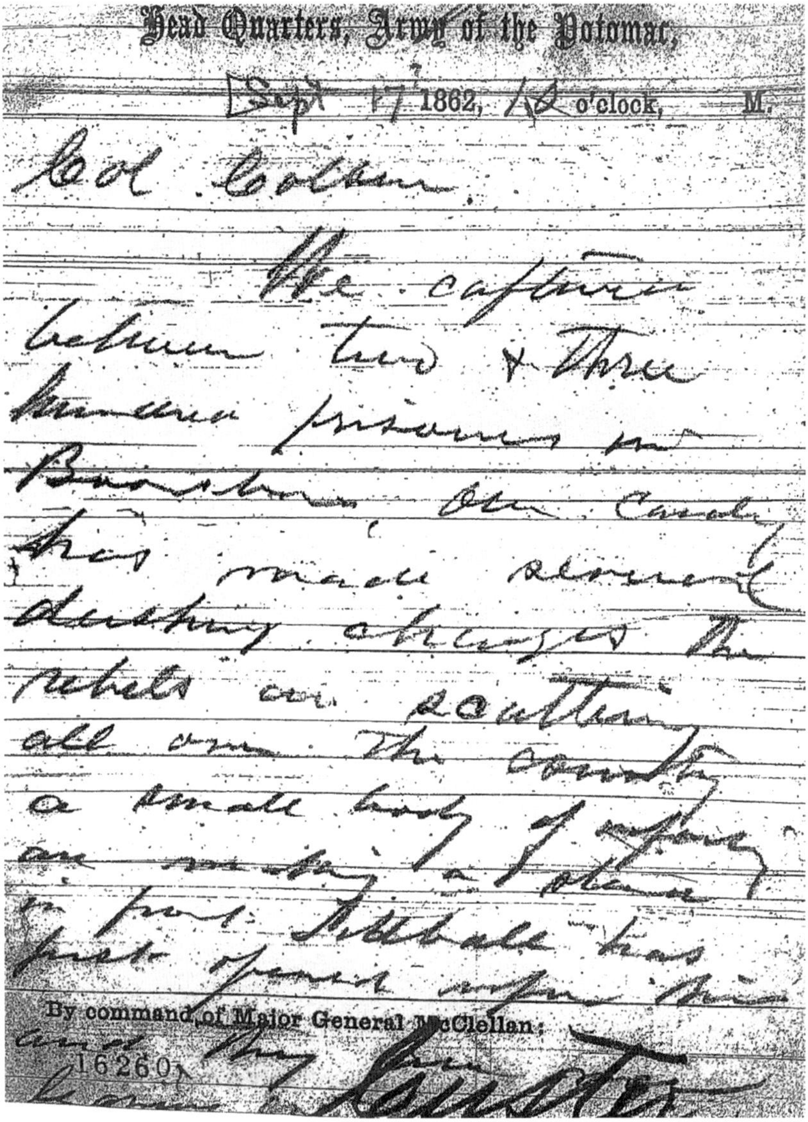
Head Quarters, Army of the Potomac,
Sept 17 1862, 12 o'clock, M.
Col Colburn:
We captured between two & three hundred prisoners in Boonsboro. Our Cavalry has made several dashing charges The rebels are scattering all over the country a small body of infantry are making a stand in front Tidball has just opened upon him
By command of Major General McClellan:
16260
Custer

Handwritten message at the front by Captain Custer, September 15, 1862. *Library of Congress.*

to his chief: "We captured between two & three hundred prisoners in Boonsboro, our cavalry has made several dashing charges The rebels are scattering all over the country a small body of infantry are making a stand in front Tidball has just opened upon him."[274]

Colonel Farnsworth also merited a commendation in Pleasonton's report for notable gallantry. Born in Green Oak Township near present-day Brighton on July 30, 1837, he was related to Michigan's attorney general and had attended the University of Michigan. He had enlisted in his uncle's Illinois cavalry regiment as first lieutenant a year before in September.[275] At only twenty-five, he and Custer shared youth and yearning for action.

McClellan's aide-de-camp remained at the front rather than return to army headquarters. Continuing with the cavalry and Richardson's advance, he soon reported, "We have just captured one three inch gun and its Caisson on the road from the Hagerst[ow]n Pike to Sharps town. Col. [Henry J.] Hunt had better send out for it. We cannot take it with us."[276] He next reported one more trophy: "We have captured another gun—a 12 pdr. brass howitzer."[277] In the afternoon, he wrote to McClellan from the advance "that we can capture the entire rebel army." It was a vivid report: the enemy was "in full view. Their line is a perfect one about a mile and a half long." He urged the army commander to forward units for an attack, promptly: "[W]e can employ all the troops you can send us."[278] Signing his messages simply with "Custer," he called on McClellan to unleash the Army of the Potomac right away.

Based on the reports of continuing success, McClellan telegraphed Washington that the Confederates were "in a perfect panic," heading for Shepherdstown on the Virginia side. He had ordered a vigorous pursuit.[279] The president replied, "Your dispatch of to-day received. God bless you and all with you. Destroy the rebel army if possible."[280]

The remainder of the Army of the Potomac, though, was not pushing with Richardson's alacrity. As darkness approached, the head of the column behind him stopped some distance away.[281] Union forces were spread out for miles back to South Mountain, with some elements having missed a key turn and continuing toward Hagerstown. The new commander of the XII Corps, Joseph K. Mansfield, had led it the wrong way and could not be located. Alpheus Williams, displaced from its command, was found and ordered the Corps to halt and prevent further distancing from the main body.[282] After riding through Fox's Gap, McClellan made his way to Richardson's front-line position around 5:00 p.m. In the fading light, he observed the Confederates occupying a position on ridges beyond the west side of Antietam Creek, displaying a significant force of infantry and cavalry with a number of artillery batteries.[283] The scene disconcerted him. Since 8:00 a.m., he had sent dispatches portraying the enemy as panicked,[284] routed and demoralized, "retreating in disorder."[285] He expected his adversary to be completing a withdrawal.[286] Now it was sunset, and the Army of Northern Virginia was standing firm on this side of the Potomac rather than returning to Virginia. What was Lee up to?

At his Sharpsburg headquarters, Lee had pondered his next step. Early in the day, he had received a message from Stonewall Jackson, written near 8:00 a.m.: the Harpers Ferry garrison would soon surrender. With most of the expeditionary force freed up, Jackson inquired "to what point shall they move?"[287] The answer: Sharpsburg. Lee had thought to abandon Maryland, but the capture of Harpers Ferry opened his lines of communications and supply. He reversed his decision to retreat. McClellan's advance had appeared across the creek around 2:00 p.m., but the Union general had never mirrored Lee's aggressiveness. Lee updated Davis during the afternoon: Harpers Ferry had fallen, and part of Jackson's corps had reached the army and gone into position, with the rest approaching. McClellan had "made no attack up to this afternoon." The Confederates had come to liberate Maryland and invade Pennsylvania. They were just wrapping up their latest victory, with the capture of Harper Ferry "a renewed occasion for gratitude."[288] Above all, this campaign could deliver Southern independence. Lee could keep the campaign alive, end up taking the offensive and deliver "the final, crushing blow to Northern morale."[289] He had come to fight. And he would do battle.[290]

Once again, McClellan confronted murkiness. He saw a major body of Confederates in his front, on what appeared to be a fairly strong position. He knew that Harpers Ferry had fallen.[291] Jackson and the other elements could reinforce Lee. Yet only a single road and ford connected the Confederates to their exit across the Potomac. Would Lee really risk a battle in this position? McClellan ordered a reconnaissance for daylight the next morning. If "found to be in position," the enemy would be attacked, he promised.[292]

Heavy fog rose from Antietam Creek at daybreak on Tuesday the sixteenth.[293] A signal station on Elk Ridge, a seven-hundred-foot elevation southeast of Sharpsburg, was inoperable until the mist cleared. Several reconnaissance parties forayed across the creek early on, but little could be determined without more effort. At his headquarters in a church on the west side of Keedysville,[294] McClellan learned early on that the Confederates who had blocked Harpers Ferry from Maryland had moved south over the Potomac. This meant—he hoped—that Lee had "abandoned his position in front of us."[295] He took it upon himself to survey the ground, and around 10:00 a.m. he took several officers with him to reconnoiter his left flank, among them his chief of artillery.[296]

Henry Jackson Hunt had graduated in the middle of the West Point class of 1839.[297] Born in Detroit, it was also site of his first posting as a second lieutenant of artillery. He won a brevet for gallant conduct in two battles in Mexico. His battery covered the retreat at First Bull Run,[298] and he was the tactical genius behind the massed batteries of Federal artillery that decimated Confederate attacks at Malvern Hill, saving the Army of the Potomac at the end of the Peninsula Campaign. He did so at personal risk, having two horses shot out from under him. He had turned forty-three two days before, even less an imposing physical specimen than ever. Characterized by "a beak of a nose" and "dull complexion, of medium height and slight frame," he lacked hearing in his left ear and spoke with a lisp.[299] "Cupid" had been his nickname at the academy.[300] His "insoluble integrity," strict adherence to the truth, personal bravery, indefatigable advocacy on behalf of the artillery arm and complete absence of cruelty made him perhaps the most popular soldier with both officers and enlisted men.[301]

McClellan trusted Hunt based on a relationship dating back to the Mexican-American War. In February 1862, he appointed him chief of the Army of the Potomac's Artillery Reserve.[302] On September 5, as McClellan sought to invigorate demoralized Union forces, Hunt had been announced in Special Orders No. 2 as chief of artillery for the army.[303] The general regarded him as "the best living commander of field-artillery," a "man with the utmost coolness in danger… an admirable organizer, a soldier of a very high order." McClellan, an organizational genius himself, praised Hunt's merit "not only in organizing his command to the best advantage, but in using it on the field of battle with the utmost

Colonel Henry Jackson Hunt, chief of artillery, Army of the Potomac, from Detroit. *Library of Congress.*

skill and power."[304] Within days and without staff, Hunt had ridden "from one part of the army to the next," ascertained deficiencies, scrounged men and materiel, refit and restructured batteries and readied the artillery arm by the time it was needed on South Mountain.[305]

Accompanying his commander on the survey meant that Hunt was again exposed to danger. They rode nearly the entire Union front line, mainly in front of the pickets. For that reason they "drew the enemy's fire frequently" but did discover the positions of many of the Confederate guns.[306] Hunt would confront more than one hundred cannons in twenty-six batteries.[307] The enemy's reserve artillery was largely across the Potomac, prepared to act as reinforcements or cover avenues of escape.[308] McClellan had given Hunt authority over battlefield deployment of all batteries, not just the reserve, as well as all staff. Having "attacked the problems with characteristic vigor" of keeping the artillery ready for use after South Mountain, he brought to Antietam Creek a total of sixty-four batteries with 323 guns.[309] At break of day, Hunt had posted the Union Artillery Reserve on the bluff east of the Antietam covering the Middle Bridge,[310] "riding furiously back and forth along the heights" to ensure the heavy "guns of position" in the reserve would provide maximum support.[311]

The Confederates remained in position when the fog dissipated. Returning to headquarters, McClellan devised an attack plan and began communicating it at 2:00 p.m. after "perfecting arrangements."[312] It commenced with a crossing at the northerly Upper Bridge to target Lee's left. One corps (Hooker's I) crossed and began to engage the Confederates that afternoon, while XII Corps would await dark before making the passage. On the left, IX Corps, including Willcox's division, would push forward to create a diversion and prevent Lee from reinforcing his right. Once one of the two flank movements achieved success, an attack would be made on the Confederate center.[313] Convinced that he faced a numerically equal (if not superior) foe led McClellan to plan for flexibility, first to probe in case Lee might respond by withdrawing and, if not, hoping to uncover the weakest part of the Confederate line against which to concentrate a successful attack.[314] Likely, II Corps—and Israel Richardson, whose division remained ready for action near the Pry house[315]—would help deliver the crushing blow.[316]

The passage of time, though, now made September 17 the day when battle could be joined in earnest. And Jackson would be present in force. Except for A.P. Hill's division, still cleaning up affairs at Harpers Ferry, Wednesday dawn would break on a reunited Army of Northern Virginia.[317] The Army of

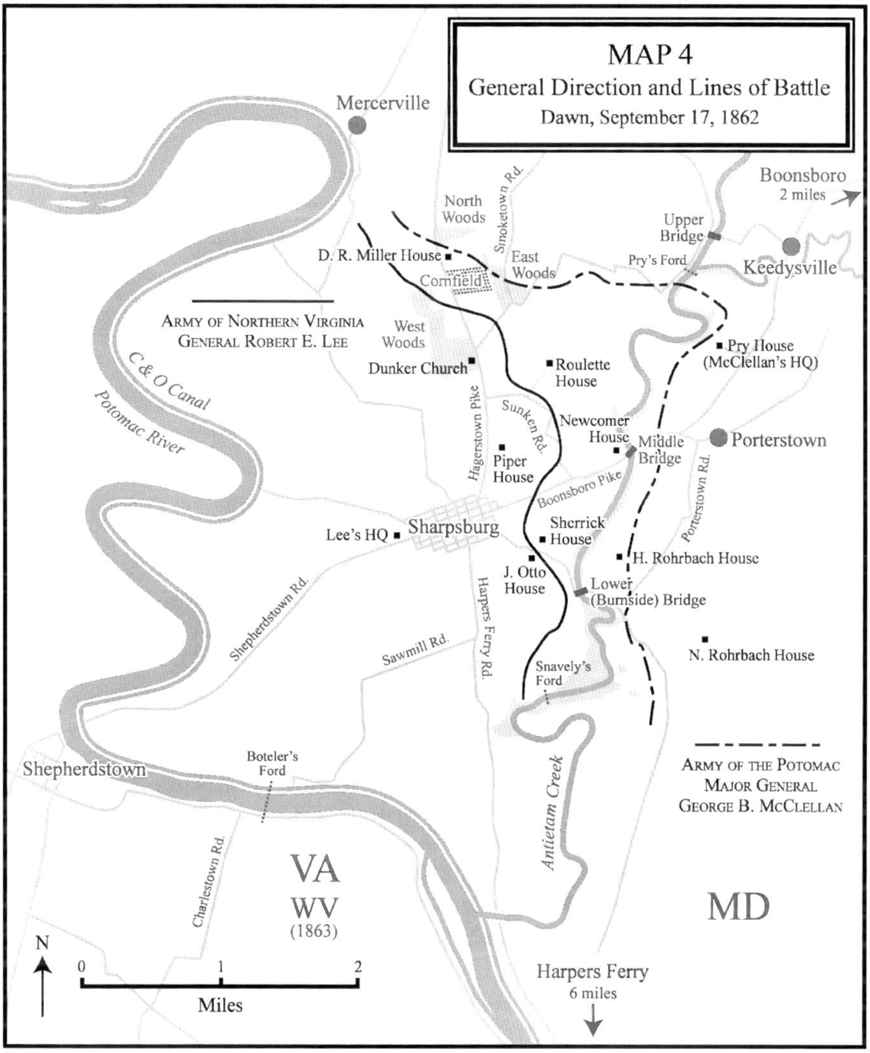

MAP 4. General direction and lines of battle, dawn, September 17. Lee's left was anchored on the Potomac and his right near Lower Bridge spanning Antietam Creek.

the Potomac faced Lee in strength, although perhaps a strong push would prompt a withdrawal.[318] More units were approaching the Antietam, such as the 4th Michigan Infantry, which had reached Keedysville and was a mile or so away, in position for a punch at the Confederate center.[319]

Williams received the order to put his 1st Division on the march around 11:00 p.m. as part of Mansfield's XII Corps.[320] He had just fallen asleep—it had been an exhausting several days. He had bedded down under a tree at 2:00 a.m. on the fifteenth and had his men on the march at daylight across South Mountain and through Boonsboro. That night, he slept in the house of "a Mr. Nicodemus"[321] and the next morning was "ordered hurriedly to the front." The division had to cross farm lots and fields in order to arrive where ordered. The sixteenth had been no different, and upon reaching the front, the men lay all day under artillery fire. After dark, Williams found a tent and "the best bed I had seen for weeks." Now, he and his men were underway in the dark along an unknown road, across the Upper Bridge, and branching off into the fields on the west side of Antietam Creek. The darkness and the heavily wooded terrain compelled a number of stops and starts as they sought their way.[322] Sam Pittman would recall the vividness of the movement:

> *To the uninitiated this night march would have been impressive in the extreme—the steady solemn tread of ten thousand men, the whispering orders of officers—the frequent halts and silent advance of one or two to examine the character of the ground ahead—the occasional fire of some miserable straggler and so forth &c all tending to make men prepare their minds for something awful upon the break of day.*[323]

When finally halted on the Joseph Poffenberger farm, Williams arranged the division for the advance at daylight. At 2:00 a.m., he found a place to rest, this time under a rail fence, but was awakened several times by picket fire and by Mansfield, who kept tinkering with the corps' alignment.[324]

"I shall not," Williams would write home, "forget that night; so dark, so obscure, so mysterious, so uncertain." Fatigue and sleep deprivation fostered "a half-dreamy sensation about it all." As troops filed into position, the soft noise of their movements and the quiet commands, coupled with erratic picket fire ahead, made for an atmosphere of unearthliness. Williams felt a foreboding. He had the distinct impression, as he lay in the field near his troops, "that the morrow was to be great with the future fate of our country."[325]

Chapter 5

DAWN OF BATTLE

Michigan Christens the Field

Between South Mountain and the Potomac, the valley of Antietam Creek forms the principal geographic feature. The creek runs past Hagerstown almost due south, looping right and left until a final swing west where it is crossed by the road from Harpers Ferry to Sharpsburg and empties into the Potomac. The creek is traversed by three bridges near Sharpsburg: the farthest south, known locally as the "lower bridge"; the "middle bridge" that carries the road to Keedysville; and the "upper bridge" that transports the road between Keedysville and its intersection with the Hagerstown Pike. The creek's banks range from practically no elevation at the Upper Bridge to steepness at the Lower Bridge. Sharpsburg was a peaceful village of some 1,200 residents set among rolling farmland, with a few woodlots separating the largely open terrain. The "charming" setting possessed "incomparable beauty."[326]

McClellan's headquarters had moved to the Pry house.[327] Close to the front, equidistant between the Middle and Upper Bridges, "the house afforded an excellent observation point for scanning the enemy positions, and the farmhouse was centrally located for communication purposes."[328] Built in 1844 by Philip Pry and his brother, Samuel, the house was a two-story, L-shaped Greek Revival brick structure set on a stone foundation with a steeply pitched roof pierced by two single chimneys. As one of the more elaborate homes in the area, located along a major road, it was slated for a special place in history. Late in the evening of September 16, Philip Pry had been "startled to see a cloud of dust coming down his farm lane. It was

The Philip and Elizabeth Pry house. Commandeered by McClellan's staff as a forward headquarters and field hospital where Lincoln visited wounded officers, including Richardson. Alexander Gardner photograph. *Library of Congress.*

caused by a column of horsemen. A dashing young officer ran up to the door and said, 'General McClellan, the commander-in-chief of the Army of the Potomac desires to make his headquarters here.'" Pry identified the officer as George Custer.[329]

The Pry family's 125-acre farm would serve as the logistical nerve center of Union operations during the battle and as a major field hospital afterward. Life as it was known for the prosperous, middle-class Union citizens would forever change as the first two Federal divisions appeared east of Sharpsburg. Although loyal citizens, occupation of their property would ultimately devastate the Prys' ability to live as they had.[330]

Historical interpretation of the battle, local lore and a "story as old as the hills" of Washington County has confirmed that Captain Custer established the Federal headquarters at the Pry house.[331] Known more for his disastrous defeat in Montana at the Battle of Little Big Horn on June 25, 1876, where he and his entire detachment of the 7th U.S. Cavalry lost their lives, Custer had a successful and illustrious Civil War career. He rose from graduating last in the accelerated four-year West Point class of 1861 to appointment as second lieutenant in the Regular Army to major general of volunteers. Custer's fearless energy, combined with determined bravado, made him one of the more colorful personalities during the war.[332] Historiography has tended to obscure important aspects of his service record, like selection of the Pry farm for a central role in the bloody day.

Alpheus Williams had no time to reflect on such matters after his brief sleep on the ground between the E.H. Hoffman and George Line farms. Skirmishers of I Corps moved to the attack while "the stars were still shining."[333] Sunrise was at 5:53 a.m.,[334] and the XII Corps arose and waited in its position a mile behind and to the east. "By a common impulse," Williams would note, "our men stood to arms" in anticipation of what was to come.[335] They did not have long to wait. "At the first dawn of day skirmishing commenced in front"; Stonewall Jackson would report that within "a short time the Federal batteries, so posted on the opposite side of the Antietam as to enfilade my line, opened a severe and damaging fire."[336]

George Hartsuff led his brigade from the I Corps forward from the Poffenberger Woods at daylight.[337] They passed through the northern part of the East Woods and then over the open ground to the west. The brigade went into action on a line running northwest and southeast with its 1,220 men. It would suffer casualties of nearly 50 percent; one of the wounded was General Hartsuff. While reconnoitering astride his horse, just beyond the North Woods, a Minié ball struck him in the left hip.[338] He remained in the saddle a few moments but grew faint. Dismounting, he put his arms around two soldiers and "tried to walk back" but was too unsteady. They laid him down on a blanket to carry him to the rear; he was put on a cot, loaded on an ambulance and taken a mile from the field to a temporary surgery. The doctor probed the wound but could not locate the projectile. Transferred to a hospital in Middletown, he was examined while still in the ambulance that evening by five surgeons, none of whom could find the bullet. Taken to Frederick, he was examined once more, this time under chloroform, without success. The Minié ball remained in his pelvic cavity.[339] His action in "bravely pressing forward his troops" would be noted by McClellan.[340]

McClellan wondered if there was a need to reinforce I Corps. At 7:20 a.m., he sent orders to Sumner to advance in order to be in readiness to provide aid. To ensure that II Corps would come up where needed, one of his aides would guide the movement: "The Comdg. General directs that you move Sedgwick and French across the creek by the fords which Capt. Custer will point out to you. You will cross in as solid a mass as possible and communicate with Genl. Hooker immediately."[341] The same message held back Richardson's Division for now.

By 7:30 a.m., bloodletting ran rampant. The I Corps of the Union army and Jackson's wing of the Confederate army had eviscerated each other.

"The Battle of the Sharpsburg from the extreme [Union] right." Waud sketch. *Library of Congress.*

Hooker's 8,600-strong corps incurred some 3,000 casualties (including Hooker).[342] Its Confederate counterpart would suffer 4,500 casualties.[343] The Confederate numbers were also a factor of the fire by Federal batteries from beyond the Antietam, positioned by Hunt, and which "proved severe and damaging."[344] From across the stream, "Hunt's rifled Parrotts, anxious to aid Hooker's attack, poured a devastating fire" on Jackson's line.[345]

The I Corps had needed help. Hooker called to Mansfield for reinforcements, and XII Corps advanced. The mode of its march stunned those with combat experience. Mansfield had none in the current war and, lacking confidence in the mass of volunteer soldiers, thought that his regiments should go into action "closed in mass"[346] (i.e., a company front to each regiment with the other companies behind within six paces[347]). They moved west across the Smoketown Road and swung to the left, marching south. Williams's 1st Division had the advance, followed by the 2nd Division. Progress was slow, as Mansfield ordered frequent halts. At 6:30 a.m., the head of the column stopped in the middle of a field "west of and adjoining the Samuel Poffenberger woods."[348]

Mansfield rode forward to investigate. Hooker's corps was "melting away."[349] "Shells and round shot" were coming thick over and around the 1st Division.[350] Thinking of his men as always, Williams ordered the lead brigade

to deploy in line of battle so as not to present a solid target. When Mansfield returned, he countermanded the order and again directed an advance *en masse*. At around 7:15 a.m., Williams took two regiments in the direction of the Hagerstown Pike, while Mansfield led others ahead. Williams led his contingent into the east part of the North Woods and deployed the units one company after another by the flank along the south edge of the trees. Ordering them forward, he "thundered into the chaos" caused among the ranks by a Confederate volley in order to settle the men.[351] Then he moved back to secure support.[352]

Within minutes, one of Mansfield's staff rode up to inform Williams of grave news: the corps commander had been wounded. Williams suddenly was back in charge of XII Corps in the midst of battle. He did not require an order from headquarters to act.[353] After Mansfield went down, Williams found Hooker, "took from him such directions as the pressing exigencies would permit, and hastened to make a disposition of the corps to meet them." At 9:00 a.m., Williams signaled McClellan by flag: "Genl. Mansfield is dangerously wounded. Genl. Hooker wounded severely in foot. Genl. Sumner I hear is advancing. We hold the field at present. Please give us all the aid you can."[354]

The men of XII Corps did not worry about the transfer of command; they knew Williams as "a very experienced brigadier and deserving of higher rank."[355] In the conference with Hooker, he learned the full gravity of the situation "amidst a very unpleasant shower of bullets."[356] The I Corps was barely holding on.[357] Williams immediately sent off his staff to inform subordinate officers of new orders,[358] directing them to advance and confront some of the hardest fighters in the Confederate army: John Bell Hood's Texans, Alabamans and Mississippians, plus D.H. Hill's division, including North Carolinians who had fought at Fox's Gap. In overall command on the left of the line was Stonewall Jackson. Hood had led an "irresistible counterattack" that had bloodied Hooker.[359] Williams's men went into the East Woods and over the forty-acre cornfield on the David R. Miller farm, where the crop was "tall and ripe and ready for harvest."[360]

In this once bucolic field between the Smoketown Road and the Hagerstown Pike, a scene developed that beggars comprehension. Through the rows of stalks the Federals advanced, some directly south and others coming from the East Woods in a flanking maneuver, firing all the way. The contest reached full pitch when a North Carolina officer spotted the side movement. "He cried out loudly that they were about to be flanked. Suddenly, all anyone could think of was Fox's Gap, and the result was mass panic. 'The most unutterable stampede occurred.'"[361] Some Confederates retreated toward the West Woods, and some withdrew "all the way to Sharpsburg."[362] For those who did not run, the result was devastating. One XII Corps regiment "succeeded in getting the first volley into the close ranks of the enemy before they could prepare for it." Another fired "four or five volleys into the corn, which swept down" the line of a Confederate unit; and the sight "was awful beyond description: dead men were literally piled upon and across each other. We had been enabled to pour a volley into an entire line, at a few rods distance and striking them in the flank at the same time." Elsewhere, the battle was equally grim: "the fighting in the northeast corner of the corn" was "fast and furious and hand-to-hand." Bayonets and clubbed guns were thrust in a bloody mêlée.[363] Hooker would write, colorfully, that "every stalk of corn in the northern and greater part of the field was cut as closely as could have been done with a knife, and the slain lay in rows precisely as they had stood in their ranks a few moments before. It was never my fortune to witness a more bloody, dismal battle-field."[364]

On the Confederate side, attempts were made to rally. Along the fences of the Smoketown Road, officers desperately entreated their men to stand and fight. On the farm of Samuel and Elizabeth Mumma and their children, with the barn ablaze, the same efforts were made, but the blue regiments pressed relentlessly.[365] Williams summed up the outcome of the XII Corps action: "When we engaged the enemy he was in a strip of woods, long but narrow.

We drove him from this, across a ploughed field and through a cornfield into another woods, which was full of ravines. There the enemy held us in check til 9½ o'clock, when there was a general cessation of musketry."[366]

Looking about the scene, Williams saw carnage everywhere. "All over the ground we had advanced on, the Rebel dead and wounded lay thick, much more numerous than ours, but ours were painfully mingled in. Our wounded were rapidly carried off and some of the Rebels." Some, not all, since the capacity to do so did not exist. Still, "hundreds appealed to me and I confess that the rage of battle had not hardened my heart so that I did not feel a pity for them."[367] The once beautiful landscape was "hellish.... The dead lay everywhere in the East Woods and the open pastures, but the toll was greatest in the Cornfield and along the Hagerstown road....Bodies were in heaps amid the broken cornstalks near the turnpike; dead men were draped over the high post-and-rail fences."[368]

Rage it had. Unlike some Union generals this day, Williams had not been overly cautious and had not held back: "The necessities of the case were so great that I was obliged to put my whole corps into action at once."[369] He followed the military adage "to strike with vigor and with concert."[370] The situation, so grave, "would permit of no reserves, and it may be truly stated that, to cover the points threatened or pressed," Williams threw every regiment against the enemy,[371] committing all seven thousand men at hand.[372] The XII Corps had charged ahead with little assistance available from I Corps after its advance.[373] For ninety key minutes, "Williams and XII Corps bore the brunt of the fighting on the Union right."[374] Williams's entire corps[375] had advanced a full mile, part of it (Brigadier General George Greene's Division) to where the Smoketown and Hagerstown roads joined near a small house of worship. The simple brick church building with plain windows and whitewashed walls would forever be known as the Dunker Church. Williams, as did Hooker, saw the position "as the key to the battlefield in his sector."[376]

This extreme point of the advance "gallantly held for several hours." Williams diligently sought to shore up the foothold, but only three regiments could be supplied. "Impressed with the importance of holding this position," he made several unsuccessful efforts to procure reinforcements from other commands. Finally, a division of II Corps under John Sedgwick advanced to his support.[377] Still, Williams had successfully "collapsed" Stonewall Jackson's position.[378] Despite leading the smallest corps, he "fought brilliantly that day, and it was no fluke that the farthest Union advance was by men of Williams' Corps."[379]

The acting corps commander and his staff were repeatedly in harm's way during the frantic hours this Wednesday morning. While conferring with

Hooker, "the dust of the ploughed ground was knocked up in little spurts all around us, marking the spot where musket balls struck." Riding over the field from one position to another, including the elevated center of the line, riders and horses were constantly exposed to enemy fire. Williams wrote that "a ball whizzed close to my horse. Two or three others followed all in disagreeable closeness to my person." Confederate artillery drew a bead on them as they traversed the Miller farm: "As I entered the narrow lane running to the right and front a battery opened a cross-fire and Pittman and myself had the excitement of riding a mile or so out and back under its severest salutations."[380] Although others had been wounded, the two Michiganders escaped.

As for Pittman, the experiences at the right hand of his general made for an unforgettable day. "Terrible was the fighting," he would write to his wife. Despite attempts to do more damage to the enemy, "we had to remain content to hold the cornfield, which our gallant Corps took at its first charge." His admiration for Williams, suddenly thrust into leadership at a critical moment, had only grown: "The command then devolved upon Genl Williams and right handsome did he carry his responsibility notwithstanding he had not been informed in the least of the plan of operations." One thing more he would observe: "[T]he 'iron hail' was so thick and my duties took me to so many different points…nothing but the protecting care of my God can have saved me from injury."

The XII Corps under Williams had done itself proud. After "a severe struggle of an hour and a half to two hours' duration,"[381] the corps had driven its counterparts and conquered this portion of the field. It was "solidly posted" though unable to send help within its own ranks or to anyone else.[382] It had "gained a good deal of ground"[383] and inflicted much damage. More, on its own, it could not do. With support, a complete Union victory could have ensued, with Lee's left crushed.[384]

Both sides were spent. As if staged, the time had arrived for the next Union corps to make its appearance. Williams dispatched a staff officer to apprise II Corps commander Edwin Sumner "of our position and the situation of affairs."[385] McClellan had directed Sumner "to be very careful how you advance" since the army's right had apparently suffered greatly, with Mansfield killed, Hooker wounded and two corps bloodied.[386] Williams was able to withdraw XII Corps units "by degrees" to resupply ammunition and reorganize. Despite the continued danger, after the advance had reached its zenith Williams "rode along where our advanced lines had been. Not an enemy appeared. The woods in front were as quiet as any sylvan shade."[387]

The lull at the West Woods meant little. The next phase of the storm was about to break.

Chapter 6

Sanctification of Sacrifice

The 7th Michigan's Destiny in Maryland

Angels have heard your story, and God knows all your names.[388]

The near universal reaction throughout Michigan in April 1861 to the bombardment and capture of Fort Sumter exhibited a combination of steadfast determination to preserve the Union, a seriousness in military response and a confidence in quick victory. Flags and other tangible elements of patriotism shadowed public buildings and adorned private dwellings. The groundswell of enthusiasm and calls for immediate action to suppress the rebellion echoed from the craggy shores of the Great Lakes.[389] The city of Monroe—one of the oldest settlements in the state, home to the Battle of Frenchtown during the War of 1812 and located forty-six miles south of Detroit on the western shore of Lake Erie—was no exception. The *Monroe Commercial* expressed the spirit of the community:

> *There is but one feeling, one sentiment, one voice; and that is, the administration must be sustained, the Stars and Stripes defended, and our government preserved. Howevermuch* [sic] *political opinions may have divided us there is no differences now. Our country sounds the bugle note of alarm, and the people respond as one man.*[390]

The firing on Fort Sumter came at the behest of Jefferson Davis. The former secretary of war and U.S. senator from Mississippi had been elected provisional president of the Confederate States of America by sweeping support and acclimation.[391] Fate would array Mississippians against boys from Monroe.

In response to the surrender of Fort Sumter, President Lincoln called for 75,000 militia to serve for three months, the maximum authorized by law. Michigan was to furnish one regiment of infantry fully armed and equipped.[392] After the Union defeat at the First Battle of Bull Run on July 21, 1861, a law of Congress of August 3 authorized an additional 500,000 volunteers for three years. Michigan's quota was 21,337. To a young state having entered the Union only twenty-four years earlier, and with a population of only 749,113 residents, this was a substantial number. With steady and vigorous recruiting throughout the state, Michigan would answer the country's call, filling regiment after regiment of citizen soldiers. By the close of 1861, Michigan had contributed 16,475 officers and men composing thirteen infantry regiments, three regiments of cavalry and five batteries of light artillery. Ten regiments, one battery and one company had been financed, uniformed and partially armed by the state. Michigan's total number of soldiers sent to the front lines by December eclipsed the prewar strength of the U.S. Regular Army.[393]

Michigan governor Austin Blair traveled from Lansing to Detroit, where he issued a proclamation in support of the president's call for troops and commitment of military aid in enforcing the laws and upholding the Constitution of the United States. The April 16 proclamation outlined Michigan's laws authorizing the raising of regiments for Federal service, the process of organization and deployment within the state and the structure and strength of command—especially with company officers and enlisted men—as well as noting that companies will "at once begin drilling according to 'Hardee's Tactics.'" It further explained that volunteers beyond what was immediately required will be formed into "additional regiments as the exigencies of the service may demand." Governor Blair's forecast of his state's response was expressed toward the closing of the proclamation:

> *It is confidently expected that the patriotic citizen soldiery of Michigan will promptly come forward to enlist in the cause of the Union, against which an extensive rebellion in arms exists, threatening the integrity and perpetuity of the government. The Adjutant General will issue and enforce the necessary orders to carry out the objects of this proclamation.*[394]

Monroe received word in the first week of August that the 7th Michigan Infantry Regiment was to rendezvous there for drill and military instruction.

Camp Monroe, as it was to be called, was the site of the old fairgrounds located north of Water (now Elm) Street. The camp took shape by adapting several various-sized buildings for use as regimental headquarters and the quartermaster department. Large tents were erected for a temporary kitchen and to house soldiers before more permanent structures—including ones for a hospital, dining hall and guardhouse—were built later that fall.[395] The decision that the city was chosen for such an encampment was fervently reported in the local newspaper:

> *The drill grounds have been selected, being the meadow fields on Water Street, on the farm occupied by David Eversol and that of T.G. Cole, adjoining, and containing together some forty to fifty acres. The grounds are beautifully level and unobstructive* [sic], *and will make the best drill grounds that could any where* [sic] *be found.*

The *Monroe Commercial* reported that the men were of excellent discipline and deportment when they were met on the streets of the town. Many of the soldiers in Company D were recruited from Monroe, and many lived in the neighborhood of Camp Monroe. Sergeant (later First Lieutenant) John A. Clark's house was about five hundred yards to the southwest. Clark was twenty years old.[396]

The community of Monroe was also pleased to learn that an esteemed local citizen, forty-four-year-old Ira Rufus Grosvenor, was to be colonel. Like many Monroe residents of that era, he came to Monroe as a young man in 1835 from New York with virtually only the clothing on his back and two dollars in his pocket. He worked as a clerk in the land office, where he quickly became head clerk. After two years with the land office, he spent the next four in study of the law and, upon acceptance to the bar, became a well-respected lawyer who developed a reputation as being a "fighter to the very end" and an "indefatigable worker in every campaign." In 1859, Colonel Grosvenor purchased a farm just north of the city. After the war, he named it Fair Oaks Farm because of its resemblance to the famous battlefield of the 1862 Peninsula Campaign in which he participated. During the antebellum years, Grosvenor had experience commanding a company and served as both a colonel and a brigadier general of the state militia. Grosvenor was commissioned colonel of the 7th Michigan on June 10, 1861.[397]

Frazey Marsh Winans of Monroe, forty-eight years of age, was commissioned lieutenant colonel. Winans brought regular army and wartime experience to the 7th. Commissioned Captain in the 15th U.S.

Infantry in April 1847, he was made brevet major on August 15 for gallant and meritorious conduct in several affairs with guerillas at Paso Ovejas, Nation Bridge and Cerro Gordo, Mexico. Major Winans resigned and was honorably discharged from service in May 1848. On June 19, 1861, he would once again enter in the service of his country, assisting Colonel Grosvenor in the leadership of the newly minted regiment.[398]

The 7th was composed of ten companies from across the state. U.S. Army Regulations outlined a company as having ninety-seven enlisted men and three officers. In April 1861, Governor Blair detailed the personnel make-up for each Michigan company as "one captain, one first lieutenant, one second lieutenant, four sergeants, four corporals, two musicians, and sixty-five privates."[399] Once a company was assembled, the unit would report to a designated location for the formation of the regiment—for the 7th, that would be the city of Monroe, where Company D was to be recruited. A recruiting office was established on Washington Street adjacent to the offices of the Wing and Johnson Bank. Three Monroe men—Captain James Darrah, First Lieutenant Sylvanias Curtis and Second Lieutenant Henry B. Landon—immediately set out to fill the company.[400]

The ten militia companies from across the state were each assigned an alphabetical designation in place of its local name: Company A, the "Union Guard" of Port Huron; Company B, the "Curtenius Guard" of Mason; Company C, the "Jonesville Light Guard" of Jonesville; Company D, the "Monroe Light Guard" of Monroe; Company E, the "Tuscola Volunteers" of Tuscola; Company F, the "Blair Guard" of Farmington; Company G, the "Lapeer Guards" of Lapeer; Company H (unnamed), from Pontiac; Company I, the "Prairieville Rangers" from Prairieville; and Company K, the "Burr Oak Rangers" from Burr Oak.[401] With the formation of the regiment at Camp Monroe complete, battalion drill was performed. After one particular dress parade, a special ceremony was conducted where twenty-one-year-old Second Lieutenant Landon presented Colonel Grosvenor with a magnificent sword on behalf of the regiment.[402]

On September 5, 1861, with a complement of 884 officers and enlisted men, the 7th Michigan left Monroe for Virginia.[403] The regiment was transported by railroad approximately twenty miles south to Toledo, Ohio, where it boarded two lake steamers, the *Ocean* and *May Queen*, for Cleveland. A delegation from Monroe led by Mayor Roderick O'Connor accompanied the men on this leg of the journey. The 7th's first casualty occurred when twenty-six-year-old Private William Thirds of Company K fell overboard and drowned. Upon the Michiganders' arrival, the *Cleveland Herald* printed "glowing praise of the appearance of the

Enlisting in Company C, 7th Michigan Infantry, Alonzo Smith of St. Joseph County was wounded during the Battle of Antietam. He would receive the Medal of Honor in December 1864 for capturing a Confederate battle flag. *Monroe County Historical Museum.*

Regiment." Transferring from the Cleveland and Pittsburg Railroad to the Pennsylvania Central Railroad, the 7th continued on to Washington, where it was assigned to Lander's Brigade of Stone's Division in the Army of the Potomac. On October 20, the 7th participated in the Battle of Ball's Bluff, serving in a supporting role "being detailed to guard the landing and man the boats." It was on the Upper Potomac that the 7th made winter camp and remained until the following spring.[404]

Within a month of arrival at the front and while camped near Leesburg, Virginia, Colonel Grosvenor purchased the regiment's United States flag, "a stand of silk regulations colors…one of the stripes was inscribed with the motto, 'Tuebor,'" Latin for "I will defend" (and motto on Michigan's flag). According to an account written nearly fifty years after the war, the 7th received another banner, probably a state regimental flag, around November 22. The memoir reads, "[W]e recieved [*sic*] a beautiful green silk battle flag, presented to us from the ladies of Monroe Michigan, which we carried on many battle fields for four long years."[405]

Like many communities both North and South, the citizens on the homefront in Monroe and throughout Michigan supported their soldiers on the front lines. Almost as soon as ranks of the early regiments filled, efforts commenced to support the men in uniform among those who could not serve directly. The women left behind waged their own form of warfare. Traditional gender roles changed as women assumed formerly male responsibilities. Concern for the soldiers from their community manifested itself by formation of ladies' aid associations devoted to supplying those needs not met by government sources. Initially, these local groups operated without a unified effort. By August 1863, the Soldiers' Aid Society of Detroit had become the Michigan Soldiers' Aid Society. As an authorized branch of the United States Sanitary Commission, the MSAS enlarged its influence and oversight to embrace the efforts of the entire state with the purpose to increase its contributions and effectiveness.[406]

Having had the regiment in their community during encampment and military instruction, Monroe's women felt a special affinity with the 7th, especially with Company D being raised among its own sons, brothers and fathers. Meeting every Tuesday evening, the Ladies Aid Society of Monroe worked diligently to bridge the gap between need and what the Federal government could provide. The *Monroe Commercial* proudly reported some of this group's efforts:

> *The Ladies Aid Society have been doing a large amount of work within the past ten days for the Seventh Regiment. The work completed and furnished to the Regiment for hospital use, up to the present time is as follows, 100 sheets, 115 pillow cases, 25 bed ticks, 3 dozen hospital shirts, 2 dozen hospital drawers, 6 dozen towels, one dozen long and 2 dozen hospital gowns, 120 bandages, 52 bags for hospital use, 12 packages of compresses, and two sacks of lint. They have also prepared as a donation to Company D (Captain Darrah's) 101 towels, and 101 housewives, and will also furnish a large additional number of housewives to others in the Regiment who have not been supplied.*[407]

Letters from enlisted men and officers alike were consistently sent home throughout the war soliciting such items of necessity and comfort. Many were directed to family members, while others were sent to and published by their community's newspaper. Often, tender letters of gratitude and appreciation from the recipients of these offerings were sent home. Once such letter to the Ladies Aid Society was published not long after a shipment of supplies reached the 7th: "To the Ladies of Monroe, I feel personally under many obligations for their untiring efforts to render comfort to my company, and many, many times will my noble boys bless them with a grateful heart."[408] The correspondence came from forty-four-year-old Monroe native Captain James Darrah. In one of the many ironic tragedies of the Civil War, he would die of disease at Fort Monroe, Virginia, on April 17, 1862.[409] He was not the first: a letter written by regimental Chaplain A.K. Strong to the *Commercial* reported earlier that winter that ten men had succumbed to disease. Most were buried at a small cemetery near the regiment's camp that was "situated in a pleasant grove and fenced in by a neat rustic fence."[410]

From breaking winter camp in the spring until the end of August, the regiment recorded forty-six killed and mortally wounded, with many times more that number wounded.[411] The death toll from disease and illness, primarily typhoid and malaria fever, further reduced the ranks of the regiment. Many soldiers fell ill during the spring and summer campaigns, having languished in the heat and humidity of the low, swampy regions on the James Peninsula enduring hardships not previously experienced. Colonel Grosvenor suffered an attack of cholera morbus, followed by a bout with scurvy. Although at times barely able to stay mounted on his horse, Grosvenor led the 7th through actions at Peach Orchard, Savage Station, White Oak Swamp, Glendale and Malvern Hill.[412] Exposure in his weakened condition took its toll. An examining surgeon informed the colonel that he "must make a speedy choice between a change of climate and a coffin."[413] Upon the surgeon's advice, Grosvenor applied for a temporary leave of absence to recuperate. The furlough request, apparently received by recently appointed general-in-chief Henry Halleck, was denied. Saddened but with little recourse, Grosvenor resigned as colonel and was honorably discharged with a surgeon's certificate on July 7, 1862.[414]

The loss of its colonel was yet another blow to the regiment. Typical of many regiments both North and South, great respect and admiration existed between officers and enlisted men due to their shared experience of martial combat. This *esprit* was especially prevalent in the early war units, where the military leadership of the unit was maintained by men who were familiar, respected and esteemed in civilian life within their local community. The correspondent of the *Monroe Commercial* expressed this feeling within the 7th over the resignation of Colonel Grosvenor:

> *Breaking his connection with his regiment alike painful to Col. G. and the regiment. The strong affection between them was mutual. He loved the regiment, and the officers and men loved him. I daily see wounded soldiers belonging to the regiment, who speak of the Colonel as they would of a father. They say he has ever been as a father to them, while the officers have complemented him with written testimonials of their high appreciation of him as an officer and as a man.*[415]

His resignation came only after he and his regiment received their baptism by fire in the Peninsula Campaign. From Yorktown in April through the

Seven Days Battles from June 25 to July 1, soldiers of the 7th died in combat. Recalling the horrors of the June 30 fight at White Oak Swamp, Private Frederick W. Oesterle of Company E wrote:

> *This was a very hot day and water was very scarce, and the sufferings that our wounded had to undergo was something terrible. Our lips were blistered from the heat and from the want of water. As soon as a man was killed he would turn as black as a Negro, and if possible some man would go and see if there was any water in his canteen and minister to some wounded comrade. The shrieks of those wounded men and their cries for water one will never forget.*[416]

When the Army of the Potomac returned to the defenses around Washington, the 7th Michigan was assigned to cover the retreat of Pope's Army of Virginia after the Battle of Second Bull Run.[417] By then, the men of the 7th had a new leader. He, too, was from Monroe County. On July 14, 1862, twenty-five-year-old Lieutenant Norman Jonathan Hall assumed command of the regiment "on the march near Fair Fax [*sic*] Virginia Court House," this being "in compliance with special orders No. 95 HQ Sedgwick Div. July 1862."[418] McClellan had authority to assign Lieutenant Hall to this post, but Governor Blair had to confirm the appointment since it was a state regiment. From his headquarters at Harrison's Landing, Virginia, Brigadier General John Sedgwick sent Governor Blair the following letter on July 12, 1862:

> *Hon. Austin Blair*
> *Gov. State of Michigan*
> *Yr. Excellency—*
> *I have the honor again to address you on the subject of the Colonelcy of the 7th Michigan Regiment. Genl. McClellan has appointed Lieut. N.J. Hall, 5th Regular Artillery, Acting Colonel of his Regiment, until your Excellency's pleasure concerning the appointment can be known. I earnestly request that you may see fit to commission this officer accordingly. I know him and can give you my cordial assurance that the Regiment will be under good and competent leadership, if the Colonelcy be given to this officer. Trusting that you may give this matter your favorable consideration.*
> *I am with high respect*
> *Yr. Excellency's mo. obt. svt.*
> *John Sedgwick*
> *Brig. Gen. Vols.*
> *Comm. of Division*[419]

The governor and Michigan adjutant general John Robertson officially signed Hall's commission as colonel of the 7th on November 6, 1862. The commission read, "Know Ye, that reposing special trust and confidence in the Patriotism, Valor, Ability and Fidelity of Norman J. Hall in the name and by the authority of the People of the State Of Michigan, I do hereby appoint him Colonel in the Seventh Regiment Michigan Infantry Volunteers to rank as such from the seventh day of July 1862."[420]

Norman J. Hall was born in New York State on March 4, 1837. While still a young lad, he moved with his family to a farm located on the south bank of the River Raisin in East Raisinville, about six miles west of Monroe. Hall received an appointment to the U.S. Military Academy in 1854. Jefferson Davis, secretary of war under President Franklin Pierce, signed Hall's admission papers. Graduating in July 1859, Hall ranked thirteenth out of twenty-two, made second lieutenant and was assigned to the 4th United States Artillery. He served in the garrison at Fort Monroe, Virginia, until being sent to Fort Moultrie, South Carolina, on September 1, 1860, as post adjutant; there he performed duties of assistant quartermaster and commissary of subsistence. With Lincoln's election and South Carolina passing an ordinance of secession on December 20, the Federal garrison under the command of Major Robert Anderson moved to Fort Sumter in Charleston Harbor the day after Christmas.[421]

Lieutenant Norman Jonathan Hall saw action at Fort Sumter before becoming colonel of the 7th Michigan Infantry on July 7, 1862. *David D. Finney.*

Hall served as an emissary to South Carolina's governor during the Fort Sumter crisis. He accompanied a Confederate commissioner to Washington, D.C., in February–March 1861, returning when the Lincoln administration refused to communicate directly with the "'so called' Confederate Government." Hall's next notoriety came during the April 14 bombardment, when the fort's central flagstaff was severed near the top. The U.S. colors fell to the parade ground, landing among the embers and fire of burning structures. Hall darted out across the parade ground, exposed to enemy fire, in order to rescue the fallen colors. Together with another soldier, they attached the flag to a spar and raised it "triumphantly by nailing and tying the pole firmly to a pile of gun-carriages on the parapet." Anderson would write of the courage of Lieutenant Hall, "to whom I was greatly indebted."[422]

Little over sixteen months later, on September 4, 1862, the 7th Michigan was in pursuit of the Army of Northern Virginia in Maryland. By September 14, the 7th was brigaded with the 19th and 20th Massachusetts and the 42nd and 59th New York infantry regiments, composing the 3rd Brigade (Brigadier General Napoleon J.T. Dana commanding) of the 2nd Division (Major General Sedgwick commanding) of the II Corps.[423] On the fifteenth, the 7th marched with II Corps west from Middletown on the National Road and through the battlefield of Turner's Gap to Boonsboro. The columns turned left near the center of Boonsboro and proceeded southwest toward Keedysville and Sharpsburg beyond. McClellan ordered the several corps to converge and mass before Sharpsburg; bivouacs for the different corps were established on both sides of the Sharpsburg Turnpike. The men of the 7th Michigan hunkered down along with the rest of Sedgwick's Division north of the pike behind Richardson's Division of II Corps. Their bivouac was on the Philip and Elizabeth Pry property. With more than five thousand men camped in and around the farm, its livestock, food stores, harvested crops and more were soon used up. Speaking of the Federal troops, one area resident said, "Locusts which settled down in clouds upon the land of Egypt could not have made things disappear before them as these soldiers did." Fencing, a readily available and cured fuel source, was especially vulnerable and was "swept away from the farm as if by conflagration." The men undoubtedly used the farm's fence rails to boil coffee and cook their rations.[424]

On the sixteenth, II Corps was held in readiness to march. Sumner asked for permission to follow Mansfield and the XII Corps, but McClellan refused. Sumner acknowledged he "had no authority to move till ordered to do so, and was given to understand that he would not receive such orders till next morning." Anxious about not accompanying Mansfield's troops, Sumner anticipated the need to have troops west of Antietam Creek at first light and sent five of his artillery batteries to bivouac with XII Corps.[425] Even the common private of the Army of Potomac sensed that the armies were jockeying for position, whether offensively or defensively, on the two days after South Mountain. Private Oesterle astutely, if not articulately, later wrote of the situation, "The 15 and 16 of Sept. were spent in maneuvering for positions for the coming battle. Gen. Lee was brought to a standstill, the whole of the army [*sic*] of the Potomac was now confronting him and every soldier of the army knew that a big fight would be on, and we were not disappointed."[426]

William W. Wade would eventually serve as regimental quartermaster, but at Antietam, he was first lieutenant of Company C, 7th Michigan Infantry. *Monroe County Historical Museum.*

The night of September 16 and early morning of the seventeenth was dark and disorienting. One soldier recalled the night being "so dark that you could make a hole in the darkness with your finger."[427] The men, some very close to the enemy, sought what shelter they could from the drizzling rain that started to fall. This night, there would be no fires to cook rations or boil coffee. The rain produced an eerie silence that was punctured by sporadic gunfire by nervous pickets and sentries. The futility of firing into the darkness at an enemy you could not see quelled each of these small firefights until the next round of anxious troops started the routine again.[428] The veterans of the 7th Michigan anticipated that a great battle was imminent. That night, Oesterle recalled, "we received 40 rounds of cartridges in our boxes and 30 additional rounds in our haversack. Many goodbyes were said and letters were sent home to dear ones. Prayer meetings were held throughout the army."[429] Thirty-year-old Lieutenant Samuel C. Hodgman of Climax[430] wrote home:

Made first lieutenant just fifteen days before Antietam, Samuel C. Hodgman of Company I, 7th Michigan Infantry, was wounded during the battle. *Monroe County Historical Museum.*

None of us feel fainthearted yet. The nearer the prospect of danger the less I seem to dread it. I know not how it will be when I come to stand face to face with it. When it is the will of God that I shall do so, I shall try and do my duty like a man, let the consequences be what they may.[431]

With no movement expected until daylight, Sumner allowed the II Corps men to sleep, if possible given the circumstance, until 2:00 a.m. The soldiers made breakfast, secured their arms and equipment and readied themselves. At approximately 5:30 a.m., first light was announced with the sound of skirmish firing from I Corps on the right. By sunrise at 5:45 a.m., the I Corps was fully engaged, followed in quick succession by XII Corps.[432] The moment finally arrived for Sedgwick's Division; Sumner received the order to march at 7:20 a.m. Although General Greene's Division of XII Corps had a temporary but precarious foothold near the Dunker Church and West Woods, reinforcements were called up. A few regiments of infantry and a battery were initially deployed, but it would take several brigades, if not divisions, to adequately maintain the ground taken. Sumner was directed to advance Sedgwick's Division, followed by French's, with Richardson's to move an hour later.[433]

Crossing Antietam Creek via the fords just south of the Upper Bridge, Sedgwick's Division advanced westerly in three columns over the William Roulette and Samuel Mumma farms, clearing fence lines as they proceeded. At about 9:00 a.m. near the Mumma house and barn (aflame from an earlier torching), Sumner deployed Sedgwick's Division in columns of brigades. Three parallel lines faced southwest, with Brigadier General Willis A. Gorman's Brigade first, Brigadier General Dana's Brigade second and Brigadier General Oliver O. Howard's Brigade third. The 7th Michigan

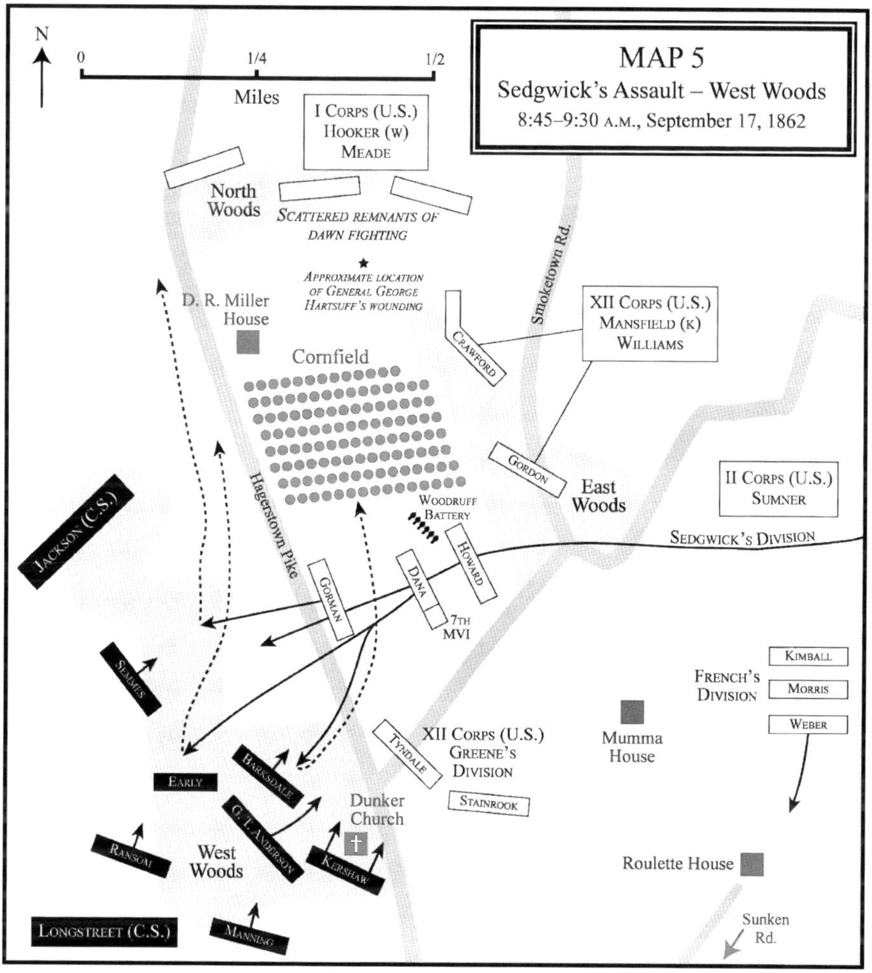

MAP 5. Sedgwick's Assault. Artillery not shown.

formed on the left flank of Dana's Brigade. Whether Sumner felt this deployment would allow him to bring each brigade to bear on the flank of each successive brigade or that his old-school "stand up and slug it" direct frontal assault would carry the day, we may never truly know. What history would reveal is that this deployment would prove disastrous.[434]

Sedgwick's Division entered the East Woods, crossed the Smoketown Road, and marched into the open fields where the earlier fighting had raged so fiercely. Gorman's Brigade emerged from the East Woods, establishing the line of battle. As it moved toward the Hagerstown Pike, it sustained casualties from concealed Confederate batteries beyond the road. The field before the brigade was strewn with the dead and wounded, displaced soldiers from various units and carnage of unrivaled description.[435] It moved across the Miller Farm pasture, and Sumner was seen on the right leading the brigade forward. Gibbon, near the southeast corner of the Miller Cornfield with the scattered remnants of his brigade, overheard Sumner call out excitedly, "Where is my second line?" Gibbon rode up and offered his assistance in executing the corps commander's orders. Sumner replied, "I will be very much obliged to you, General, if you will see my chief of artillery and pick out some positions for my batteries." Gibbon galloped away and eventually placed a battery on a rise adjacent to the Smoketown Road.[436]

Gorman's Brigade pressed onward across the field littered with enemy dead and wounded. Exposed to enemy artillery fire, the brigade "passed over it at a rapid charge," crossed the Hagerstown Pike and charged into the West Woods. The Hagerstown Pike was lined on both sides along this stretch with sturdy post and rail fences, but this did not inhibit the advance as the men quickly crossed. Once over the second fence, heavy lines of Confederate infantry were spotted in the open woodlot in front of them. The momentum of the Federals swept the front of the Confederate line, which "retired in considerable disorder." Within moments, the whole front "became hotly engaged, giving and receiving the most deadly fire it has ever been my lot to witness," reported Gorman. The advancing Federal infantrymen were checked in place by opposing artillery fire and remnants of Confederate general Jones' Division.[437]

The 7th Michigan and Dana's Brigade had been directed to keep pace behind Gorman's line by seventy-five yards and Howard's that distance behind Dana. However, the intervals were lost in the advance through the East Woods, and Gorman's Brigade outpaced Dana's by a considerable margin. As his line emerged from the East Woods, Dana saw a line of troops lying on the ground in the open field before him. Assuming this was Gorman's Brigade and that he should do likewise, he halted the brigade and ordered the men to lie down. No sooner had the men done so than the order was countermanded with a directive to Dana to "move forward at double quick and enter the [West] woods."[438]

This was a critical point in the course of this phase of the battle. Had Dana's Brigade, and ultimately Howard's behind, remained a distance back, Sumner could have directed the bulk of Sedgwick's Division to the flanks or to plug any breakthrough of Gorman's Brigade. The distance between the West and East Woods would have given ample opportunity to assess the unfolding situation and deploy accordingly. Furthermore, the high ridge at

Artillery Hell (Sedgwick's Assault), the painting by observer Vermont captain James Hope, does not represent a single moment in time but rather a series of events. *National Park Service, Antietam National Battlefield.*

the summit of the slope rising from Antietam Creek, which runs somewhat parallel to the Hagerstown Pike, creates a visual barrier between the two areas of that section of the battlefield. Thus, once Sedgwick's Division was on the westward side of the ridge, ultimately, it was completely out of sight from the rest of II Corps. This ridge, literally and metaphorically, cleaves the traditionally accepted first and second phases of the battle.[439]

Although Sumner would be heavily criticized afterward for the manner in which he deployed Sedgwick's Division in column of brigades, not all general officers in the vicinity thought it so far out of the ordinary or a recipe for disaster. Gibbon, a West Point graduate, wrote, "When I saw Sedgwick's Division going into action in such splendid style I felt that was destined to carry everything before it." In testimony before the Joint Committee on the Conduct of the War months after the battle, Sumner removed himself as the culprit for the disaster during this phase of the battle. Instead, he blamed McClellan for committing the army piecemeal rather than in force, which Sumner was confident would have collapsed the Confederate left and ultimately defeated Lee's army.[440]

The 7th Michigan had been ordered to advance at the double-quick over the David Miller farm. The men were impeded by the number of fallen soldiers from the earlier fight; that section had exchanged hands at least six times.[441] Private Oesterle recalled:

> *Part of our corps had been driven back from distance and the second division to which our brigade belonged was hurried up to check the enemy, which we did at a fearful cost. It was almost impossible to advance, the ground was covered so thick with dead and dying men of both sides, as the field had been fought over twice previous to our advance.*[442]

While convalescing from his wounds two months after the battle, Sergeant Hodgman recalled the terrible destruction the men of the 7th endured during the advance:

> *The bursting shells were the most terrible and grand part of the scene. Before we got into the fight I saw a battery in front & to the right of us throwing shell at our advancing lines about sixty or seventy rods to our right. The first shell struck among a group of ambulances knocking one or two of them to atoms and causing the rest to move to the rear double quick. The troops were advancing in two lines about ten or twelve rods apart. The next shell exploded directly in front of the first line at not more than six or seven feet from the ground and perhaps 20 or 30 feet in front of the line. The third exploded directly in the second line about breast high. In both cases the lines never wavered for an instant but pressed on regardless of the storm of iron and lead which soon began to tell so fatally on their ranks.*[443]

George W. LaPointe, Company D, 7th Michigan Infantry, was commissioned second lieutenant on September 18, making colonel by war's end. *Monroe County Historical Museum.*

Advancing up the slight incline, the brigade crossed over the Hagerstown Pike and entered the West Woods. Dana described this point of the assault: "The outline of the woods was irregular, presenting a salient point where the left of my line first entered." The leftmost regiment, the 7th Michigan, was the first of the brigade to enter the West Woods at this salient. With Gorman's Brigade "hotly engaged in front," a Confederate counterattack emanating around the Dunker Church had "succeeded in crowding back the troops of Gen. Greene's division." Without the support of Greene's Division on the left, Sedgwick's column of brigades was now exposed

James McPherson of Fentonville was second lieutenant of Company F, 7th Michigan Infantry, at Antietam. *Monroe County Historical Museum.*

on the flank and rear. Anderson's and Kershaw's Brigades of Longstreet's Corps and Early's Brigade of Jackson's Corps pressed the Confederate advantage, causing great alarm among the troops in Dana's and Howard's left.[144]

In spite of the situation to their left, Dana's Brigade pushed forward with Howard's Brigade, now also over the turnpike and into the West Woods, at the specified interval between sixty to seventy-five yards. Just moments after the 7th Michigan entered the woods, a Confederate line of battle, nearly perpendicular to the regiment, opened a devastating fire to the front and left flank of Dana's Brigade. The Michigan men were at the mercy of Mississippians from Barksdale's Brigade. Seeing the threat developing on the left, Sumner sent word to Howard to change front to the south to check the enemy advance. Unable to effectively return fire due to the column of brigade deployment, Howard's Brigade crumbled and gave way to the right and rear under the withering fire.[145]

Deeper in the West Woods, Dana addressed the dire situation. Barksdale's Brigade was on his front and left flank. A retreating Union regiment passed through the Michiganders' lines; once unimpeded, the 7th commenced firing at the left oblique. Without waiting for orders, Dana ordered the 42nd New York and 7th Michigan "to change front to the left and meet the attack which had apparently broken through the first line on my left and front, and was now precipitated with fury on my left flank." Private Hodgman described the devastating situation now faced by the 7th:

> *It was perfectly awful where we were. Infantry in front and in flank. Artillery in flank and in front all pouring in upon us a terrible storm of iron and lead. It seemed almost a miracle that any escaped. I did not feel in the least degree any desire to get out of the way until after I was wounded. I then had to turn my back to the enemy and was not very ambitious to see how long I could stay amongst the balls. They were flying all around each side, over, in front, and behind me and like plums in a pudding the shells were bursting in every direction, still there seemed to be a clear spot for me to escape in as though it was specially ordered for my benefit. I could not help admiring the scene terrible as it was and full of danger at every step.*[446]

While the 42nd New York maneuvered as instructed, the Mississippians closed up. Dana reported that "the fire poured upon it and the Seventh Michigan was the most terrific I ever witnessed." The 7th Michigan attempted to make a second stand, but Barksdale's men, "after firing several volleys into their ranks, drove them through the woods and into an open field beyond." Caught in terrible crossfire, the two regiments began to retreat in disorder. Dana stayed with the New Yorkers and Michiganders in an effort to stem the tide of Confederates cascading through the West Woods. He then accompanied them back across the turnpike and into the open fields over which they had advanced less than an hour earlier. Dana defended the retreat in his after-action report: "I bear them witness that it was after nearly half the officers and men were placed *hors de combat.*" Still in danger close to the pike, Dana ordered the brigade, or what was left of it, to re-form about 350 yards northeast of the West Woods.[447]

Private Roland E. Bowen of the 15th Massachusetts Infantry in Gorman's Brigade described the panic and chaos that all the Federal soldiers realized as Sedgwick's Division began to crumble: "I heard a voice in the rear crying out 'Fall Back.' I turned around and said, what does that mean, ain't [*sic*] the rebs falling back themselves. But again, the cry 'Fall Back.' Now someone yelled out, 'we are flanked, the rebels are in our rear.' I looked and Ah, it was true." As the flank of all three brigades, unable to support one another, began to dissolve, officers struggled to keep their men on line and in order. Bowen continued, "In a moment all was confusion, it was every man for himself. We all run like a flock of sheep." An anonymous soldier in Dana's Brigade detailed the precarious nature of the three brigades stacked up so closely together in the West Woods: "One single shot of an Enfield or Springfield rifle could hit a man in the front rank of the first brigade and go through to the rear rank of the last brigade."[448]

Taking advantage of the rock ledges and outcroppings on the western edge of the West Woods, Semmes's Confederate brigade pulverized Gorman's front and drove that lead element back and to the north. The unrelenting and withering fire from the enemy to the front and now steadily on their flank and rear inflicted severe casualties unlike anything in the II Corps' experience. A Massachusetts officer metaphorically recalled his men being mowed down "like grass before the scythe." Private Bowen, now swept up in the retreat, wrote, "No God D--- Southerner is a going to catch me unless he can run 29 miles an hour. That's my gate [*sic*]." As was the case earlier in the battle, Confederate soldiers seemed to rise out of the ground and appear everywhere.[449]

Captain James H. Turrill of Lapeer was killed at Antietam while leading Company G, 7th Michigan Infantry. *Michael Hogel.*

Having attempted to make a stand along the turnpike with the 7th, Colonel Hall saw Dana riding slowly to the rear. In a moment, a staff officer galloped up to inform him that Dana was wounded and "that I [Hall] should take command of the brigade." Not until later did Hall understand that Dana intended for him to take command of "this wing of the brigade" and "to reform the two broken regiments and assume command of them until he rejoined the brigade." Howard, who would take over command of the division, also believed that Hall was now in command of the brigade.[450]

Hall emerged unscathed from the West Woods. For others in the 7th Michigan, the intensity of enemy fire was so severe that a number were struck multiple times. Oesterle described several near-misses: "I had the button of my cap shot off, one ball went through my blouse pocket and tore my dictionary to pieces, another cut my leg just over the knee and another crazed [*sic*] my right arm." Twenty-five-year-old First Lieutenant Robert C. Knaggs was one of many so wounded. A *Detroit Free Press* correspondent wrote of the regiment's valor, calling out Lieutenant Knaggs specifically:

> *The behavior of officers and men was, without exception, magnificent. Three color-bearers in quick succession were shot down, when acting Adjutant Robert C. Knaggs sprang from his horse, seized the colors, and waved them triumphantly in face of the enemy, receiving almost instantly two bullet wounds, fortunately neither of them severe.*[451]

The situation of the 42nd New York was not triumphant. The regiment essentially dissolved, and its colors were carried to the rear. Hall rallied the 7th Michigan and focused on yet another stand near the edge of the East Woods. Searching for regiments to assist in stemming a Confederate advance, Hall found troops "in line of battle about 150 yards in rear of the edge of woods, under command of Brigadier-General Gibbon." The 7th re-formed inside the East Woods. It moved back to the western edge once Hall received instructions to form there along with the bulk of the division. In the process of this movement, Hall met Colonel William R. Lee of the 20th Massachusetts Infantry. He stated that, as senior colonel, Lee was now in command of the brigade. However, Colonel Lee "positively declined to relieve me, and repeatedly desired me to give such orders as I saw fit, and he would obey them." Learning that Howard was now in command of the division after Sedgwick had left the field wounded, Hall reported as temporary brigade commander to the temporary division commander.[452]

The 7th took additional casualties south of the Miller Cornfield as it attempted to rally in the field north of the Smoketown Road and east of the turnpike.

Howard had the unenviable task of picking up the pieces of the shattered and dispersed division after Sedgwick's wounding. The division commander had experienced a horse shot out from under him and was wounded three times before being taken from the battlefield unconscious.[453] Howard praised the "officers of every grade in this division in rallying and reorganizing their commands, all having suffered more or less confusion in the change

Right: Norman Jonathan Hall of Raisinville, colonel of the 7th Michigan Infantry at Antietam. *Archives of Michigan.*

Below: Southern portion of the D.R. Miller farm, where Sedgwick's Division attacked in column of brigades from right to left. Alexander Gardner photo. *Library of Congress.*

of position."[454] Sumner ordered several regiments sent to support Federal batteries that were holding back potential Confederate assaults in the face of enemy artillery to the front and right.

The opening phase of the battle was now subsiding. Men of the 7th, like the other units decimated this morning, searched for their comrades, cared for the wounded, resupplied as possible and tried to form a semblance of their former regiment. With the exception of occasional artillery or musket firing, this portion of the field was now very quiet.

Samuel Hodgman attempted to communicate the carnage of the battle to his father: "I suppose that there never has been, in any battle ever yet fought more terrible fighting, and in pro-portion to the number engaged more slaughter than in the battle of Antietam[.] None avoided the contest all fought like heroes, both union & rebel." Having survived the battle and the war, Frederick Oesterle wrote years later:

> *My company went into this fight with 36 men and in thirty minutes we only rallied 15. The regiment took into this action 636 men and in one hour afterwards we could not muster 140. We lost 6 captains, 2 lieutenants, and our company lost every non-commissioned officer but one. Our brigade was again driven back over the same ground, only to swell the list of the slain. This was the key of the position of the battle of Antietam, consequently the heaviest firing concentrated here.*[455]

The tragedy of Company K's Captain Allen H. Zacharias, all of twenty-eight, is full of poignant irony. Born in Clear Spring, Washington County, Maryland, he relocated to Michigan at a very young age. He graduated from the University of Michigan in June 1860 and became a professor and principal of the State Military Institute in Brandon, Mississippi. On September 17, Captain Zacharias was wounded in the county where he was born by soldiers from the state where he had been an instructor and administrator. Found on the field near the Hagerstown Pike, he held in his hand an envelope on which he had written to family back in Michigan:

> *To Peter K. Zacharias, Monroe, Michigan: Dear Parent, Brothers and Sisters,—I am wounded mortally, I think. The fight rages around me. I have done my duty; this my consolation. I hope to meet you all again. I left the line until nearly all had fallen and colors gone. I am getting weak; my arms are free, but below my chest all is numb. The enemy trotting over me, the numbness up to my heart. Good-bye all. Your son, Allen*

Twenty-one-year-old Tower S. Benham of Company K, 7th Michigan Infantry, was wounded on September 17 but survived to become major by November 1864. *Monroe County Historical Museum.*

He would succumb to his wound on the final day of the year.[456]

The shockwave of grief reverberated home in the form of personal correspondence and, more immediately, newspaper accounts. The anxiety and uncertainty over the fate of a family member on the front lines could be intensified by such articles. The *Monroe Monitor* reported in its October 1, 1862 edition the following:

> *This Regiment* [7th] *suffered severely in the recent fighting in Maryland. It is said that about half of the 500 engaged are killed, wounded or missing. Among the killed are Lieut. John A. Clark, son of Thos. Clark of this city, and probably Capt. Zacharias, son of P.C.* [sic] *Zacharias, esq. of Ida. Lieut. Col. Baxter, of Jonesville, well known to many of our Monroe people, is among those severely wounded.*[457]

The *Free Press* correspondent reported on the fate of Zacharias:

> *Capt. Zacharias of the Seventh Regiment—it is supposed that Capt. Zacharias was mortally wounded in the Maryland Battles. His father is residing in Ida in this county* [Monroe] *has received a letter in which was enclosed an envelope written in his hand writing, his last words. The letter was found by a Main* [sic] *soldier. Capt. Z. enlisted in the 7th Regiment we believe as a corporal, and by his good behavior promoted until he became a Captain of Co. K. His numerous friends in Monroe county* [sic] *will mourn his death as a loss to the army and to our community.*

The same writer also reported, "Lieutenant John A. Clark, of Monroe, a gallant and worthy young officer, was shot through the head and instantly killed."[458] Other accounts tell of the regiment's sacrifice at Antietam: "The 7th Regiment, whose ranks were seriously thinned out on the Peninsula, is now left with a bare handful of men—less than one hundred and fifty fit for duty. Listed among the dead are Captain J.H. Turrill, Lieutenant J.P. Eberhard, Lt. John A. Clark and Captain Allen Zacharias, a Monroe native."[459]

For his actions at Antietam, Hall would receive a brevet captaincy in the U.S. Regulars for "gallant and meritorious service." Howard made special mention of Hall, among a few other officers, for successfully "drawing off their regiments without breaking." The survivors of the 7th Michigan, though punished and driven from the field, remained relatively intact.[460]

After enthusiastically leading Sedgwick's Division into action, by that Wednesday evening Sumner was deflated and somber. McClellan sent a staff member to Sumner for a status report on the condition of II Corps. He merely responded, "Go back, young man, and tell General McClellan I have no command." Sumner's after-action report was relatively short and lacking in detail, revealing his melancholy: "I regret to report that the loss in my corps was very heavy, which is to be accounted for by the long and furious contest that my divisions had to maintain in the center against the most determined efforts of the enemy." McClellan registered the corps commander's moroseness by writing, "Gen. Sumner expressed the most decided opinion against another attempt during that day to assault the enemy's position in front, as portions of our troops were so much scattered and demoralized."[461]

The II Corps sustained the highest casualties of any Federal corps that day. Of the 15,000 effectives present for duty, 5,138 became casualties. Nearly half of these casualties, totaling 2,183, were in Sedgwick's Division. Of the three brigades in the division, Dana's suffered the highest loss of

William Asher Churchill, sergeant major of the 7th Michigan Infantry, was killed in action on September 17, 1862. *Monroe County Historical Museum.*

Martha Archer Fleet was recognized by the 7th Michigan Infantry Association for her indefatigable service in erecting a memorial tablet after the war to the regiment in Dundee, Michigan. *Monroe County Historical Museum.*

any brigade in the Army of the Potomac, recording 369 killed, 652 wounded and 104 captured or missing. The 7th Michigan went into battle that morning with approximately 636 men. Within an hour, the regiment could account for only 140 men. As displaced soldiers eventually found their way back to the unit, a final count of losses was made. In just a few hours, it lost more than one-third of its strength, reporting 39 killed, 178 wounded and 4 captured or missing, totaling 221. It suffered the highest losses of its brigade.[462]

Little did the 7th Michigan recruits anticipate, as they trained on the beautifully level meadow fields of Monroe, what was to come at Antietam. Just over a year later, they marched over the rolling fields and into the woodlot known as the West Woods beyond the farms of David R. Miller and Samuel Mumma. On this land along Antietam Creek, more men of the regiment were killed or mortally wounded than in any other battle during their service.[463]

The most eloquent testimony to the men who sacrificed so dearly on the fields of Antietam can be the closing words of Howard's after-action report: "The above list stands for itself a record of almost unparalleled loss during a single battle. They have poured out their blood like water, and we must look to God and our country for a just reward."[464]

Chapter 7

AT THE BLOODY LANE

Richardson's Breakthrough

After the first two divisions of II Corps went into action, one remained: the 1st Division commanded by Israel Richardson. It was composed of three brigades and numbered about 4,300 soldiers.[465] The men were awakened at 2:00 a.m. to prepare for the day's events.[466] They had to wait hours before seeing action this Wednesday, but when the division moved out, it was because its presence "was sorely needed."[467]

Corps commander Sumner had received McClellan's order at 7:20 a.m. to move out. His first two divisions marched almost immediately, but the 1st Division had to wait until an hour later because of the prerequisite that its place be taken by a division of Fitz John Porter's V Corps.[468] McClellan wanted his center in solid shape before allowing Richardson to leave. By the time he released the division, the situation it headed toward "was becoming exceedingly desperate."[469]

The Michigander personally[470] led the men east on the Keedysville Road and filed to the left. At 9:30 a.m., they crossed Antietam Creek at the same ford, Pry's, as their predecessors.[471] The general sat uncomfortably on his horse, all the while urging the soldiers to keep together as they splashed into the stream.[472] He told an officer, "No straggling today, Colonel! Keep your men well up and in hand."[473] After a pause to allow them "to wring the water from their socks,"[474] the men climbed the muddy slope and reached high ground. Richardson could hear the sounds of battle emanating to his southwest.[475] He had no specific orders from either the army or corps commander, no courier or officer appeared to provide directions, and he had to employ his

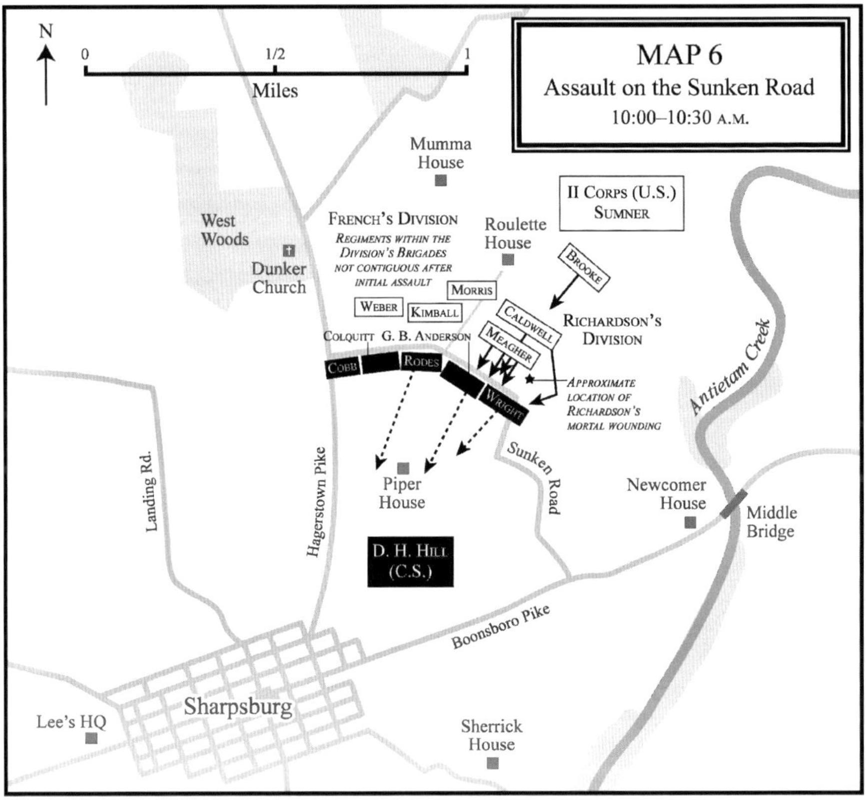

MAP 6. Assault on the Sunken Road.

own judgment.[476] Deciding to head in the direction of the noise, he marched the division south in parallel to the creek near the Henry Neikirk farmhouse. Halting in a nearby ravine, the men piled knapsacks and blankets and formed their regimental lines east of the William and Margaret Roulette house. To the southwest lay the wagon path nicknamed "Sunken Road."[477]

Anticipating that the Federal army's approach would be from the east, the Confederate center formed in line of battle on a ridge at the easternmost part of the Sunken Road where it turns sharply to the south. Upon hearing the early morning fighting and learning that at least two Federal corps were positioned to the north, the Confederates redeployed to face in that direction, taking advantage of the ready-made ditch for protection. They removed the rail fencing on the southern side of the road and built up the north edge as additional defensive protection. The Union infantry would confront Alabama, Georgia and North Carolina troops under D.H. Hill.

The Confederate contingent comprised the brigades of Robert Rodes, George B. Anderson, Alfred Colquitt, Howell Cobb and Samuel Garland—several thousand "first-class troops" who were "well led."[478]

Richardson led the men forward "at a rapid pace," rushing them "hastily" forward "under cover of the rising ground and depressions which intervened" between the division and the enemy.[479] He had the soldiers' "confidence and affection, and they willingly followed him" into conflict.[480] Once the lines were dressed and bayonets affixed, Richardson gave them a final encouragement: "Men, follow me and where I will not go I will not ask you to go."[481] They saw "his countenance is stern, and when he gives an order, he means it; but, he is a man, every inch of him. He never puts on any extra airs or style but delights to be around his men in citizen's dress."[482] With their leader at the front, the division marched into combat.

The 1st Division went into action on the heels of the "disaster" that had befallen the rest of the corps. Sumner had placed himself with the lead division, John Sedgwick's. He then ordered the 2nd Division under William French to come to the aid of the 1st. By the time Richardson's reached the Roulette farm, French's Division had "launched a series of frontal assaults against the Sunken Road that were handily and bloodily repulsed." From the Pry home, McClellan watched as the day went from promising to "an exceedingly anxious time."[483] He had ordered IX Corps under Burnside to attack on the Federal left in order to assist the right, but no progress was being reported. As he observed the battle, the commander of the Army of the Potomac could only wonder whether the next development would mean triumph or defeat.

At about 11:00 a.m., Richardson's was the only fresh Union division near the undented enemy center.[484] He placed the 2nd ("Irish") Brigade on the right, the 1st Brigade on the left slightly behind and the 3rd Brigade in rear of the 2nd. His men were about eight hundred yards north of the Sunken Road, arranged in line of battle largely parallel to the lane.[485] The Irish Brigade, commanded by Brigadier General Thomas Meagher, confronted rising ground that culminated in a ridge overlooking the road, after which it sloped for an additional fifty to seventy-five yards. Samuel Mumma's cornfield covered the first one-third of the distance, and then came a pasture with a plowed field to its east before reaching the ridge. Three split-rail fences impeded the route. "All final preparations having been made," Richardson ordered the two lead brigades to advance toward the ridge.[486]

Moving through a cornfield and into the pasture subjected the Irish Brigade to artillery fire, with losses mounting. As they neared the ridgeline, they fired several volleys and forced Confederate skirmishers to retreat to the safety of the Sunken Road. At the summit, silhouetted against the sky, the brigade took heavy casualties but also inflicted a number. Losses became so severe and its ammunition so low that Meagher ordered a withdrawal in order to regroup.[487]

Richardson assessed the situation from a vantage point immediately behind the Irish Brigade. He wanted to keep the pressure on Hill's troops. Ordering a staff officer to bring up Francis Barlow's two regiments from the 1st Brigade, Richardson rode off to find the rest of that command and ensure its advance. The prospects for this second wave were better since the terrain would shield it for much of the way from the Confederates, who lay primarily to its right. Barlow could come in at the end of the Confederate line in the Sunken Road, flanking the enemy and turning the position.[488]

After advancing and finding no enemy immediately in front, Brigadier General John Caldwell had commenced to wheel his three regiments "cautiously to the right," until he encountered Richardson and received an order to expeditiously[489] "relieve the line of General Meagher, which had fought the enemy gallantly and suffered severely."[490] The brigade moved by right flank in rear of Meagher's line and, according to Caldwell, passed it "to the front in the most perfect order, under a severe fire of musketry." Another reporter contended that the movement was not made with such precision; rather, "the brigade was running when it reached Meagher's line and, without slacking pace, dashed through his ranks."[491] With them was the general commanding: "Swinging his hat and shouting, and without slackening pace," Richardson "dashed through his ranks, passing the line by simply pushing its way through, Meagher's men quickly conforming to the movement."[492]

Joined now by elements of the Irish Brigade, the two front units of the division advanced with support of John Brooke's 3rd Brigade. Richardson's aide, Major Norvell, brought them the order to do so.[493] Richardson also drove some of French's men into the fray.[494] The natural trench had been strengthened by three to four thousand troops of Major General Richard Anderson.[495] On the far right, however, waited the 30th North Carolina of Anderson's Division, where "as far as the eye could reach to the right (300 yards), there was no support."[496] A brigade of one Alabama and three Georgia regiments filed into the road, extending the line but leaving it unanchored.[497]

Richardson's main assault would prove effective. The Confederate collapse began on its right, where his division overlapped the enemy flank. Barlow came in where his position provided "peculiar advantages for attacking in flank this part of the enemy's line." His two regiments "advanced and obtained an enfilading fire upon the enemy."[498] Barlow had changed front, quickly withdrew from the ridge, moved to the left under its cover and came on rapidly.[499] The Federal soldiers fired down the length of the Confederate line. The result: "Seeing the uselessness of further resistance, the enemy, in accordance with our demands, threw down their arms, came in in large numbers, and surrendered."[500]

In the center, the Federal firepower also overwhelmed the Sunken Road defenders, especially at the angle where the road turned southeast. One of Meagher's regiments hit that apex, and the sudden dash "so startled the enemy that their fire visibly slackened, their line wavered, and squads of two or three began leaving the road and running into the corn"—the field of Henry Piper south of the wagon road.[501] These Confederates had seen the disaster unfolding to their right: one lieutenant colonel reported to Rodes that "the right wing of his regiment was being subjected to a terrible enfilading fire." Within a few moments, all of Rodes's command was "retreating in confusion."[502] They had become increasingly nervous as "word came for the command to keep lookout on the extreme right." They watched as "masses of Confederate troops in great confusion were seen," and the right flank "broke beyond the power of rallying."[503] Their position was untenable; Federals seemed to be firing from all directions except the rear, and to the rear is where Hill's line ran, since surrender was the only alternative.[504] Barlow had taken "about 300 men and 8 commissioned officers, among them an aide to General [Jeb] Stuart," as captives.[505] Brooke reported the capture of two battle flags, two thousand stand of arms and "a great number of prisoners."[506] Caldwell added to Barlow's count "six stand of colors"; one of his staff officers "captured several prisoners with his own hand."[507]

The triumph of Richardson's Division came in significant part because of its leadership.[508] One regimental commander attributed his unit's success to that key factor: "Animated by the presence of both its brigade and division commanders, the regiment moved forward with a determined enthusiasm I have never seen excelled." The soldiers of the division "had cleared the ditch of every living enemy, and were driving them in great disorder through the corn field beyond."[509] True to his military ethic, Richardson had brought all to bear. It was an awful scene:

> *The Federals drew their line partly in front of and partly behind the sunken road—the road itself was so full of dead men, so horrible with its torn fragments of flesh, its congealing pools of blood in ruts and hollows, that it could no longer be used as a trench.*[510]

The country road emerged from the battle with a new identity: Bloody Lane. The soldiers of Richardson's command had used up to sixty rounds per man during the fight.[511] The center of the gray line "was wrecked."[512] One Confederate officer thought "Lee's army was ruined and the end of the Confederacy was in sight."[513]

The division's achievement did not go unnoticed. At the Pry home headquarters, V Corps commander Porter sought to hurry forward one of his arriving divisions under Brigadier General Andrew Humphreys, still miles away, messaging at 12:30 p.m. that "all goes well, and we are driving the enemy."[514] To the Michigander went the credit: "Richardson's success was visible from army headquarters and, although not a part of his [McClellan's] plan, was eagerly welcomed by a commanding general for whom the past few hours had brought nothing but bad news."[515] At 1:25 p.m., McClellan telegraphed Halleck:

> *We are in the midst of the most terrible battle of the war—perhaps of history. Thus far it looks well, but I have great odds against me. Hurry up all the troops possible. Our loss has been terrific, but we have gained much ground. I have thrown the mass of the army on the left flank. Burnside is now attacking the right, and I hold my small reserve, consisting of Porter's (Fifth) Corps, ready to attack the center as soon as the flank movements are developed. I hope that God will give us glorious victory.*[516]

Richardson had presented the army commander with just such an opportunity. But McClellan's expression of "hope" betrayed uncertainty, further revealed in the first draft of the conclusion: "It will be either a great defeat or a most glorious victory. I think & hope that God will give us the latter."[517]

Porter's V Corps had taken serious losses at Second Bull Run. It still comprised nearly thirteen thousand soldiers,[518] including four units from the Great Lake State: the 1st, 4th and 16th Michigan Infantry and the Michigan Sharpshooters, Brady's Company. Porter's corps had been held in readiness to take part in the Battle of South Mountain, but its services were not called for. On the fifteenth, his troops had passed through Burnside's command, which had halted on South Mountain, and moved on the road to Sharpsburg as far as the Middle Bridge. Here they took position behind the heights to the left of the road approaching the span and posted the artillery. At 2:30 p.m., Porter urged Humphrey on again: "The rebels are desperate. We have driven them some distance, but it is of vital importance to get up all our troops. Come on as soon as possible, and hurry up with all haste. Do not render the command unfit for service, but force your march."[519]

Later in the afternoon, at about 4:00 p.m., Porter dispatched two brigades to the aid of Sumner's Corps. One was the 2nd Brigade, including the 4th

Michigan, and the other the 3rd Brigade, which included the 16th Michigan and Brady's Company. The two brigades moved a half mile to the right, where they were halted by McClellan, "with directions to remain there until further orders." When those orders arrived "just before sunset," they were to return to their morning positions. Thus, none of these units saw action on the seventeenth.[520] None reached Richardson's hard-won foothold in the center of the Confederate line. None was deployed to help push on to Sharpsburg.

The opportunity remained to press Lee: "Shortly after one o'clock the Federals finally held the key to the field" when Richardson's Division overran the Sunken Road.[521] After taking control of "Bloody Lane," the surviving complement advanced beyond the road into the Piper cornfield and orchard, passing by the stone slave quarters.[522] The Confederates had fled across the property toward the Hagerstown Pike to regroup and now opened on Caldwell's Brigade "a terrific fire from a fresh line of infantry, and also poured upon us a fire of grape and canister from two batteries, one in the orchard just beyond the corn-field, the other farther one to the right."[523] A force concealed behind a ridge in the cornfield aimed to turn Caldwell's left flank. The Union infantry changed front, "received the advancing enemy with a volley, which checked him and drove him back. He soon rallied, however, and, moving by the right flank, endeavored to turn our left." Two regiments "drove back the enemy with great loss," capturing the colors of a North Carolina regiment. By moving to the left to avoid being flanked, an opening had been created. Brooke's 3rd Brigade moved forward to plug the gap.[524]

At the same time as the movement toward the left, enemy infantry was discovered moving around the right. Barlow ordered "right shoulder shift arms," and his men moved to the right oblique to a hill about three hundred yards beyond the lane and commenced firing. After about twenty rounds, the Confederate line "broke in perfect disorder and ran in every direction." At about the same time, a sharp musketry firing commenced on the left as the Confederates advanced another line through the Piper cornfield. The brigade moved through the field despite canister fire, pressing forward, driving the Confederate infantry before it until ordered to halt. Barlow received a wound from an artillery round, and no more forward momentum existed. Richardson's Division held the position—for the remainder of the day, as it turned out—and was not engaged again.[525]

A primary cause for the lack of forward movement lay with Richardson himself. Battery K of the 1st U.S. Artillery arrived from Henry Hunt to fulfill Richardson's request for armament to retake the offensive.[526] The general had been all over the field, placing himself close to the front, where danger always loomed. He was "exceedingly popular with his men, inspiring them by his own example"[527] in leading from the tip of the spear. One officer remembered well Richardson's vigor as they were advancing this day:

> *I looked over my right shoulder and saw that gallant old fellow advancing on the right of our line, almost alone, afoot and with his bare sword in his hand, and his face was as black as a thunder cloud; and well it might be, for some of our own men, turning their heads toward him, cried out, "Behind the haystack!" and he roared out, "God d--- the field officers!"*[528]

Battery K took position about eighty yards north of the Sunken Road on the left of Richardson's Division. Richardson was standing "about thirty yards behind his most forward units" directing the battery's fire and trying to reorganize his command, personally placing one regiment for attack,[529] expecting to advance.[530] "A very sharp fire of shot, spherical case, and shell" came from Confederate guns in "concentrated" reply. The gunners of Battery K discovered that most of the enemy artillery was beyond their range; recognizing its plight, Richardson "wished to save the battery as much as possible in order that it might advance with his division."[531] He ordered the guns to retire north of the road. "It was at this time that the general commanding was dangerously wounded." A fragmented "ball of spherical case" from a Confederate artillery piece struck him in the left shoulder. He went down.[532]

Major General Richardson was gravely wounded. He was carried off the field to the Pry house, to an upper room, and gingerly placed on a bed. To the surgeon he said, "Tell General McClellan I have been doing a Colonel's work all day, and I'm now too badly hurt to do a General's."[533] His day of combat had ended, but his men did not forget him.[534] He was one of more than 1,100 casualties in his division this brutal day.[535] Contemporaneous newspaper accounts accorded Richardson credit for directing "the murderous flanking fire" that had crippled the Confederate center.[536]

The center of the Union line held. For corps commander Sumner, that would be enough, especially since he had not been involved and was ignorant of prospects for a further advance.[537] Without vigorous leadership and fresh reinforcements, the II Corps could make no more progress despite being only half a mile from Sharpsburg. The task now fell to the IX Corps and its effort over on the left. Complete victory still offered itself to the Union arms on the west bank of Antietam Creek.

Chapter 8

WILLCOX AND THE FINAL HOURS

Near Complete Victory

On the Union left, Wednesday was to be a signal day in the war. McClellan initiated battle on the right, but he envisioned throwing his other flank against Lee at a key point. Accordingly, IX Corps readied itself early. Having fought just three days prior at Fox's Gap, Orlando Willcox and his men marched out of camp to the hill overlooking Antietam Creek before the Lower (or "Rohrbach's") stone bridge that took the road to Sharpsburg. His orders, received from corps commander Ambrose Burnside in person, were to cross over after the span had been secured following three other divisions. Willcox then would form the right of the corps in its attack on the Confederate lines in front of the town.[538]

At 9:10 a.m., McClellan ordered Burnside to open his attack on the left.[539] For the rest of the morning, IX Corps sought to take the crossing, secure the heights on the west bank and press on toward the Confederate position in front of Sharpsburg. About five hundred Georgia soldiers under Brigadier General Robert Toombs held off two successive Federal assaults to cross the bridge. Four hours later, success was achieved when Union soldiers rushed across the bridge and stormed the rifle pits above the creek. Two brigades of Rodman's Division crossed downstream at Snavely's Ford and pressed northward toward the same position. On a normal fall day, the elegant bridge and its surrounds evoked peace: "Water-willows, like silvery clouds, follow the bend of the stream, and sycamores with dappled trunks and broad leaves lean over the water."[540] Today was all mayhem.

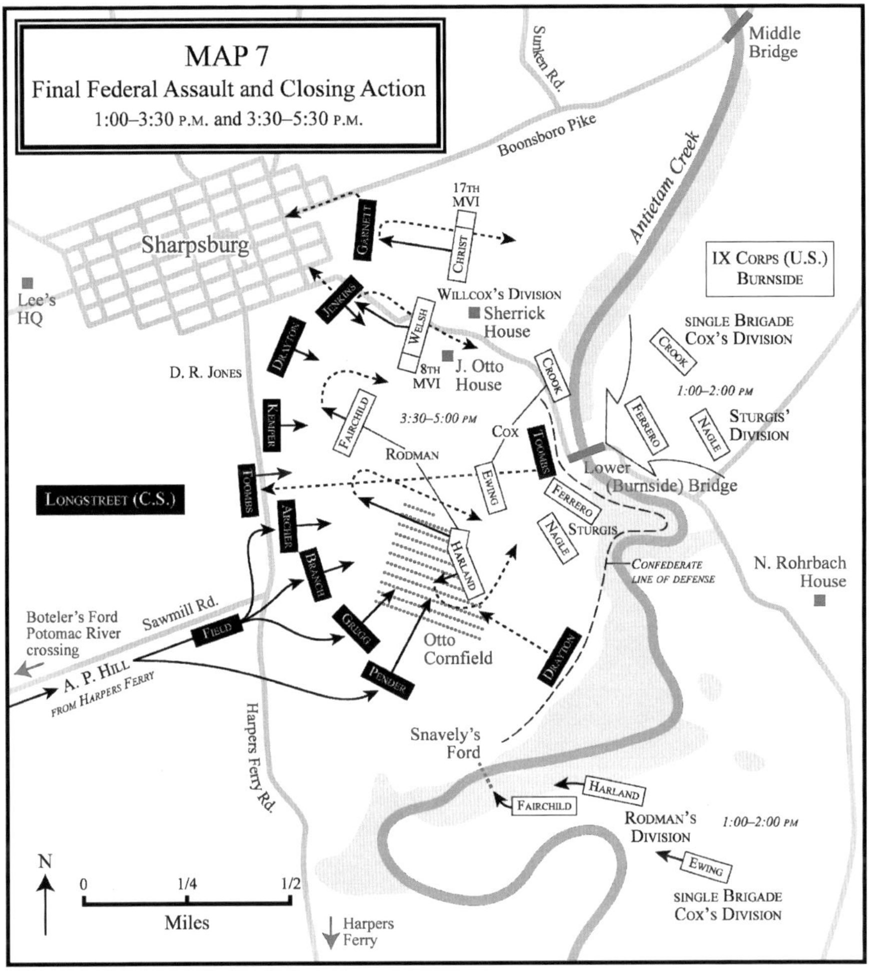

MAP 7. Final Federal assault and closing action.

After securing the bridgehead, Burnside organized the corps for the next stage of the advance. He now brought up Willcox from about three-fourths of a mile away on the east side of the creek;[541] the 1st Division crossed the Antietam at 1:00 p.m. with "reasonable alacrity."[542] It moved through a cornfield on the east side and then marched up the road to the bridge, across the structure and along the road on the west bank to where it left the creek. At about 3:15 p.m., IX Corps was arranged and moved forward.[543] The 3rd Division was on the left, or more southerly part of the advance, and on the right was the 1st Division with its two brigades. The 1st Brigade included the 17th Michigan; the 8th Michigan was part of the 2nd Brigade. They faced a single Confederate division—the only obstacle between the bridge and town. From Sharpsburg only a few miles remained before reaching Boteler's Ford on the Potomac and cutting off Lee's route of retreat.

That short distance, however, possessed some imposing terrain. Across the bridge, the road turned sharply to the right, paralleled Antietam Creek for about two hundred yards and then turned to the left into an open ravine overlooked by heights on both sides. Once on the heights, the country was rolling and intersected with wood and stone fences. Confederate sharpshooters were posted behind the fences and haystacks of the several farms, and an artillery battery commanded the road and ravine down to the crossing. More Confederate artillery defended the outskirts of the town to compensate for the paucity of infantry on this part of the field.[544]

Willcox put across the 1st Brigade, and it filed up the road, across the ravine and up onto the crest on the right of the road. One regiment served as skirmishers, and the other three regiments formed in line of battle. The 17th Michigan, Colonel Withington in command, was posted on the right of the brigade and thus formed the far right of the division. The 2nd Brigade moved onto the heights to the left of the road in similar fashion, with the 8th Michigan, Captain Ely, farthest south. Willcox had posted the two Michigan regiments on the ends of his advance, protecting his flanks with units in which he felt confidence. He also took along two artillery pieces from a Massachusetts battery.[545]

The IX Corps presented an imposing sight to the Confederates and a thrilling one to Union headquarters, from which its advance could be seen. Willcox and his counterparts "surged forward from the Antietam toward the ridge on which Sharpsburg and the Harpers Ferry Road's intersection with the road to Boteler's Ford stood."[546] They began to take casualties from the very first moment of the movement.[547] One private in the 17th received a shoulder wound before even firing a shot. Despite "a most galling cross-fire which raked our ranks severely," the regiment continued on.[548] Willcox's "two brigades gallantly advanced over the plateau toward Sharpsburg"[549] in compliance with Burnside's order to move directly upon the town.[550]

Willcox had ridden up the road from the bridge, while his infantry turned from the creek toward the town and watched as they went forward on both right and left. The 1st Brigade went into action first, attacking a force of the enemy infantry along its front and driving it steadily.[551] The action "was a fierce one from the moment Willcox's men showed themselves on the open ground."[552] The Federals reached the vicinity of a small apple orchard on the southern slope of a nearby hill with a "stone house and mill on the

Sherrick's house near Burnside Bridge. Willcox's Division, including the 17th Michigan, passed by the house during its advance toward Sharpsburg. Gardner photograph. *Library of Congress.*

road to Sharpsburg."[553] This was the Joseph Sherrick house; across the road sat the John Otto farm. The division's success put it at some risk, since the unit got about three hundred yards[554] in advance of the rest of the line and was without proper support. As the men halted to let the remainder of the division come up, they took fire from three directions: artillery on their left, infantry from a cornfield in front protected by a stone fence and from another battery farther up in front beyond the cornfield.

The 2nd Brigade lagged a bit on the left since it "had a greater distance to move, and over much more difficult ground."[555] On its left, the 8th Michigan initially got entangled with a New York regiment of Zouaves but soon swung to the right and, with the rest of the brigade, drove the enemy from a stone wall on the town side of a ravine south of the Otto house. The brigade went into the ravine, climbed the slope, crossed over the wall and continued to engage the Confederates posted near the orchard, house and mill.[556] Willcox brought the two artillery pieces forward, moved them up the Otto farm lane and directed their position near the barn in order to fire on the Confederate artillery posted near a cemetery on a rise located just east of town adjacent to the Boonsboro Pike.[557] The infantry continued to press, nearing the orchard of John Avey on the southeastern outskirts of Sharpsburg.[558]

The 1st Brigade also continued its forward momentum, advancing past the Sherrick farm on the north side of the road. A Confederate battery with its supporting infantry was playing havoc on the right wing, and the 17th Michigan was ordered to make a charge on the position.[559] Seeing the Michiganders approaching, the Confederates "limbered up" their guns and escaped when their opponents were only one hundred yards away.[560] An intervening hill temporarily prevented the 17th from firing on the fleeing Confederates.[561] "The charging party was ordered back—an order very reluctantly obeyed by the 17th Michigan," for Withington had seen that the hill was abandoned.[562] The 2nd Brigade's commander witnessed the charge and would issue a written commendation that the 17th Michigan "sustained the brunt of the battle with a bravery and constancy seldom equaled in modern warfare."[563]

Willcox continued forward with his men, issuing instructions and commands as the action unfolded.[564] He kept the 2nd Brigade moving ahead toward the 1st Brigade, "so that by the time we entered Sharpsburg the greater part of my division was on the right of the road and extended across the hollow, up the side hill, and on the plateau." The division commander would report his front-line presence, noting how he was "able both to see and assist my division at every part of the ground."[565]

On the southeast edge of Sharpsburg, on the elevation on the right of the road, was an orchard in which the Confederates, pushed all the way by Willcox's troops, made a final stand. The position in the orchard soon collapsed:

> *Willcox concentrated his artillery fire upon it, and his infantry was able to push forward and occupy it. They now partly occupied the town of Sharpsburg, and held the high ground commanding it on the south-east.... The struggle had been long and bloody.*[566]

Some of Willcox's men had actually stepped onto the first street in Sharpsburg, with some going beyond the Avey house.[567] It was about half past four o'clock, and ninety minutes had been required for the 1st Division to advance to the town, "driving the rebels" before it.[568] The situation presented a golden opportunity for taking Sharpsburg and preventing the Confederate army from escaping through its streets. The division "had carried the heights of Sharpsburg, and rested partly in the town and partly on the hills. The enemy kept up a desultory fire along our line, but at a respectful distance." Willcox's officers "had great difficulty in restraining the ardor of [the] troops, who seemed anxious to charge through the town and capture the batteries beyond."[569] Unfortunately, the division was low on ammunition and was securing the more than one hundred prisoners it had captured.[570]

Complete success arising from the advance by IX Corps seemed within McClellan's grasp. Unfortunately, two factors combined to prevent capture of the town.

First came overcaution. Willcox was prepared to take Sharpsburg when an order from Burnside arrived "forbidding the move." Incredulous, Willcox dispatched an aide to explain and advocate for the opportunity—"a clear front and signs of confusion at Sharpsburg"—and to convince the corps commander "to insist upon our going ahead." The aide returned, unsuccessful. Burnside had McClellan's concurrence in the halt.[571] By one account, it took three directives to dissuade Willcox from his plan.[572]

The other factor involved the 3rd Division having placed its greenest unit on its left flank. Unlike the 17th Michigan, which had demonstrated amazing competence in its initial combat, the rookie Connecticut regiment was attacked at about 4:30 p.m. by leading elements of the only remaining Confederate division under A.P. Hill, which had raced the seventeen miles from Harpers Ferry in order to reach the battlefield at nearly the precisely needed moment. Panicked by the assault, the Federal left broke and retreated. On the right, Willcox's Division did not panic.[573] Further, the bulk of V Corps stood intact only a short distance away, in which the 1st Michigan, though reduced in numbers from its full strength, prepared to fight. Lieutenant George Lockley, a twenty-six-year-old from Ann Arbor, felt "gay. Guess we'll whip them." His regiment had been ordered "to be ready to move at a minutes notice. Guess we'll give them the best we've got for [Second] Bull Run."[574] But McClellan felt he had no infantry to spare.[575] Burnside's corps was on its own.

Willcox had "fetched up some cartridges" to replenish his men's ammunition in preparation for taking the town. Now he was called on to help save the day for IX Corps. He retired the left of his line, swinging back "in perfect order," uniting with reinforcements that had come up from the creek and forming "on the left flank of the whole line." The steadying movement prevented further chaos, loss of more prisoners and retreat beyond the bridge crossing. Instead, IX Corps could "lay that night upon their arms" on the ground it had won just shy of Sharpsburg.[576] The 1st Division was ordered back toward the Antietam by corps command.

Obeying the directive, "every regiment marched back in perfect order." Willcox had seen to a successful advance and similar regrouping. He did so at great personal risk.

On the high ground to the left, the Confederates occupied a cornfield in opposition to Brigadier General Jacob D. Cox's Kanawha Division. The Federals had taken shelter behind a stone wall, seeking to hold their position. A regimental commander looked to his right and witnessed an amazing sight:

> *To our right a short distance was Gen. Willcox, aiming a gun in person, all his men gone. He sent out word to us to know why in hell we were not advancing. Just then Col. Scammon came up from my left. He was in temporary command of our division, and sent word back to Willcox that if he would give him written orders, he would march.*[577]

The Michigander wrote home in a few days about the event, recounting how he responded:

> *Tell Father I am really careful & never expose myself unnecessarily. When poor Rodman was shot his division at once became partially demoralized & probably nothing but my presence prevented it from falling back disastrously. Scammon who commanded Cox's old division stood manfully by me. My right was all secure but Rodman & Scammon were pressed & the extreme left, Sturgis was in danger. I told Rodman's brigade commanders that we could hold the ground & would & agreed with them & Scammon to assist the left by a charge bayonet (our ammunition being exhausted) along the whole line, when we were ordered to fall back near the bridge. I had my Washington horse killed in the same battle; he was being led with my escort. I called him "Reno." Another horse, "Burnside" was disabled, & Roebuck came up just in time. Burnside* [the horse] *is nearly well. Arndt keeps them in splendid order. Adieu.*[578]

Willcox concluded the letter placidly: "God bless you & the children.... Also send me 3 flannel drawers & 3 thick flannel shirts."[579]

Others in his command did not fare as well, staff officers included. Adjutant William Richards had gone down with two wounds, "a piece of shell fearfully bruising him in the groin, and a Minie ball shattering his leg near the ankle." Surgery immediately afterward did not remove the fragment.[580]

As IX Corps consolidated its position, "nightfall put a welcome end to the bloody day"; "the Confederate army was worn & fought to a perfect frazzle."[581] The Union army was bloodied, yet several major units had seen no real action. For those that had, their casualty lists told a tale of valor. Willcox was proud of the sacrifice and performance of his division. It had "ejected" the enemy "from the fields and orchards overlooking the roads leading westward to Sharpsburg," clearing the way for McClellan to have cut off Lee's retreat.[582] The general's performance would merit corps command.[583] The conduct of his troops had been "gallant beyond criticism."[584] He sought particular notice for "all the officers and men" in his command: "There is no officer or man among them who cannot feel proud of having been engaged in the battle of Sharpsburg." He recommended that each regiment of the division be authorized to inscribe "Sharpsburg" and "South Mountain" on their colors. On his personal staff, he cited First Lieutenant James W. Romeyn, 4th Michigan Infantry, "for promptness and fearlessness in carrying orders."[585] Romeyn had been born in Detroit on March 18, 1839, the son of one of the city's most prominent attorneys and Democrats, Theodore Romeyn. He graduated from Columbia College in New York City, studied law and began practicing in 1860. Romeyn was the senior aide on Willcox's staff,[586] only twenty-three years old. And he had almost witnessed one of the most spectacular moments of the war: a rout of the formerly unbeaten Army of Northern Virginia.

If but a single reserve division had been employed on the right of the corps as it fought its way toward town, the IX Corps' "movement into Sharpsburg could not have been checked."[587] McClellan would come to the same conclusion years later, regretting that he had not put into position a more aggressive overall commander on his left.[588] As it was, the ground gained on the left was nearly relinquished. Late that Wednesday evening, Willcox chatted in his tent with another officer when Burnside entered. To their shock, they soon heard the wing commander reveal his plan to withdraw to the east side of the Antietam, yielding the day's hard-won gains. Willcox responded sternly: "General, your troops must remain where they are and must hold their ground." Braced by his subordinate, Burnside relented.[589] The "complete victory" of Willcox's Division was preserved, precariously.[590] Ralph Ely summed up the afternoon: "[D]rove them on our front and right the division on our left gave way and they came in on our flank, which obliged us to fall back." They remained in position "all night" and until 4:00 p.m. on Thursday.[591]

That evening, the general from Michigan could speak firsthand of the brave soldiers and staff of his division. Miles away, looking out a window of the White House toward the Potomac, the president of the United States used the eyes of his imagination to envision continuing success by his Army of the Potomac. Lincoln had to wait for definitive news until McClellan's telegrams of 8:00 a.m. the next day[592] and 8:30 a.m. on the nineteenth.[593] As of late Wednesday, the only messages over the wires from the army commander were to request a replenishment of artillery ammunition.[594] This Wednesday evening, anticipating victory, the president worked on the draft of a document that he had been preparing for a number of weeks.[595] He needed to be ready should a Union triumph enable issuing the final version.

The paper was the preliminary Emancipation Proclamation. The time devoted to it this night, honing its language, was well spent.

Chapter 9

Pursuit to the Potomac

The Battle of Shepherdstown

September 18 was a rainy Thursday, as if the heavens wept for those no longer in the ranks.[596] At 6:30 a.m., Robert E. Lee was busy reporting to his superior on his version of events. It was his first communiqué to Richmond in some time. He wrote to President Davis to recount the artillery battle on the sixteenth and the battle on Wednesday, during which "large masses" of Federal troops "threatened to overwhelm" the Confederate army. The contest had raged fiercely, the Confederates being driven and then counterattacking successfully. The letter ended on a rather positive note that the Army of Northern Virginia maintained its ground at day's end.[597]

McClellan began the day by reporting on Wednesday's events to those most important to him. At 8:00 a.m., he telegraphed his wife, "The battle of yesterday a desperate one. We hold all we gained. The contest will probably be renewed today."[598] He followed with a letter to wife Ellen expanding on his assessment. He regarded the seventeenth as successful, "but whether a decided victory depends on what occurs today."[599] To his immediate superior, Henry Halleck, he sent an 8:00 a.m. telegram with similar thoughts:

> *The battle of yesterday continued for fourteen hours, and until after dark. We held all we gained, except a portion of the extreme left; that was obliged to abandon a part of what it had gained. Our losses very heavy, especially in general officers. The battle will probably be renewed to-day. Send all the troops you can by the most expeditious route.*[600]

He also directed the acting I Corps commander, Brigadier General George Meade, to ready his troops either to mount an attack or to resist one. Meade was ordered to "keep a good watch of the movements of the enemy, and report everything of importance,"[601] betraying McClellan's primary concern as to what Lee might do. Other orders from Union headquarters directed reconnaissance by cavalry for the same purpose of ascertaining whether the Army of Northern Virginia would renew the contest.[602] McClellan was content to await his opponent's initiative. He would later develop his rationale as to the reason that no Union infantry movements were to occur before dark on this Thursday:

> *The* [Wednesday] *night, however, brought with it grave responsibilities. Whether to renew the attack on the 18th or to defer it, even with the risk of the enemy's retirement, was the question before me. After a night of anxious deliberation, and a full and careful survey of the situation and condition of our army, the strength and position of the enemy, I concluded that the success of an attack on the 18th was not certain.*[603]

Instead, daylight was invested on the Federal side in "collecting the dispersed, giving rest to the fatigued, removing the wounded, burying the dead, and the necessary preparations for a renewal of the battle" on the nineteenth, when, apparently, McClellan posited that the likelihood of success would greatly improve.[604]

McClellan ordered Richardson's replacement, Brigadier General Winfield Scott Hancock, not to precipitate hostilities.[605] Those still in line, like the 17th Michigan, had pulled picket duty during the night and now remained poised, according to their colonel, as skirmishers "in plain sight of the rascals all of the time." They, like most of the men in ranks, believed that the conflict would be renewed. Only at close of Thursday were they withdrawn, enabling Withington to enjoy "a good night's sleep on a bundle of luxurious straw."[606]

McClellan did not plan for an all-out advance for Friday either. Rather, he directed several elements to push pickets forward "at an early hour in the morning" of the nineteenth to ascertain the enemy's dispositions—more specifically, "whether the enemy is in force in your front."[607] The morning of Friday dawned sunny on the warmest of all the days on the Maryland side of the Potomac.[608] The setting was quite different in other ways. McClellan had an inkling of this change overnight, having sent a message to Sumner at 4:00 a.m. specifying what to do if, indeed, the enemy was "retiring."[609] At

4:30 a.m., he wrote to three corps commanders that Sumner was reporting "the enemy is moving his artillery to the west, and felling trees behind him," directing them to prepare to move.[610]

The Confederates had, in fact, departed the battleground. The Union commander was delighted. He telegraphed his wife, "Our victory complete. Enemy has left his dead & wounded on the field. Our people now in pursuit."[611] To Halleck he telegraphed at 8:30 a.m.:

> *But little occurred yesterday except skirmishing, being fully occupied in replenishing ammunition, taking care of wounded, &c. Last night the enemy abandoned his position, leaving his dead and wounded on the field. We are again in pursuit. I do not yet know whether he is falling back to an interior position or crossing the river. We may safely claim a complete victory.*[612]

Two hours later, he reported to Washington that his cavalry "is driving the enemy across the river. Our victory was complete. The enemy is driven back into Virginia. Maryland and Pennsylvania are now safe."[613] Another three hours elapsed, and McClellan dispatched a celebratory telegram to Halleck: "I have the honor to report that Maryland is entirely freed from the presence of the enemy, who has been driven across the Potomac. No fears need now be entertained for the safety of Pennsylvania."[614] He wrote to Ellen on the twentieth, again asserting that his enemy was completely defeated: "Our victory was complete & the disorganized rebel army has rapidly returned to Virginia.... I feel some little pride in having with a beaten and demoralized army defeated Lee so utterly, & saved the North so completely."[615]

Now that the Maryland Campaign was apparently concluded, McClellan initiated a different contest to vindicate his performance and to safeguard against criticism that he had let Lee escape. This effort included enlisting the aid of friendly reporters. The *New York Times* reported on Thursday, for example, that "had the rebels remained, a general engagement between both armies would have taken place this morning."[616] It also headlined how the battle had been won by "consummate generalship" on the Union side.[617]

While his cavalry was pressing toward the Potomac early Friday, McClellan ordered the infantry to advance but cautiously. The unbloodied V Corps under Major General Fitz John Porter took the lead. Believing that the retreating Confederates had left obstructions in their wake—and rear-guard positions that could play havoc with pursuit—McClellan directed all other corps commands to push out pickets and, "if the enemy appears to be retreating," mass their troops "in readiness to move in any direction."[618]

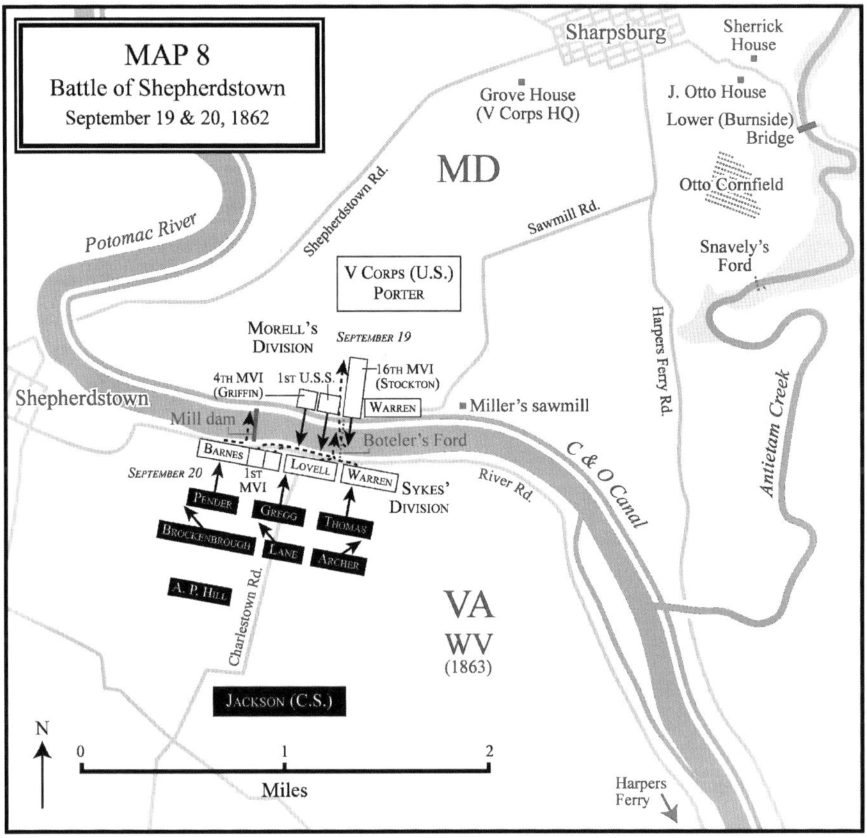

MAP 8. Battle of Shepherdstown.

Two divisions of the VI Corps advanced through Sharpsburg, one reaching the Potomac opposite Shepherdstown, Virginia.[619] Williams and XII Corps moved out, the 2nd Division in the direction of Harpers Ferry and the 1st Division marching behind it through Sharpsburg east to Brownsville.[620] The I and II Corps nursed their wounds in place. At the close of this day, McClellan would seek to consolidate his army and prepare for the twentieth. The I Corps was instructed to cover the far right between the Hagerstown Pike and the Potomac; VI Corps ordered to its left; XII Corps positioned adjacent to II Corps, which would rest its left on Sharpsburg; V Corps directed to rest its right on the town; and IX Corps posted on the far left to reach the Potomac downstream.[621]

Porter would report that, at first, "the Fifth with other corps was directed to take up a position in line beyond" Sharpsburg. Next, he was ordered "to

Thomas Baylis Whitmarsh Stockton, West Point class of 1827, was commissioned colonel of the 16th Michigan Infantry in September 1861. *David D. Finney.*

pursue the enemy and give aid to the cavalry brigade, then in advance."[622] Upon reaching the Potomac, he verified that Lee had crossed his entire force. The enemy had not gone far, though, still "defending the fords with artillery well posted." Lee had left his Artillery Reserve and some infantry under Chief of Artillery William Pendleton to guard the crossings across from Shepherdstown, where the bridge had been burned, and at Boteler's Ford just east of town.[623] Porter saw opportunity: "I determined to clear the fords, and, if possible, secure some of the enemy's artillery." He had significant forces to choose from in this mission, including three Michigan regiments. The 1st Michigan Infantry was part of the 1st Brigade, Colonel James Barnes commanding, in the 1st Division under command of Major General George W. Morell. Captain Emory W. Belton was regimental commander. The 4th Michigan under command of Colonel Jonathan W. Childs formed part of the 2nd Brigade, Brigadier General Charles Griffin commanding. The 16th Michigan under Lieutenant Colonel Norval E. Welch and Brady's Company, Michigan Sharpshooters, Lieutenant Jonas H. Titus Jr. commanding, were in the 3rd Brigade, with Colonel Thomas Baylis Whitmarsh Stockton in command.

Belton, Childs, Welch and Titus were all experienced officers who had stepped forward to lead Michigan units in the first six months of the war. Belton had enlisted in Company D of the 1st Michigan Infantry's ninety-day regiment on April 29, 1861, with the rank of sergeant. He was only twenty-three. After his initial enlistment expired, he accepted a commission as first lieutenant of Company F. On April 22, 1862, he was commissioned captain in Company G. Because regimental commander Horace S. Roberts had been killed at Second Bull Run, Belton now had succeeded to its leadership.[624] Childs entered service from Washtenaw County when the 4th Michigan organized on June 20, 1861, age twenty-eight, as its major. He was

Ezra Brown of Clinton was promoted to sergeant in Company K, 4th Michigan Infantry, on July 1, 1862. *Monroe County Historical Museum.*

commissioned lieutenant colonel on September 25, 1861, and colonel on July 1, 1862.[625] Welch enlisted on August 22, 1861, as major of the 16th, age twenty-six, from Ann Arbor. He was commissioned lieutenant colonel on July 6, 1862.[626] Titus was the oldest, age thirty, from Detroit, and had been commissioned second lieutenant on September 16, 1861. On May 18, 1862, he had been made first lieutenant.[627]

Stockton commanded the 3rd Brigade and was colonel of the 16th Michigan. A graduate of the 1827 class at West Point, he had served as lieutenant and quartermaster until 1836 and volunteered again during the Mexican-American War. In civilian life, he superintended harbor improvements on the Great Lakes. Prewar activities included membership on the board to help organize Michigan's militia. He helped raise the 16th Michigan and entered service on August 22, 1861, for three years, age fifty-nine. He had been taken prisoner at the Battle of Gaines's Mill on June 27, 1862, and was exchanged on August 12. A month later, he was leading his troops against the same Confederate enemy.[628]

The 4th Michigan, all three hundred strong, had marched into Sharpsburg to a very positive reception by the townspeople despite the battle's destruction. As twenty-four-year-old Lieutenant John Milton Bancroft noted in his journal, "nearly every house struck with solid shot or shell. Things look rough. Rebels have stripped houses of everything. Union sentiment is strong. As we go through women point out houses of those who have given the Rebels shelter and where rebel flags are concealed. Children swear vengeance."[629] After enjoying the fête, the regiment continued on past the site of Lee's headquarters and arrived in position near Shepherdstown at about 1:00 p.m.[630] All along the route, the Michiganders passed houses, barns and tents "filled with secesh wounded."[631] More casualties were to come; an artillery duel ensued as the Union troops neared the Potomac, with the 1st Michigan "loaded up and ready for use" while hostile shells shrieked overhead.[632] George Lockley had been ready to "go in" and felt "first rate."[633]

Porter sought to clear the approaches across the Potomac: "I caused the banks of the river and canal to be well lined with skirmishers and sharpshooters, supported by portions of their respective divisions (Morell's and [Brigadier General] George Sykes's), while their artillery and that of the reserve was posted to control the opposite bank."[634] He threw out a number of units as skirmishers, including two companies of the 4th.[635] Their job was to "drive the enemy from the banks."[636] To aid the effort, the V Corps artillery was positioned so as to concentrate on the Confederate guns across the river. Henry Hunt offered to help and directed the guns, which did "a devastating artillery fire across the river."[637] Their fire proved so powerful that the Confederate gunners took many casualties and their counter-fire became sporadic. With what might be a panic ensuing, it appeared that several of their pieces might be vulnerable.[638]

Although it was now 4:30 p.m., Porter saw opportunity arising from the Federal artillery bombardment. He ordered the 4th Michigan "to cross the river and take" the abandoned ordnance[639] after Childs volunteered to do so.[640] The colonel directed his regiment to discard extra gear in preparation for the river crossing. They marched down a ravine to an open space between the Chesapeake & Ohio Canal and the Potomac, where they were subjected to hostile shot and shell. The regiment would be joined by other units in this expedition across to the south side; initially, it acted in support of the 1st U.S. Sharpshooters by firing volleys over the heads of the marksmen and into the enemy positions up the embankment on the other side of the river.[641] Rushing to the safety of the virtually dry canal, they formed for the water trek. Childs motioned toward Virginia, shouting, "Boys, are you willing to cross and take that battery?" Although they knew not the force awaiting them, the Michiganders could imagine the difficulty of wading into the current while Confederate bullets rained down.[642]

Urgently, Childs cried out, "Battalion, forward double-quick-march!" The 4th climbed up the canal bank, rushed down into the flowing water and began to move toward the opposite shore. As enemy fire began to find its mark, the Federals discovered that they were west of the ford and in rushing water more than waist deep. Bancroft would report on the harrowing ordeal,

The 4th Michigan crossing into Virginia (now West Virginia) near Boteler's Ford, from the John Milton Bancroft diary. *Auburn University Libraries.*

a nearly one-thousand-foot crossing: "Sharpshooters along the bank. Capt. Gordon is wounded. While going down to the river a fragment of a shell strikes the man in front of me taking the top of his head and killing him instantly. We lose but few men in the crossing." Emerging onto the Virginia shore, cartridge boxes wet and several colleagues absent, the regiment re-formed preparatory to climbing the embankment, accompanied by soldiers of the 1st U.S. Sharpshooters.[643]

Twenty-five-year-old John A. Gordon of Detroit was a casualty of the crossing. Wounded in the right shoulder by a musket ball at the Battle of Malvern Hill on July 1, 1862, he had spent weeks convalescing in the Judiciary Square Hospital in Washington. Promoted from his lieutenancy on September 2, now he had suffered a second grievous wound, the "ball passing downward and forward through the upper left lung causing difficulty of breathing and spitting of blood." Thankfully, Assistant Surgeon David Palmer Chamberlin of Hudson was nearby and treated him on the battlefield. Gordon was soon back in Washington convalescing once more.[644]

The havoc played on the Confederates by Union artillery proved to be telling. McClellan's headquarters would report how Hunt had "opened nineteen guns on the enemy…and kept up his fire until night set in."[645] Under cover of the guns, the 4th Michigan scaled the embankment overlooking the river, finding hardly any enemy present. Left behind were "cannon, muskets, mess-chests, sick, wounded, &c." The men broke out in cheers "for the Union" and their gallant colonel, the sounds resonating across to the Federal positions on the far bank.[646] Believing that they were expected to hold the foothold, the soldiers began to make camp. Around 8:30 p.m., however, they were ordered back to the north bank. As the 4th made its way toward the crossing, seven horsemen mistakenly rode into their midst. They were "some members of General Lee's Richmond reporters." The Michiganders took their prisoners back across the Potomac.[647] Other Federals remained on the south bank.

The day had been something of a Union success. At 10:00 p.m., McClellan's chief of staff directed the Union cavalry to "be at the river by daylight without fail" because "Colonel Hunt thinks that you should be."[648] At 10:45 p.m., McClellan's headquarters issued Porter directives for a profitable September 20. The V Corps would cross to Virginia again at daylight, supported by Pleasanton's cavalry.[649] The commanding general intended to ride to the Potomac and see for himself the condition of affairs.[650] Saturday would be warm and sunny[651] and might evolve into an energetic pursuit and renewal of wider hostilities.

The 4th Michigan was up at first light and moved across the river before breakfast. Crossing Boteler's Ford with the 62nd Pennsylvania and Hazlett's Battery D of the 5th U.S. Artillery, once more the Michiganders climbed the heights on the Virginia side. Once again they encountered no significant opposition, and the hungry men foraged for flour, geese and turkeys.[652] They had been sent over for bigger game—recovery of abandoned Confederate cannons. Returning to camp at about 8:00 a.m., the regiment and its accompaniment brought over "three guns, several caissons and one battle-flag, picked up on the field."[653] Porter had ordered Morell and Sykes to cross at about 7:00 a.m. to follow the early morning incursion. By dispatch at 9:15 a.m., he had received word from Sykes that the skirmishers of his advanced guard had encountered an enemy brigade advancing from the south on the Charlestown road.[654]

Troops of the 1st Brigade, 1st Division, including the 1st Michigan, had made the crossing just about at that hour and filed to the west toward Shepherdstown.[655] Lockley had taken off his boots "and rolled up my pants and got across with all my clothes dry." The brigade halted and, under orders from Sykes, maintained its presence close to Boteler's. The 1st Michigan and two other regiments were directed to ascend from the ford and to form below the top of the ridge; "these movements were all promptly executed, and in good order." Lockley recorded simply that "we move up a large ravine and form a line of battle."[656] The brigade advanced its skirmishers, being now in position to withstand an attack. It soon came: "[N]otwithstanding the vastly superior numbers of the enemy, every man stood his ground firmly, and the line exhibited an undaunted front." The Federal batteries on the north side of the river "opened a heavy fire with good effect."[657] As the Confederates approached, the 1st Michigan "gave them such a shower of bullets that they had to leave us & flank off to our right" where the 118th Pennsylvania stood.[658]

The V Corps commander left his headquarters on the Stephen Grove farm just west of Sharpsburg and went down to Boteler's Ford to see the situation for himself.[659] It was not pretty: only a small part of his corps, including the 1st and 4th Michigan, had made it over to the far bank.[660] Sykes advised Porter that "the Virginia side of the river was no place for troops until a proper reconnaissance had been made."[661] And so Porter concluded that it was impossible to move over and form a sufficient force in time to withstand the "large" Confederate advance. He gave the order for a general withdrawal, and all units but one did so with little injury. The Michigan cohorts and the rest of the expedition "conducted the withdrawal skillfully and with little loss."[662] The urgency in crossing back onto the Maryland shore created an unlikely route for two regiments. While the 1st Michigan crossed back over at the ford, the right two regiments of Barnes's Brigade—the 13th and 25th New York—crossed the milldam located to the west.[663]

Lockley was now not scrupulous about remaining dry: "We plunged into the river and waded across. This time I did not wait to pull off my boots or anything else." When halfway, "something hit me in the back and knocked me head over heels into the water. I got up and plunged on." Whatever the cause, he was unwounded.[664] Only the 118th Pennsylvania took significant casualties.[665] Colonel Barnes exhibited pride at his brigade's performance: "[F]inding themselves suddenly and unexpectedly attacked by a force so vastly superior, there was no sign of intimidation on the part of any one, and when the order to retire was given it was received with evident disappointment."[666] They were covered in the crossing by accurate fire from the sharpshooters.[667]

The V Corps infantry and artillery did not continue their withdrawal beyond the Potomac but rather continued to man positions on the Maryland side. The 4th Michigan, in fact, had made its camp only to return to the river to cover the withdrawal of the rest of Porter's reconnaissance.[668] McClellan had not wanted to incur a general engagement. His orders to Porter had been to detach "a reconnoitering party in greater force" than the day before to verify how far Lee had retreated on the Charlestown and Martinsburg roads toward Winchester; to Pleasanton, it was to push the enemy, using artillery to damage them, but not to incur "too much risk to your command."[669] The intentions of his adversary were again not obvious. Enemy movement toward Williamsport was reported, and Porter's reconnaissance had produced unhappy intelligence when Hill's troops of Jackson's corps reappeared and precipitated the Federal withdrawal from Virginia.[670] That night, McClellan reported to Halleck on what he knew of Lee: "I think he has a force of infantry near Shepherdstown."[671]

McClellan's confusion had a basis in reality. The retreat of the Army of Northern Virginia on the eighteenth had been rapid, but not because its leader considered the Maryland Campaign to be over.[672] Lee had first ordered Stuart to turn the Federal right that morning, but the Potomac was so close and the Union artillery so capable that the plan was abandoned.[673] After the Union army failed to attack and provide an opportunity for further bloodying, Lee developed an improvement on the notion of turning its right. The Army of Northern Virginia would return, temporarily, to its home state only to revisit Maryland via Williamsport, thus executing a turning movement that would involve crossing at Boteler's Ford, marching west to Martinsburg and then north to Williamsport over the Potomac and be once again on Maryland soil. By the twentieth or the day following, this movement would be completed, with the Confederates coming in on the rear of McClellan's right flank.[674] Accordingly, Lee ordered Pendleton to prepare for the army's crossing.[675]

Stuart would go to Williamsport. His cavalry crossed the Potomac into Virginia during the night of the eighteenth, moved back into Maryland the following day and joined up at Williamsport on the afternoon of the nineteenth.[676] Back at Shepherdstown, A.P. Hill had been ordered by Stonewall Jackson to expel the Federals. His division was in the lead, followed by those of D.H. Hill and Jubal Early. Only the first division would be necessary to check the Union incursion. Among the Confederate gains was twenty-two-year-old Private Newton Storm Bibbins of the 1st Michigan, captured along the bank of the river before he could scamper across.[677]

Although the Confederate army faced no immediate threat, General Lee's views on its prospects had suffered. The Potomac had not proved to be a significant barrier to his enemy; the earliest report on the situation caused him to think that he had lost his entire rear guard and all forty-four guns of the Artillery Reserve. McClellan's army was not immobilized after the seventeenth.[678] The action at Shepherdstown the evening of the nineteenth found its way into Lee's letter to President Davis the next morning, written from near Martinsburg (now West Virginia). The tenor was less sanguine than the message sent two days earlier. The Federals had not attacked on the eighteenth, and "our position being a bad one to hold with the river in rear I determined to cross the Army to the Va. Side....the morning of the 19th, found us satisfactorily over on the south bank of the Potomac near Shepherdstown." Lee's goal was to move northward to Williamsport and threaten McClellan's right. Because the enemy had crossed over to the same bank near Shepherdstown, he indicated that a return eastward to that area was necessary to drive the Federals back.[679] If the whole Union army was across, though, "an attack would be inadvisable."[680] By dark, he had ordered Stuart back into Virginia.[681]

The next day, Lee sent another letter to Davis. It revealed an altogether different state of affairs. The general had believed the objectives of the Maryland Campaign still obtainable after completing "a successful change of base."[682] He reported that "the march of the army toward Williamsport was arrested" by the Federal incursion to the south side of the Potomac. After driving the enemy back into Maryland the previous day, "this army resumed its march." He complained of straggling by troops during the recent invasion, and then the letter admitted to a situation of quiescence: "[T]he army is resting to-day on the Opequon, below Martinsburg."[683] No promise of an advance to Williamsport was repeated. Two days later, still from his "camp on the Opequon," Lee again raised the issue of straggling in a report to Davis. He also discussed the related subjects of recruiting and replacing incapacitated officers, giving this as "the main cause" of the army's "retiring from Maryland." Without mentioning the battle on the seventeenth or its effects on his army's strength, Lee went into some detail on the issue of subsistence.[684] Not until a letter of September 25 arrived via an aide who was one of Lee's sons did Davis actually read that in the recent conflicts his principal Southern army, still immobile near Martinsburg, "got the worst of it."[685] The army commander addressed a communication to Davis that day indicating that he had hoped to return to Maryland, but the condition and strength of his troops prevented it since the "hazard would be great."[686] Instead, the army moved south near Winchester,[687] being capable only of a defensive posture.[688]

Over the course of these communications, Lee was laying the ground for conceding that his vaunted Maryland Campaign had ended. Nearly one year later, he admitted that the Battle of Antietam had gone badly and the losses very costly: "[T]he condition of our troops now demanded repose."[689] His goal now proved very modest: "[I]t is still my desire to threaten a passage into Maryland." Locating the army around Martinsburg constituted only a feint; perhaps he could draw the enemy into the Shenandoah Valley and attack them to advantage. Offensive operations, however, were over.[690]

September 21 dawned a sunny day. When John Bancroft recorded this Sunday in his journal, the account was brief: "Beautiful day. All quiet in the morning."[691] Succeeding days found no mention of hostilities, only going into camp, standing picket duty and, as the calendar turned the page to October, a presidential visit to the army with conditions having made it safe. McClellan did not seriously consider further pursuit across the Potomac. Three weeks had elapsed since his resumption of command, and the Army of the Potomac had accomplished much. It had defeated Lee and sent him across the Potomac back into Virginia and had done so "with a patchwork force—including a fifth of its men so green they made McDowell's soldiers at Bull Run look like seasoned veterans."[692]

On the twentieth, the XII Corps under Williams was in and about Harpers Ferry, occupying Maryland Heights and Sandy Hook, a site on the Potomac east of the river fork.[693] Two days later, the II Corps occupied Harpers Ferry.[694] From the twentieth on for several weeks, McClellan consolidated his forces, content to stand guard on the north bank of the Potomac and occupy the key river junction. He would be prepared to attack should Lee attempt again to cross into Maryland.[695] The watch phrase in the ranks: "[A]ll quiet on the Potomac."[696]

Confederate expectations had been very high. Under a headline "Our Army in Maryland," the *Richmond Daily Dispatch* on the day of the battle published a hopeful report despite the affair on South Mountain. It was too early for the newspaper to tell readers of Antietam or Shepherdstown results.

> *The intelligence which we have received, thus far, from our army in Maryland, is meagre, unsatisfactory, and made up from Yankee papers. The mortal terror of the Yankees, however, affords ample proof that the blow has been struck in the proper place, and that, if properly followed up, it will not fail to tell.*[697]

Far different accounts appeared in Detroit newspapers during and after the campaign. Jackson's *Weekly Citizen* reported with hometown pride that the 17th Michigan "had covered itself with glory" at South Mountain. A subsequent piece hailed the "Michigan 'Invincibles'" who had routed and nearly annihilated an enemy brigade. Several accounts included different nicknames for the unit:

> *A "Stonewall" Regiment—One of the new regiments from Michigan, during one of the battles in Maryland, after fighting like veterans… charged over a stone wall upon Drayton's South Carolina brigade…. The Seventeenth Michigan is the "Stonewall" regiment, and the South Carolinians will long remember with grief those "raw recruits from country towns."*—New York Post

> *Stonewall Jackson will now have to divide his sobriquet with the doughty Michigander, who performed such gallant service in the late battles in Maryland.*—Boston Transcript

> *The 17th Michigan, out only two weeks, fought until their ammunition was exhausted, then retired to the wagons in good order, refilled their boxes, returned and made a terrible charge over a stone wall and into the timber, almost annihilating Drayton's South Carolina Brigade.*—New York World

Letters from Withington were reprinted, providing a front-line vantage point for readers. Similar telegraphic accounts had prompted communications to the colonel, such as a letter from General Willcox's brother, Eben: "Our city is wild with delight at telegraph news that your Regt destroyed a whole South Carolina Brigade in the fight of Monday."[698] Stories on the major battle contained McClellan's dispatches under breathless headlines like "A Great Victory Over the Rebel Forces—They Retreat in a Panic to the Potomac" and "McClellan's Great Victory." Accompanying these triumphant accounts (of varying accuracy) were sobering casualty lists. In several, Withington was reported wounded, causing unnecessary distress to his family. He emerged unscathed, but duty called him to write letters to the loved ones of those who had not fared as well. On September 21, he wrote to the father of Sergeant James H. Tuttle of his son's death four days earlier:

> *I cannot allow the sad bereavement which the battle of Sharpsburg has visited upon your household to pass, without saying how deeply my*

> *sympathies are with you, and giving my testimony to the noble bearing of your son, James, in the battle of south Mountain and Sharpsburg. In both he proved himself a brave soldier. At the former his hat and clothing were cut by two shots; at the latter he gave his life to his country. I saw him on the field after he had received the fatal shot, and taking his hand asked him if he knew me. He said he did, and asked me if I would procure his discharge.... Words are vain as consolation to yourself and his mother. God alone is our refuge, and to him I know you will look.*
>
> *The conduct of your son as a soldier in the regiment was ever exemplary, and his death was heroic. He fell with face to the foe, fighting for his country's preservation.*[699]

The letter arrived on the heels of one the sergeant had written on the fifteenth to his family: "I am slightly wounded but will get along. If I should get sick, or wounded dangerously, so that I could be of no further service here, I will get my discharge, if possible, and come home to you, as I promised you I would."[700]

Not all news from the front had such a sorrowful ending. Newton Bibbins was paroled after nine days of captivity.[701] Publications in Michigan's largest city also reported on the favorable outcome of the campaign. The *Detroit Free Press* published on September 24 a reprint of a *New York Tribune* story. The headlines read, "From the Potomac. The Fourth Michigan. The Rebels Failed at Williamsport. Bravery of the Fourth." The story acknowledged how, as the regiment was preparing to cross the river, an enemy battery opened on it: "[A] slight movement resembling a panic at first manifested itself." Once the order was given "to cross the stream, ascend the hill and take the battery, a shout went up which echoed and re echoed through the gorge." The Michiganders waded through the four-foot-deep waters, and up they charged: "The hill was gained in the face of a deadly fire, the guns reached, the gunners shot or bayoneted, the entire battery in our possession." The correspondent regarded it one of the bravest charges of the war.

Because accounts arrived erratically for days following the main event, the paper also included a wrap-up of the campaign now that Lee had taken his army back to Virginia:

> *We have not crushed or annihilated the rebel army, as many have demanded of the commanding General, but we have whipped him upon ground admirably selected by himself, and compelled him to make a*

> *precipitate retreat from the State he came to dragoon into the service of his rebel Confederacy.*

Two brilliant victories by our brave soldiers in blue, the author opined, had been added to the glorious history of the republic.[702]

As for Lee, his full and final campaign report would not be finished until August 19, 1863.[703] By that time, he had attempted a second invasion of the North, seeking to achieve what his Maryland Campaign of 1862 had not.

Chapter 10

AFTERMATH

A Proclamation and Its Price

The Battle of Antietam had ended. The Maryland Campaign had ended. The invasion of the Union had ended. The Union army, though bloodied, had gained many trophies. On September 27, George A. Custer wrote to a friend, "Enclosed I send you a small strip of silk which I tore from a rebel flag at the battle of Antietam."[704] Edwin Sumner's report sought commendations for Williams and Richardson, "who were distinguished for their zeal and devotion."[705] Sumner informed Williams that "he had mentioned my name and had recommended me for promotion."[706]

On September 30, General-in-Chief Halleck congratulated McClellan on South Mountain and Antietam, terming them "hard-fought battles, but well-earned and decided victories":

> *The valor and endurance of your army in the several conflicts which terminated in the expulsion of the enemy from the loyal State of Maryland are creditable alike to the troops and to the officers who commanded them. A grateful country, while mourning the lamented dead, will not be unmindful of the honors due the living.*[707]

Willcox issued a congratulatory order to his men reflecting "his entire satisfaction with the manner in which they fought in the bloody battles of South Mountain and Sharpsburg."[708] Hard-fought, they were; bloody, no one could contest. Williams had visited the Sunken Road at battle's end and witnessed how the Confederate bodies "lay as thick as autumn leaves along a narrow lane cut below the natural surface, into which they seemed to have tumbled."[709] Many lives had ended, but the war went on. Northern attempts to develop a winning strategy also continued.

On July 17, 1862, President Lincoln signed the Second Confiscation Act.[710] This "Act to Suppress Insurrection, to Punish Treason and Rebellion"[711] had taken nearly the entire seven-month Congressional session before passage. No member stood more staunchly in favor of the bill than Michigan senator Jacob Merritt Howard. In lengthy remarks on April 18, admitting that the legislation "is one of novelty in this country," Howard defended it on constitutional, legal and historical grounds given the "novel times." He adjured his colleagues "to come up to the work" required to save the nation.[712] As ultimately passed on July 12, the measure directly emancipated slaves within Union lines of those engaged "in any rebellion or insurrection" against the United States and authorized the president to proclaim emancipation of the enslaved in seceded territory beyond military control.[713] When the final vote came—after the president had objected to an aspect of the bill adopted the day before[714]—Howard took the floor to announce that he would, despite concerns, vote yes. Far better this than a veto:

> *Language scarcely enables me to express the feelings of deprecation with which I contemplate that contingency. I foresee that should it happen, it would create a most serious embarrassment in the prosecution of the existing war; that it would tend greatly to divide opinion and so to arrange parties in the free States that it would be extremely difficult, not to say impossible, that all the energies of the loyal people of the United States shall be used for the suppression of this rebellion....anxious especially that we should have a united North in the suppression of this rebellion, I must waive any pride of opinion which, under other circumstances, and in peaceful times, might induce me to vote against this measure, at such a moment as this.*[715]

The greater cause demanded Howard set aside his desire for more radical action. Voting "aye," he sought to secure emancipation and thus "to destroy slavery completely in the seceded states."[716]

So, too, did all of Michigan's Congressional delegation, all voting in favor. On May 24, Congressman Fernando C. Beaman of Michigan's 2nd District had spoken bluntly in favor of confiscation, convinced of "no impediment" to the legislation. The average American knew, he said, "that his Government has been wickedly assaulted and besieged by traitors" and "that his native land is being fertilized with the heart's blood of his country." The rebellion was "unconstitutional violence" and the war against the United States "unconstitutional murder." Since "the original and continuing cause of the rebellion is slavery, and all attempts to conceal or disguise the fact are simply absurd," confiscation and emancipation were critically necessary to strike at the root of the war. Consequently, he avowed, "I am in favor of liberating the slaves of rebels."[717]

The day of the final vote, Lincoln told his secretaries of state and navy that he favored issuing the proclamation that the legislation sought.[718] But he needed a Union victory to undergird the action. On September 22, just five days after the sun set on the Sharpsburg battleground, he took the step and signed the preliminary Emancipation Proclamation. As of January, 1, 1863, "all persons held as slaves within any State, or designated part of a State, the people whereof shall then be in rebellion against the United States shall be then, thenceforward, and forever free." The president's action was momentous; it also fulfilled a vow:

> *When the rebel army was at Frederick, I determined, as soon as it should be driven out of Maryland, to issue a Proclamation of Emancipation such as I thought most likely to be useful. I said nothing to any one; but I made the promise to myself, and (hesitating a little)—to my Maker. The rebel army is now driven out, and I am going to fulfill that promise.*[719]

After discussion and a few revisions, the document was finalized. In addition to providing for emancipation on January 1, it called attention to military commanders that the Second Confiscation Act required protection of escaped slaves.[720]

September 22 saw the penning of a different document from Washington. Detroiter John J. Bagley wrote to William Withington a poignant letter:

> *Dear Sir, I found in a barn near the battle field of Wednesday George Newman of your regiment wounded in the leg. I took him to Boonsboro and got him in a private house where has good care and attention.…I believe he is not dangerous though he has a bad wound.*

Bagley urged Withington to secure the wounded soldier's commission and "make him a Lieutenant.…He is the only son of his widowed mother—and I hear he is brave."[721] Newman had enlisted at Detroit in the 17th Michigan on July 29, 1862, age twenty-two, with the rank of private. The officer's

Engraving of President Lincoln reading the draft of the Emancipation Proclamation to his cabinet, September 22, 1862, from Francis Carpenter's 1864 painting. *The Henry Ford.*

commission he expected would be delayed until September 26, when he was mustered as second lieutenant to date from September 4.[722]

Bagley had gone to Sharpsburg as representative of the Michigan Soldiers Relief Committee. On the nineteenth, he sent the committee a report from Boonsboro, "4 Miles from the Battle Field," indicating that he and party "have been here and to the front for two days." He could "not describe the scene to you. I thank God that we were able to come.…Such a sight I never saw before." The loss in wounded was heavy: "I suppose we have dressed 400 wounds yesterday and today. Tell our people to hurry down hospital stores to our association at Washington." Among the wounded aided by the committee were Major George Collins Lyon and Lieutenant Rowen Summers of the 17th Michigan. Bagley also mentioned hearing that the regiment's lieutenant colonel, Constant Luce, "was saved by his watch" apparently deflecting a bullet.[723]

Back in Michigan, the proclamation was hailed by many and reviled by some. Governor Blair signed a letter along with other Northern state chief executives expressing solid support to the president: "We hail with heartfelt gratitude and encouraged hope the proclamation of the President issued on the 22d." It was, the governors wrote, a decision that was designed "to strike at the root of the rebellion." Blair supported Lincoln in prosecuting "with the utmost vigor this war for the preservation of the national life and the hope of humanity."[724]

Many Michigan soldiers concurred with the step, such as David Lane of the 17th Infantry: "I hail with delight the President's proclamation. I believe it is a step in the right direction."[725] Other Michigan men in blue supported their governor and exhibited state pride. Private Eugene Deverny Young of the 8th Michigan, all of nineteen, wrote home to tell his parents how he had been in both battles "and we beat them every time and drove them out of the state."[726] Captain J. Benton Kennedy of the 1st Michigan wrote to his father on October 10 from near Sharpsburg: "I think Gov. Blair has done nobly as a general thing for Mich. and no better man could be chosen for the position in the State....If the soldiers could vote, Blair would get a big vote I think from the army." He was proud of being a member of the "Western" troops in the Army of the Potomac:

> *O that we had all western men in our army here. The eastern city troops cry "enough" too soon but the western boys never. I have noticed the difference on the field. When the eastern men are in a hot place and are suffering, the* [sic] *want to get out, and generally back out but the western boys, when they are in a warm spot, they get out of it by going out toward the enemy.*[727]

Men from "the West" between the Great Lakes were answering the call to "go out toward" the Confederate military.[728] The 20th Michigan arrived at the Antietam battleground soon after the bloody day, remaining there until October 6. Among its complement was a young man from Waterloo, Michigan, named Anson Croman. On July 29, 1862, he had signed enlistment papers at the recruiting station in Marshall for a three-year term. Croman became one of those participating in the midsummer "surge" who had not volunteered in the heady first weeks of the war. In his case, a compelling reason existed: he was underage. Croman had been born in December 1844; he was seventeen years and seven months old at enlistment. His first acquaintance with death came as the regiment assisted in burial of nearly 3,700 dead.

At the Pry house, pressed into service as one of the numerous field hospitals treating the thousands of wounded soldiers, Israel Richardson lay in an upper bedroom. His division had camped on these very grounds on the nights of the fifteenth and sixteenth.[729] Doctors sought to remove the shell fragment, but it was embedded too deep in his chest. Notified of her

Citizen volunteers assisting wounded on the field of battle, sketch by battlefield artist Alfred Waud. *Library of Congress.*

husband's condition, Frances Richardson traveled from Washington to aid his convalescence.[730]

Among the surgeons working on the grounds was Abner Hard. He had moved to Livingston County from New York when thirteen years old, about 1833, later taking up the study of medicine and spending winters teaching school near Detroit. In 1851, he moved to Aurora, Illinois, continued to study with his brother and graduated from the medical department of Iowa State University in 1854. He was serving as surgeon of the 8th Illinois Cavalry, an appointment owed to the regiment's colonel, John Farnsworth, former Livingston County resident.[731] During his grim work at Antietam, he encountered Clara Barton ministering to wounded soldiers on the seventeenth and afterward.[732]

The future founder of the American Red Cross would be one of many civilians to visit Antietam. President Lincoln arrived on October 1, and one of his reviews included the 17th Michigan. A diarist noted, "I saw the long geared President.... Old Abe looks better than his portrait & a good deal more pleasant."[733] On October 2, as the president reviewed troops, twenty-one-year old Franklin Benjamin Marsh of the 8th Michigan wrote a letter home from "Spring hospital" a mile in rear of the Rohrbach Bridge (now Burnside Bridge) on the left of the Union line where Willcox had crossed. He wrote, with phonetic spelling:

> *I have bin so busy since I came to the Hospital.... we have bin in two very heavy battles. the battle of South Mountains & the one on the 17th of Sept Oh you can't have any idea what a sight it is to pass over a battle field and see the dead I saw the rebs at South Mountains whare they lay so thick that you could walk all around on the dead and in other places around a stone fence whare they lay three & four deep whare our boys charged on them and gained the ground, our 17th Mich did noble work at the sunday fight.*[734]

On the third, the president inspected troops, including Willcox's Division, along with McClellan and Burnside, the latter proclaiming that it "looked the finest." Lincoln was impressed, asking both generals, "Is not Gen. Willcox a very faithful officer?"[735] Several days later, the Michigander would be honored with command of IX Corps.[736] A correspondent identified as "J.T.M." wrote an account of the review that appeared in the *Detroit Advertiser and Tribune* regarding another exchange between Lincoln and the army commander:

> *As they passed the 17th, McClellan informed the President it was the Stonewall Regiment, and a smile, which we deemed a smile of approval, took possession of the homeliest countenance your correspondent has met in his limited travels, but we felt as we rode with his escort that we were in the presence of a* great *man of future history, a man whom the future biographer would compare with* [Andrew] *Jackson and Washington, and whose memory would be cherished with that of the Father of his country.*[737]

The reporter likely was Lieutenant James T. Morgan of Muskegon; no other regimental officer possessed such initials. The writer openly castigated the general commanding: he was no idol of the soldiers, and "I have heard men of high and low rank express their utter want of confidence in McClellan."

The 24th Michigan had arrived from the capital in Frederick on October 2, and the next day, it marched to the Antietam battlefield and set up Camp Harbaugh a mile southeast of Sharpsburg.[738] The 1st, 4th and 16th Michigan regiments camped nearby. The wounded filled field hospitals all around the countryside.[739] Three physicians arrived with the 24th and contributed their services while the regiment remained in camp. Regimental surgeon John H. Beech, a Coldwater native, was a founding member of the Michigan State Medical Association and had just turned forty-three. He was to become the surgeon-in-chief of the Iron Brigade.[740] Charles C. Smith was the assistant surgeon, a resident of Redford, thirty-four years of age and an experienced practitioner.[741] Forty-year-old Alexander Collar of Wayne, who had presided at one of the regiment's organizing meetings in Detroit,[742] also served as an assistant surgeon.[743]

An article appeared in a Michigan newspaper on October 9 telling of how the 24th had seen "some of the horrors and devastations" on the two battlefields. The men had spent six hours on the South Mountain ground, visiting "the stone wall over which the Seventeenth charged; here, the lane into which they forced the South Carolina brigade." The landscape bore the evidence: "[E]very bush and shrub is riddled with shot and shell, and huge trees cut entirely off by shell." Battle detritus lay all around, including hats and canteens "with two and three bullet holes in each."[744] Abel Peck, color bearer in the regiment, wrote home on October 24 of his impressions:

> [W]*e camped a bout one mile from the Burgh and went over the batelfield it was a sight that I hope you will never see and yet I should like to have you see it but it is a harde sight thare is one trench whare they say thare is one hundred & 50 Rebels buried and the graves are plenty whar our men ly but the friends of our men have few and removed some of them Houses and Barns are destroyed and one Church is badley rideled it is a brick one and will have to be rebilt if ever any thing is don with it the wods a round the Church look as if it had haled cast iron it is sayd to have bin the hardest batel ever fought on the Continant that is thare was the most heavy artilery used.*[745]

The 24th arrived just in time to see the president depart for Washington. The regimental historian recorded the scene:

> *On October 4, President Lincoln passed by our camp, from a visit to the recent and neighboring battle-fields. He stood at the rear of his train, bowing to us as it slowly moved by. His head was uncovered and he looked careworn from the weighty matters upon his mind. We gave him some Michigan cheers as the train moved slowly by.*[746]

Alpheus Williams had a more private encounter and came away largely impressed: "I had quite a long talk with him, sitting on a pile of logs. He really is the most unaffected, simple-minded honest, and frank man I have ever met. I wish he had a little more firmness."[747] A soldier in the 17th liked his appearance: "He looks much better than the likenesses we see of him—younger, and not so long and lank."[748]

Lincoln, McClellan, Hunt (behind Lincoln near tent), Custer (far right) and other officers of the Army of the Potomac at Grove Farm, photo by Alexander Gardner. *Library of Congress.*

The president had come for consultations on the state of the army. On the third, he and McClellan reviewed IX Corps in the vicinity of the Antietam battleground, moved on to a visit of V Corps, went over the battlefield by following the II Corps route (seeing the Dunker Church and Bloody Lane)[749] and then spent time at McClellan's tent to confer about forthcoming strategy, enabling photographers to capture the scene.[750] On October 4, the two leaders "visited such of the wounded as still remained in the vicinity, including…General Richardson" in the morning. Next they visited the South Mountain battleground, after which Lincoln and his party returned to Washington from Frederick.[751]

The president had come to visit those who had sacrificed much and sought opportunities to console wounded soldiers. What passed between the president and Richardson went unrecorded for decades; the account, based on the recollection of twenty-one-year-old Charles Stuart Draper of Pontiac, himself recuperating from a wound nearby, had the president promising army command once the general recovered.[752] The two leaders had already made contact in another way that neither of them likely knew. During the photo opportunity session at headquarters near Sharpsburg, one image captured the two men inside McClellan's tent with a captured Confederate battle flag on the ground nearby.

The colors were seen by a delegation to McClellan's headquarters a few days after:

President Lincoln and General McClellan in the general's tent, with the flag on the ground captured by Richardson's Division. Gardner photograph. *Library of Congress.*

> *This flag was about four feet square, red ground, with blue stripes, about four inches wide, running diagonally across, or from corner to corner. On these stripes are twelve white stars, representing the twelve States claimed by the rebels as belonging to their confederacy. It was very badly torn and blood-stained. From a written paper sewed on it, I learned that it had been the battle-flag of the Eleventh Alabama regiment, captured by the Fifty-seventh New-York volunteers, Richardson's division, Sumner's corps, at the battle of "Antietam," September seventeenth, 1862.*[753]

Ironically, the twelfth star represented aspirations for Maryland becoming a member of the Confederacy, a hope dashed by the Union victory epitomized by the capture of this flag.

Several similar banners were described in this inventory, including one taken by a VI Corps regiment that had come up to reinforce Richardson and one captured by the "Seventh New-York volunteers, Caldwell's brigade, Richardson's Division." Another, having an "orange-colored fringe"—from

Florida, perhaps—also came from the same part of the field, taken by the "Sixty-first New-York volunteers, Caldwell's brigade, Richardson's division." A uniquely designed pennant, large and dark blue, with two female figures holding a staff, liberty cap and scroll, the colors of the 4th North Carolina Infantry, had also been taken by the "Fifth New-Hampshire volunteers, Colonel E.E. Cross, of Caldwell's brigade, Richardson's division."[754]

In all, some twenty Confederate colors were viewed, but only a handful could have been the specific flag in the photograph with the president. Of those, all but one were from Richardson's Division.[755]

After the president visited the South Mountain battlefield, he arrived in Frederick at about 4:45 p.m. His first stop was the residence of Mrs. Ellen Tyler Ramsey at 119 Record Street to visit George Hartsuff, "who lay wounded" there.[756] By the time he was finished, a crowd had gathered to hear remarks. Lincoln offered a hundred words, concluding, "I can only return my sincere thanks for the compliment paid our cause and our common country." A few moments later at the railway station, he again was importuned to speak. This time he sought to pay appropriate thanks to the men in uniform he had seen:

> *Fellow-Citizens: I see myself surrounded by soldiers, and a little further off I note the citizens of this good city of Frederick, anxious to hear something from me. I can only say, as I did five minutes ago, it is not proper for me to make speeches in my present position. I return thanks to our soldiers for the good service they have rendered, for the energies they have shown, the hardships they have endured, and the blood they have so nobly shed for this dear Union of ours; and I also return thanks not only to the soldiers, but to the good citizens of Maryland, and to all the good men and women in this land, for their devotion to our glorious cause. I say this without any malice in my heart to those who have done otherwise. May our children and our children's children to a thousand generations, continue to enjoy the benefits conferred upon us by a united country, and have cause yet to rejoice under those glorious institutions bequeathed us by Washington and his compeers. Now, my friends, soldiers and citizens, I can only say once more, farewell.*[757]

The commander in chief had gone out of his way to visit with the three wounded Michiganders. Hartsuff would visit with the president again on April 3, 1865.[758]

The 17th Michigan had suffered much. Of the survivors, none had a story superior to that of James Van Kleeck. Born at Exeter, Monroe County, on September 26, 1846, he was fifteen years old when, in June 1862, his "boyish patriotism" led him to enlist in Company D as a drummer boy.[759] He incurred two wounds on September 17; in the second incident, "a ball was lodged in his side, and he was left on the field supposedly dead. Taken to the hospital, he remained for a number of months in the Frederic [*sic*] City Hospital in Maryland, and was finally discharged in December, 1863, for disability. For one year after his wound he was unable to walk."[760] Several years later, according to a Bay City newspaper story, he received a memento of that bloody day:

> *Mr. Van Kleeck's sister, who lives in Washtenaw county, received the missing book from a Captain Theodore Gregg of Co. F. Forty-fifth regiment, Pennsylvania Volunteers, who explained that he had picked it up on the battlefield and finding between the leaves a letter from the lady to her brother considered the matter of sufficient importance to forward the book to her address....Some of the leaves are badly stained. "That is my blood," said Mr. Van Kleeck, "but only a small portion of what I lost on the memorable day I missed the book after the battle and made an effort to find it, but could not secure any trace of it."*
>
> *On the fly leaf of the book is written, "Found on the battlefield of Antietam while a hot engagement was going on Sept. 17, 1862, in which the union troops were victorious."*[761]

Adjutant William Richards wrote a letter for publication while in Detroit recuperating from his serious wound. "Young men of Michigan," he encouraged, "turn out" and join the ranks of the 17th. It was now a complement of 437 men out of the 960 who had left for the front. Of 287 sick and wounded, he named several officers: Edmonds, loss of arm; Thayer, home in Battle Creek recovering; Clarkston, visiting friends in Maryland, the same; Luce, suffering from illness and fatigue; and Lyon, so far recovered as to think he will soon resume his post.[762]

In terms of sheer numbers, the 7th incurred the most casualties. Thus, the impact was felt heavily in Monroe. But other communities bore their burden of sorrow. From rural Napoleon Township south of Jackson, five young men were killed in the Maryland Campaign: Sergeant Oscar E. Miller, age twenty-three; Corporal George Myron Hawley, twenty-four; Private Alonzo D. Palmer, almost twenty-four; Private Gilbert B. Peck, age twenty-five;[763] and Private Dwight C. Slack, twenty-four. Their remains returned by train to Napoleon. Following a service with military honors at the Township Park with more than two thousand in attendance, interment occurred in a single grave in Maple Grove Cemetery south of the village. The five names were later inscribed on a monument as a perpetual reminder of the community's loss.[764]

One of the 7th's alumni was Cyrus Bacon Jr., who had enlisted on April 16, 1861, only four days after Fort Sumter, and was appointed assistant surgeon. Born in Ontwa Township in Cass County in 1837, he first studied medicine with a local doctor and then graduated from the University of Michigan in 1858[765] at the age of twenty-one. After a few months demonstrating his skill, in April 1862 Bacon was promoted to the position of a surgeon in the U.S. Army.[766] His service with the Army of the Potomac in the Peninsula Campaign resulted in serious illness. On leave, he made his way to Detroit, where he boarded a Michigan Central train for Niles. In his sleeping berth, he "slept like a log"[767] until reaching Niles at 4:05 a.m. Receiving his commission on August 3, two weeks later he was back on the "forenoon train for Detroit" expecting to travel to the front. It took until September 13 for his orders to arrive specifying that he was to report at Washington.[768]

On Tuesday, September 16, Bacon left home at 9:00 a.m. for the journey to the nation's capital. He arrived there on the nineteenth and reported for duty the next day. He was ordered "to be ready within perhaps two hours to proceed to Frederick, Maryland in charge of a train of ambulances, (12) loaded with Hospital Stores, to proceed as expeditiously as possible.... [The ambulance] train did not leave 'til 2:15 p.m. Drove all night, had a wagon master along. After sundry mishaps [we] reached Frederick at 7:30 the following morning." He began his medical duties on the twenty-second at the Novitiate General Hospital at 200 East Second Street.

Despite fatigue from the trip and a fever, twenty-five-year-old Bacon began his work that Monday. Caring originally for eighty soldiers, the number kept increasing as more wounded were brought from the battlefield, almost all of whom became surgical patients. After only a few days, he reported, "I get tired easily, and have to work very hard. We have operations every day, some days several. This is hard work. I put a man in my wards under chloroform for the extracting of a bullet." Operations took place regularly; one involved excising "nearly all the Carpal & part of [the] Metacarpal bones of [the] right hand of one of my patients." The next day, he amputated a leg; another time he "performed a partial excision of the radius (rather was a resection)." Then there was "the circular amputation of a thigh. Also the flap amputation of the leg."

On November 9, he received orders to report to General Hospital Camp A just outside the city. This site housed a thousand wounded and sick. He repeatedly complained of not being as healthy as would be possible with exercise, indicating the degree of work required daily. For one example: "In a ball which I removed from the muscular tissue of [the] thigh of one of my patients here, was found a hammering out flat, quite as if it had been upon the anvil under the hammer. It did not appear to have struck the bone, yet was in the leg deep and spread out flat and thin almost as if intentional." On the twenty-sixth, pursuant to orders, he left Frederick for a post closer to the Army of the Potomac. En route, he passed through the capital and "placed my chest in store in Washington at the rooms of the Michigan Soldiers Relief Association, in the basement of the Patent office." His humanitarian role at Antietam had concluded.

Depositing his property at the patent building might seem curious, but Bacon had an excellent reason to do so. The Relief Association established its office there since it served as a hospital, notably the second floor. Walt Whitman wrote about his experience as a nurse there.[769] So, too, did a young woman from Michigan.

Julia Susan Wheelock had moved to Michigan in 1854 after the death of her parents. She attended Kalamazoo College and was teaching in Palo, Michigan, outside Ionia at the inception of the Civil War. Her brother, Orville, a farmer, enlisted on September 23, 1861, in the 8th Michigan. At the Battle of Chantilly he suffered a serious leg wound. On the tenth, Julia was in class "in the old red school-house" when, at about 3:00, "there is a gentle tap at the door—a little girl steps upon the threshold; her eyes are red with weeping, and, in great agitation, she says: 'Orville is wounded; his limb is amputated. He has sent for Anna, and she starts for Washington tomorrow!'"[770] Julia decided to accompany Orville's wife, and the sister of her brother's wife also went along to care for her wounded husband in the 8th Michigan. They departed Ionia the next day, taking the Detroit and Milwaukee Railroad to Detroit, boarding a steamer for Cleveland and then taking the train to Washington only to discover that their soldier had died on the ninth. Anna and Mrs. Peck went home to Michigan, but Julia had discovered a new life purpose: "My mind is at length made up to remain, and engage in the work of caring for the sick and wounded, as my desire to do so has increased with every day and almost every hour since our arrival." Twenty-eight years old, Wheelock began nearly three years of service to the wounded of Michigan that day.[771]

She did not have long to wait before newly suffering Michigan soldiers arrived in the capital:

The 25th, I saw for the first time the wounded as they came from the battlefield—the bloody field of Antietam. They were taken to the Patent Office Hospital. Oh! those bloody, mangled forms will long be fresh in memory. Some were able, with the help of a comrade, to crawl up the stairs, while others were carried up on stretchers. A few moans were heard, but no complaining, and no loud groaning, as I expected to hear.

Her resolve to serve those afflicted by combat immediately met a severe test. On the heels of losing her brother came the flood of broken soldiers whose lives would never be the same:

The sight was too much for me; I was completely unnerved, and found it impossible to conceal the emotions so deeply stirred in my inmost soul. I returned to my room to weep over the sufferings I was powerless to alleviate. Oh, cruel, cruel war![772]

"Michigan's Florence Nightingale" would minister to them over the remainder of a horribly grievous war, leaving "job, home and family" to serve for five dollars per week (covering her board) in "makeshift, often dirty, ill-equipped, and crowded hospitals."[773] A fellow Michigander, forty-six-year-old Elmina Brainard, who had come to the capital to serve the needs of her son and his comrades in the 7th Michigan, also worked for the Michigan Association alongside Wheeler.[774]

The recovery of the wounded could be incomplete. Alpheus Williams would note one soldier in his command "whose left arm was so disabled at Antietam that he could only carry his musket in his right hand."[775] Before reaching Sharpsburg, the 24th Michigan experienced the pathos of comrades brought all the way to Washington for treatment:

Our heart was stirred with deep emotion at this time. These massive walls of the Nation's council chambers were lighted from basement to unfinished dome, within which, on cots of anguish and pain, lay hundreds of our country's defenders, brought from the recent battle-fields up the Potomac.[776]

One officer in the 17th Michigan came home to Jackson "with a painful wound…from which he has suffered much." Twenty-six-year-old Second Lieutenant Benjamin B. Baker of Company K had been shot in the hand, the ball entering "at the back of his wrist, and came out at the ball of his thumb." Amputation seemed inevitable, but a month after the battle "it is hoped that he will not lose his hand."[777]

The female relief agents combed all over Washington and environs in search of Michigan soldiers to succor. Fourteen hospitals in twenty different buildings and numerous camps housed the wounded and ill. Wheelock sought out the inhabitants of each one, faithfully. Her efforts and those of the doctors paid off; she was able to record that by the end of October only four soldiers from Michigan, two in the 8th Infantry, had died of their wounds.[778] Women, too, served in vital ways.[779]

November saw the same. Some recovered and others succumbed. Draper, Richardson's aide, would live but be too disabled for further active service.[780] His general's story took a different turn. Thought initially to have a recoverable wound, by November 1 his condition had deteriorated. Pneumonia, infection and perhaps depression sapped his strength. At 7:30 p.m. on Sunday, November 3, with his wife by his side, Richardson died.[781]

"It is with a sad heart we announce the death of one of the bravest men of the nation, Major General Israel B. Richardson," the *Free Press* reported:

> *He was wounded in the terrible battle of Antietam so severely that he could only be removed to the hospital on the field of battle, where he lingered until the evening of the 3d of November, when he expired.... Gen. Richardson*

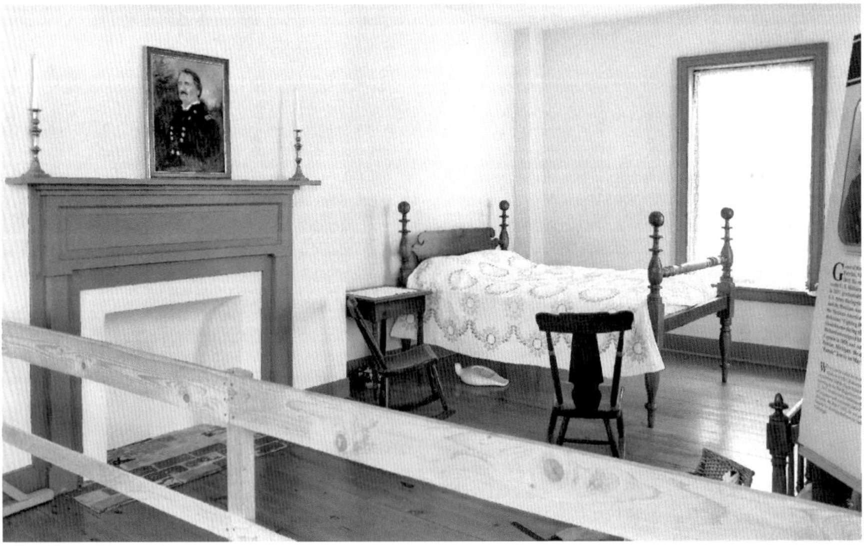

The bedroom at the Pry house where General Richardson died of his wound. *National Museum of Civil War Medicine.*

> *was known and recognized throughout the army as one of the best of our fighting Generals. Wherever the battle raged the fiercest, there he was the most at home.... There was no braver man in the army, and few whose death will be more sincerely regretted than that of Major General Richardson. He was ever held to be one of the bravest of the brave.*

The general's remains arrived at the Michigan Central Railroad dock in Detroit on Saturday morning, November 8. The coffin was met by a "Committee of Reception and Escort." At 12:30 p.m., the procession moved onto Jefferson Avenue and then on Brush Street to the Detroit and Milwaukee Railroad depot for a special funeral train to Pontiac. Pallbearers included U.S. Senator Zachariah Chandler, Detroit mayor William C. Duncan and Michigan Republican Party chairman William A. Howard. On Monday, visitors paid their respects as the coffin rested in state in the Pontiac Courthouse surrounded by American flags draped in mourning. A newspaper reported that the general's "features were as natural as life, though he looked somewhat worn down, owing to loss of blood, and the pain to which he was subjected, prior to his death."[782]

The funeral was held in Pontiac on November 11. Mourners came from Detroit and other Michigan communities by train and horse. Major Norvell of his staff came on leave, as did Major William A. Throop of the 1st Michigan. Services began at 11:00 a.m. with a eulogy from Reverend Azariah Eldridge of the Fort Street Presbyterian Church in Detroit. The cortege proceeded solemnly to Oak Hill Cemetery followed by a concourse of citizens to the accompaniment of martial salutes. Upon arriving at the grave site just inside the cemetery entrance, "a beautiful and impressive service of the Episcopal Church was read [by Reverend John O'Brien of Pontiac], after which the coffin was lowered into its receptacle." An honor volley was fired by the Detroit Light Guard, and the crowd slowly departed.[783] Richardson's funeral was the largest of its kind in Michigan history. Two who could never leave the grave behind were Richardson's young wife and their only son. Married in 1861, General Richardson was forty-six at his death.[784]

No matter the number, those grieving had to come to grips with their loss. In November, Withington received a letter from the mother of twenty-four-year-old James H. Tuttle, sergeant in Company K. He had been killed in action on September 17 just a month from his mustering in on August 16. His remains were brought home to Jackson by his father, Dr. James B. Tuttle, on October 8. Tuttle's funeral took place on Sunday afternoon from the Congregational Church; the procession to Mount Evergreen Cemetery

Grave of Israel B. Richardson at Oak Hill Cemetery in Pontiac, Michigan. *Author collection.*

was headed by the Jackson Grey's Band, playing a mournful funeral dirge. Full military honors were bestowed; a detachment from the 26th Michigan Infantry escorted the remains to the "patriot's tomb." Attendance "was quite large."[785] Mrs. Tuttle's letter wrote to seek "the particulars of his death, as far as you know them." Withington's September 21 note was not enough.[786]

George McClellan continued in command of the army until November 7. After Shepherdstown, he did not move with the alacrity expected by the administration. Before being relieved, he revised the command structure and appointed a new leader for XII Corps. Passing over Alpheus Williams, who had performed so capably and had saved McClellan from ruin on the north end of the field, Henry W. Slocum, a West Point graduate in VI Corps, was appointed to corps command.[787] Williams returned to division command, his bravery and leadership unrecognized in McClellan's reports.[788]

While recovering from his wound, George Hartsuff would serve on a military commission that produced the famous "Lieber Code" prescribing standards for military conduct.[789] Another wounded Michigander played a significant post-campaign administrative role. Forty-one-year-old Christopher Columbus Augur served on the commission charged with examining the capitulation at Harpers Ferry,[790] the largest surrender of U.S. troops in the nation's history. Augur had been appointed to West Point from near Ann Arbor, graduating sixteenth of thirty-nine in the class of 1843 ahead of U.S. Grant. Veteran of the Mexican-American War and on the frontier, he was commandant of cadets at the Military Academy at the war's beginning. In the Battle of Cedar Mountain, he suffered a serious wound and was convalescing during the Maryland Campaign.[791] The commission issued its final report on November 3. Ultimately, the members decided that Harpers Ferry was prematurely surrendered, that its resistance would have saved Union lives at Antietam and that holding out would have saved the position and likely produced a greater victory.[792]

On January 7, 1863, Governor Blair sent his annual message to the legislature. After extolling positive conditions within the state, he pointed to the real crisis still at hand: "Our one great need is national peace, and the only road to that leads through the gate of victory." That goal, he believed, had been mightily advanced by two great national tactics, "emancipation and confiscation." No longer would the United States be duty-bound to uphold "the claim of a white traitor to compel a black loyalist to aid him in destroying the government." Rather, the days-old Emancipation Proclamation "has by a single blow struck the shackles from nearly 3,000,000 of slaves, and added them to the loyal free people of the Republic." This act, he trumpeted, "will be memorable as long as history endures." After all, the war had but one cause: slavery. Now, "in the smoke and flame of battle"—such as at Antietam—American slavery would be destroyed, "struck dead by the resistless arm of its conquering antagonist, *Emancipation*."[793]

The governor also encouraged universal affection be paid to those in uniform: "I commend the Michigan troops to your active sympathy and support. By their heroic endurance of the hardships of war, and by their splendid bravery in battle, they have crowned the state in glory." More than sympathy, though, was required:

> *We have already a long list of immortal heroes dead in battle. I hope you will in some appropriate way place upon the enduring records of the State your appreciation of the valor and patriotic devotion of these brave men. Let us hand down their names to posterity upon an illuminated page, that they may be revered as examples for all time to come. They belong to history now. We must take care that it is rightly written.*[794]

Chapter 11

MEMORY

Michigan and a Monument

The gruesome landscape surrounding Sharpsburg—devastated farm fields overflowing with battle debris—also sheltered an inestimable legacy. Thousands of temporary graves of those who had fought their last fight marked grievous locations. A new name for the old wagon road, "Bloody Lane," served as a powerful reminder that men had died in scores and singly. No other day could be like September 17.

In 1864, the State of Maryland commenced the process of establishing a central resting ground for the dead of the campaign. A March 1865 law decreed that Maryland would hold cemetery land in trust, under governance by a specially appointed board, for any state that would contribute. Within six months, the board had purchased eleven acres east of Sharpsburg on the Boonsboro Pike and begun to devise the cemetery design.[795] Each state participating would have a designated section for its dead.[796] Of a total cost of nearly $86,000, Michigan's portion amounted to $3,344.88.[797]

Because the statute, and thus the initial cemetery plan, did not limit interment to the Federal deceased,[798] several Northern states withheld financial support. The Michigan legislature "refused to pay at all" if the design went unchanged.[799] Once the decision was made to inter Confederate remains elsewhere, Michigan relented. All such messages were conveyed by the state's representative on the Antietam Battlefield Commission, John Judson Bagley.

Bagley was an obvious and appropriate choice to represent Michigan. A leading Republican figure, he had been a delegate to the Chicago convention

John Judson Bagley, member of the Michigan Soldiers' Aid Society and of the Antietam Cemetery Commission, as well as future governor. *Archives of Michigan.*

in 1860. His commercial acumen made his tobacco company among the largest in the Midwest, and he also served as president of the Detroit Safe Company, was an organizer and president of the Michigan Mutual Life Insurance Company of Detroit and was a director of the American National Bank, among other interests. His public service career began in 1855 with election to the Detroit Board of Education. He served on the Detroit Common Council from 1860 to 1861.[800] Beyond politics, his focus was diligently working for the Soldiers' Aid Society of Detroit. Bagley's charity was renowned: "[W]hen the war came he was lavish of money and personal exertion in supporting the government and contributing to the comfort of the troops and of the sick and wounded. His face was familiar in camps and hospitals, and he never visited either without a full supply of articles welcome to the men."[801] His heart went out to his fellows: "[T]o him every wounded Michigan man was a friend and brother, and he never was as happy as when administering to their wants."[802] Of all the qualifications, one stood foremost: he had been on the ground, at the front, during that awful day. "I arrived on the battlefield of Antietam Wednesday noon, but was engaged all of the evening and Thursday, caring for our wounded soldiers."[803] He secured appointment in 1866 from Governor Henry Howland Crapo. At the June 1867 meeting, he reported that Michigan had made its appropriation.[804]

The cemetery work culminated in 1867, when dignitaries including President Andrew Johnson, Generals U.S. Grant and George McClellan, several governors and state representatives such as Bagley attended the dedication.[805] Not until 1877, when the secretary of war assumed its charge, did the site become a national graveyard.[806] The lack of an organized veterans' constituency, as well as distrust of Maryland for its early openness to co-interring the dead, hampered greater care of the cemetery or attention to the battlefield.[807] Bagley became a member of the Executive Committee in 1869 and served on the Commission until 1874.[808] His tenure was one of the longest among all of the delegations. He endeavored to fulfill what was becoming a Michigan postwar tradition: "The State of Michigan has always been ready and prompt to respond to calls made for means to improve cemeteries for the heroic dead of the nation, and to raise permanent works of art and beauty in their honor and to perpetuate their memories."[809]

The cemetery served as the first step in preserving memory of the bloody battle. In 1868, an extraordinary set of conversations revealed Robert E. Lee's recollections of that fateful season. Serving as president of Washington College, and still fairly reticent about sharing his views on the war, he engaged in postmortems, first recalling his opponent to be "an able but timid commander." Based on that assessment, he expanded: "I went into Maryland to give battle, and could I have kept Gen. McClellan in ignorance of my position and plans a day or two longer, I would have fought and crushed him." The "distinct and emphatic impression" garnered out of the discussion "was that Gen. Lee attributed without hesitation the loss of the campaign to the 'Lost Dispatch.'"[810] That is, "Sharpsburg was forced on him by McC. finding out his plans and moving quickly in consequence."[811] One of Lee's chief aides recalled that "General Lee frequently expressed his inability to understand the sudden change in McClellan's tactics which took place after we left Frederick."[812] Another participant similarly attributed a major reason for the defeat to factors beyond any human control. McClellan, usually so "slow & cautious," had become unusually aggressive thanks to the Lost Order: "[I]t was a shabby trick for fate to play us."[813] James Longstreet, Lee's "war-horse," cited the Confederate loss at the Battle of South Mountain as having dissipated "the moral effect of our move into Maryland." Even more than that, he regarded Antietam as the beginning of the end for the Confederacy: "[A]t Sharpsburg was sprung the keystone of the arch upon which the Confederate cause rested."[814]

One of Orlando Willcox's recollections centered on his fellow general from Michigan. He wistfully recalled having encountered Israel Richardson in the early days of the war. Governor Blair had directed Willcox to size up the Oakland County farmer:

> *He went about Pontiac looking queer perhaps and certainly unsociable. But in talking over old days, the Mexican war and the coming strife, I found him clear and alert and up to the occasion. It did not take me fifteen minutes to "size him up," and returning to the governor I reported most emphatically: "That is your man, not for major, but for colonel, the man to drill your Second regiment."*[815]

The common soldier remembered him with similar pathos:

> *It was with a feeling of a personal loss that we parted with General Richardson. He was not a fuss and feather soldier. He usually wore a soft hat and fatigue dress, and looked oftenest like a uniformed farmer. But a study of his features revealed intelligence, determination, and a quiet force of character and fatherliness that made his men believe he was one of them. There has always been a halo around his head since Antietam, for the double reason that he, a general, was killed in battle at our side, and also that he was the first general officer thus lost to us.*[816]

Thomas Livermore would become famous for compiling numbers and losses of the war. He, too, recalled the tragedy: "[N]o one but a soldier can understand our sorrow at seeing him carried off the field.... I shall never cease to admire that magnificent fighting general who advanced with his front line, with his sword bare and ready to use, and his swarthy face, burning eye, and square jaw."[817]

In the late 1880s, Michigan veterans congregated to remember their deeds of valor. Willcox went back to Fox's Gap on September 14, 1889, for the dedication of the monument to Jesse Reno, his commander in the Battle of South Mountain. As a trustee for the monument and grounds, he delivered the keynote address to the IX Corps vets.[818] Jackson had been the scene for a similar reunion of 17th Michigan veterans in September 1886. More than one hundred of them attended to hear an address by William Withington, who openly expressed his bond with those he had led up the slope: "[No man] could welcome you as I welcome you, with a comrade's affection and out of a heart swelling with admiration." Those who had worn the "17" on their hats were, to him, "the bravest and best." They knew their duty, "of marching up to the Rebel line behind the stone wall, charging over the wall and driving the enemy from it." Although newspapers had overlooked the regiment's advance, "its deed was the talk of the army." Their Jackson host was also the subject of reminiscence, as one soldier recounted at South

Mountain that there was "a large tree, and a conspicuous mark in the form of an officer at the foot of the tree. The enemy observed this mark also, and a shot shattered the tree, and the officer {Gen. Withington} remained seated on his horse and his coolness had a salutary effect on the raw material, of which the regiment was composed."[819]

Several years after these reunions, Congress acted to create the basics of a national battlefield at Antietam. It appropriated funds for "the purpose of surveying, locating, and preserving the lines of battle" outside Sharpsburg and "acquiring land for marking the position of each of the commands of the Regular Army engaged in the battle with suitable tablets." In subsequent years of that decade, appropriations were made to mark the position of all commands that fought at Antietam, Harpers Ferry, South Mountain and Shepherdstown.[820] In 1894, Michigan responded favorably to a request for representation to assist the Antietam board in marking the positions of units. The principal aim was "to show the extreme advance of the Union on the 17th of September" and thus mark "how far the Confederates were driven from the positions they held on the morning of the 17th." The officers who went over the ground were to locate the extreme advance of the Michigan commands and "where they did their hardest fighting."[821]

Remembrance brought debate about causes and circumstances, which continued after the turn of the century. Could McClellan have moved more quickly after the Lost Order? Sam Pittman thought so. Although his assessment may have been influenced by other accounts, Pittman recalled that "to the few of us who did know [about Special Orders 191], it was puzzling, if not distressing, that more vigor was not from that moment shown.…we could see that there were no movements being made that were fitting under the circumstances."[822] And they could not complain of it, for secrecy had to be maintained about possessing the enemy's marching orders.

Pittman did remember something very personal about his role:

> *It would be difficult to describe the sensations in having in possession that most important document. Those sensations have continued until this moment, the thrill is perpetual. Think of it:* That *information in possession of the Great Army of the Potomac, which had been for six weary months marching, fighting, retreating, practically at the will of that masterly officer, Robert E. Lee. Surely now has come the golden moment when Lee in his turn can be crushed, and then: Why, the end of the rebellion in sight if not in hand.*[823]

"Alas," Pittman summed, Lee was not crushed. George Lockley had that conviction contemporaneously. In his pocket diary for September 18, he had written, "I wonder why Little Mac dont pitch in again today. Now is his chance to wipe them out before they get over yesterdays licking."[824] The war would continue and the casualty lists would grow and grow until some 750,000 Americans would not return home after the last gun was fired.

Antietam languished in the shadow of Gettysburg in part because of its indecisive outcome. Commemorations were far less attended. The fiftieth anniversary did not compare to the festivities at the larger and more well-known Pennsylvania park. Northern veterans had come to view Gettysburg as the high-water mark of the Confederacy; by contrast, the Battle of Antietam was a missed opportunity. The seventy-fifth anniversary commemoration again paled by comparison to that of Gettysburg, being largely the province of a local county organization.

Within two more decades, though, Antietam had begun a transformation "from small backwater battlefield to a significant national park."[825] Part of this change was due to a historian from Michigan. The campaign had no popular historical analysis until, in 1957, "Bruce Catton drew Antietam back into the historical spotlight....Catton's widely read account of the Union side of the Civil War, *This Hallowed Ground*, proclaimed Antietam, not Gettysburg, as the turning point of the war." The book aided efforts to improve conservation of the battlefield, for "Catton's spotlight attracted considerable attention to the Maryland campaign."[826]

Catton's treatment of the bloody day came in a section entitled "High-Water Mark" in a chapter called "Turning Point." His thesis opposed the "Lost Cause" mythology—indeed, the book's subtitle, "The Story of the Union Side of the Civil War," sought to demonstrate that the war was occasioned by slavery and for no other primary cause. The civil rights movement had yet to find its legs, but Catton would advocate for Antietam a hallowed place in American memory:

> *Incomplete and imperfect as it had been, Antietam was a decisive Union victory. It had broken the great southern counteroffensive, it had given Lincoln the opening he needed, and it would change the character of the entire war, turning it openly and irrevocably into a war against slavery. As the long gray columns crossed the river and started plodding down the Virginia roads, the South's high tide had begun to ebb.*[827]

Michigan Historical Marker commemorating the Stonewall Regiment at Fox's Gap. *Author collection.*

Soon, the centennial of the Civil War and a new line of thought about the battle's significance would prompt the federal government to acquire more land and assemble the contiguous battlefield that exists today, in many ways untouched from its wartime appearance. Neglect was a blessing in disguise; failing to appreciate the full import of the campaign meant tawdry commercialization went elsewhere. The centennial also brought a renewed attempt to encourage states that had not erected monuments to take that step (Maryland had erected its contemporaneous with the Spanish-American War), and for those that had done so to rededicate them.[828] Georgia was the first to respond in 1961, Delaware the next year and Texas in 1964. On August 23, 1963, Dr. Martin Luther King Jr. would deliver his most famous speech on the steps of the Lincoln Memorial, invoking the Emancipation Proclamation as a "momentous decree" that brought hope to millions of enslaved Americans. The role of the battle in enabling Lincoln's action could never again be overlooked.

Michigan did not officially respond. In 1996, a Michigan Historical Marker honoring the Stonewall Regiment—sponsored through private donations—was dedicated at Fox's Gap.[829] A related marker went up in Ypsilanti in 2012. A marker honoring artillerist George A. Woodruff was erected in

Marshall in 2007 (see Appendix D). Other Antietam-related monuments in Michigan went up in Jackson County, one in Napoleon and the other in Springport,[830] and in Kent County in downtown Grand Rapids.[831] During the sesquicentennial, the Michigan Historical Commission accepted an invitation from the National Park Service and held a "Michigan at Antietam Day" to commemorate its role.[832] On November 3, 2012, the commission held a solemn tribute ceremony to the memory of Israel Richardson at his graveside in Oak Hill Cemetery in Pontiac. A chilly and overcast day served as a fitting scene for remarks concerning the loss of Michigan's highest-ranking military officer in the Civil War.

Antietam today is home to nearly one hundred "silent sentinels," composed of regimental monuments, state monuments and monuments to individuals. The majority are Union. The location of where six (three Union, three Confederate) generals fell is marked by a mortuary cannon, an inverted cannon barrel embedded in a block of stone. One marks the spot of Richardson's mortal wounding. None of the ten monuments to individuals commemorates a Michigan person. Ten Northern states, other than Michigan, have erected at least one monument. As the Civil War sesquicentennial winds down in 2015, that omission is about to be rectified.

At 5:26 p.m. on Tuesday, June 3, 2014, co-author Jack Dempsey was sitting in a rocker on the front porch of his home in Plymouth. His cellphone rang; it was Brian James Egen, fellow member of the Michigan Historical Commission. Dempsey answered, "Hello, my friend." "Hello," was the reply, "are you sitting down?" Egen had just received a call from the surviving owner of land at the epicenter of the Antietam battle, thanks to good work by a Maryland attorney representing the Michigan Civil War Association, a nonprofit corporation created for the purpose of erecting a Michigan monument at Antietam. Sitting down? Dempsey held his breath for a moment, wondering if it might be bad news. "Yes," he replied to Egen, both hopeful and concerned.

"The MCWA is now the owner of a portion of the Antietam battlefield," Egen said brightly. There was silence for a moment; Dempsey had nothing to offer except a quiet, "Wow." "I talked to Mrs. Wilson. I called her to extend our condolences." She had recently lost her husband. "She appreciated that and then said she had signed the paperwork." And so, after months of hoping, planning, working and praying, a simple phone call conveyed that people of Michigan had, after over a century and a half, returned to hallowed ground, where their ancestors struggled, fought, bled and died and now had acquired a four-hundred-square-foot easement on which to erect a memorial to that unselfish service.

Tears welled in Dempsey's eyes as they talked a bit more. He felt grateful to God, to the Wilsons, to the National Park Service personnel who had cooperated in finding the location and assenting to the effort, to those working with the two commissioners within Michigan's history structure and to Egen, whose investment in Antietam was unparalleled in Michigan. Dempsey said that he was in awe of the moment. He struggled to find words. It was a moment to cherish.

The story of Egen's connection to this section of the battlefield and the Wilson family goes back to 1991, when as a young college student he first met "Lil" Wilson. Having been born and raised in Monroe, Egen had a special affinity for the 7th Michigan—notably Company D, raised almost exclusively from his hometown. He had done extensive research on First Lieutenant John A. Clark of that regiment, killed on September 17. Clark's hastily marked grave was well known from the Alexander Gardner image taken shortly after the battle. Egen was planning the dedication ceremony for a military tombstone at the officer's forgotten final resting place in a Monroe cemetery the following May. In 1991, he was the same age as Clark when the soldier was killed in action.

Prior to the ceremony the following spring, Egen desired to visit the site of Clark's grave on the battlefield. Thanks to the 1978 classic *Antietam: The Photographic Legacy of America's Bloodiest Day*,[833] he knew the location. Egen made the drive to Sharpsburg in November 1991. Since that section of the battlefield was in private hands, clearly identified on the National Park Battlefield brochure, he required permission from the landowner to walk the ground. Summoning courage, Egen proceeded up to the front door of the postwar house on the old Hagerstown Pike. He speculated that the owners received hundreds of such solicitations and anticipated a cool or even disagreeable response. Overcoming his other concern of disturbing the family, he knocked on the exterior storm door. Immediately, the loud barking of a large dog erupted inside. As his heart rate slowly settled, the vacuum of the inner door opening drew the storm door closed with authority. His heart raced again. A woman opened the storm door slightly; tongue-tied, Egen tried to explain the purpose of his call. With graciousness, the woman—Lillian Wilson—granted permission for access to her land. On that brisk November afternoon, Egen walked solemnly over the ground where his fellow townsman had fallen.

Discussions about a monument to Michigan on the Antietam battlefield acknowledged that it would need to be on private property due to park regulations. Egen recalled the triangular piece of farmland he had been privileged to visit twenty-two years ago. He discovered that a group from Mississippi had recently secured an easement on this land to erect a monument to their state's participants. Not knowing if Mrs. Wilson still lived in the farmhouse or was even connected to the property, Egen determined to make another unannounced visit. After attending a conference in Gettysburg in March 2013, Egen and his wife, Jody, drove directly to the farmhouse outside Sharpsburg. Proceeding to the same door he had approached in November 1991, the same thoughts and emotions coursed through his mind. His knock on the door produced an equally instant and sustained dog barking, this time from a small, apparently feisty lap dog. Egen's wife, familiar with the story and assisting in the monument effort, stood beside him—making it less odd that an unfamiliar man was at the door. Once again, a woman opened the inner door, and the vacuum with the storm door drew it inward.

Egen identified himself as a member of the Michigan Historical Commission, introduced his wife and mentioned his purpose. The woman was receptive, open to hearing more and acknowledged that a Mississippi group had worked with her and her husband. Having a fairly good understanding at this point that she was the woman who greeted him when a college student, Egen said, "You may not remember me, but I knocked on your door twenty some years ago and"—before he could continue, the woman interrupted. "You were wearing a blue coat! Oh, my gosh! My husband and I have often said to each other, 'I wonder what ever became of that young man who was doing a study of the soldiers who fought on our land.'" Egen remembered that he was wearing a reproduction sky-blue Federal Great Coat on that chilly November day in 1991. As if it were a family reunion after many years apart, joyous smiles and hugs abounded.

They had met only once, a score of years ago. Yet Egen felt a special bond as the woman affirmed it would be a "noble thing to honor these soldiers." She was "supportive of what you are trying to accomplish." She would discuss with her husband offering a piece of their land for a home to a monument. As the Egens left for Michigan, they felt anticipation and deep gratitude to "Lil" Wilson, who would become a key ally in the effort to erect Michigan's monument at Antietam at long last.

In the spring of 2015, the Civil War Trust announced a fundraising campaign to acquire the tract of land surrounding the location for the Michigan monument. Calling it the epicenter of the bloody battle, the trust noted it as the most blood-soaked ground on that entire battlefield.

Conceptual sketch of Michigan monument at Antietam. *Author collection.*

On September 18, 1910, Samuel Pittman wrote to his wife a lengthy letter from the Hotel Hamilton in Hagerstown. He was now nearly eighty, but age was not yet an impediment to revisiting the scenes of a half-century prior. On Thursday the fifteenth, he had hired a horse, a buggy "and a native boy as driver" to tour sites and scenes. They went "direct to Keedysville through which hamlet we passed the P.M of Sept 16th 1862 and bivoucked in the fields adjoining," pursuing Pittman's plan to "drive all around just as the [XII] corps marched." He recounted I Corps having "heavy skirmishing" that night while getting into position for the main action. Then he recalled how at 11:00 p.m. Williams's Division "made a stealthy march on a long circuit around to the right and rear of Hooker to be his support for the battle to come next morning."

But the scenery had changed too much, the boy was too young and Pittman too old; they had to seek directions from a farmer plowing a nearby field. Resuming his tour, Pittman located "the fields where we slept," "the fields and woods we marched at early morning," "where our several regiments fought at and through the famous cornfield and around the famous Dunker Church." The buggy stopped "time after time" so that Pittman could alight "to read the numerous bronze tablets descriptive of our part" and the inscriptions on monuments. He attended the commemoration at the National Cemetery and engaged in reminiscence with comrades and their descendants. Concluding, he told his wife, "I am glad I took that ride alone, for one gets but little of the general going about in a body in carriages."

The old adjutant added a telling anecdote. The helpful ploughman, born at a farmhouse nearby, "as a boy of 16 witnessed the battle from the top of a nearby hill." His reaction after being asked for assistance pleased the old Michigan soldier: "When he found who I was he took the greatest interest in me and yesterday brought his wife, daughter and grand children over to the gathering at the 'Cornfield' and Dunkard Church to see me."[834]

Some fifty years after the terrible affair, a boy who drove the touring buggy, a farmer who had been a boy in 1862 and an old man from Detroit who had been in the bloom of youth that September day crossed paths. For Samuel Pittman, memories remained important. His letter home reported that the XII Corps reunion commended the Michigan Commandery of the Loyal Legion for "its movement toward the erection of the Williams monument" on Belle Isle, an effort spearheaded by Pittman as former adjutant general. Hometown newspaper the *Detroit News* had supported the effort, reminding readers that "had Williams given way before the terrific onslaughts of the enemy the whole federal line would have been pierced and Antietam would be remembered as a federal defeat."[835]

Another decade elapsed before the statue of Pittman's friend would rise in the island park in the Detroit River. Its unveiling took place on October 15, 1921, as "an old man sat in an open motor car" to witness a dream finally fulfilled. Pittman's infirmity, soon to end his life, prevented speaking or even rising from the automobile:

Civil War Veteran, Company Official Who Is Dead

COLONEL S. E. PITTMAN

Civil War veteran, who died at his home Thursday. Colonel Pittman was 91 years old but had been actively engaged in business as secretary of the board of directors of the Detroit Steel Products Co. until shortly before his death. Funeral services will be held Mon-

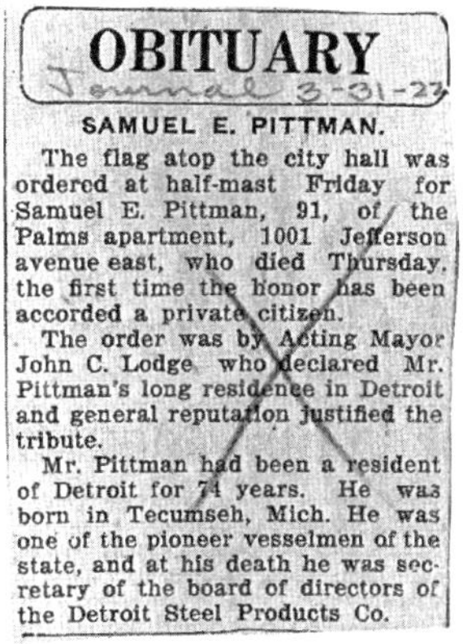

OBITUARY

SAMUEL E. PITTMAN.

The flag atop the city hall was ordered at half-mast Friday for Samuel E. Pittman, 91, of the Palms apartment, 1001 Jefferson avenue east, who died Thursday, the first time the honor has been accorded a private citizen.

The order was by Acting Mayor John C. Lodge who declared Mr. Pittman's long residence in Detroit and general reputation justified the tribute.

Mr. Pittman had been a resident of Detroit for 74 years. He was born in Tecumseh, Mich. He was one of the pioneer vesselmen of the state, and at his death he was secretary of the board of directors of the Detroit Steel Products Co.

tors of the Detroit Steel Produc Co., died at his home at the Palr Apartment, 1001 Jefferson avenu late Thursday night, following short illness.

Until a few months ago, Mr. Pit man went to his office daily and

COL. S. E. PITTMAN.

was only a few days ago that he lost hope of being able to return to his work.

Col. Pittman has been activel connected with many Detroit indus tries. He formerly was associate with the Detroit Linseed Oil Co., an

Newspaper obituaries for Samuel Emlen Pittman, aide to Alpheus Williams and key to authenticating the Lost Order. *Burton Historical Collection, Detroit Public Library.*

> *But those who watched the bowed form of Col. Samuel E. Pittman that day, who caught the eager upward turn of the silvered head to the monument, who heard his murmur that this was the happiest moment of his life, they could not know that the cold, towering figure to him was not a statue, but the living form of his commander and his life-time friend.*

Less than six months later, the old veteran entered his "last bivouac," as a Detroit newspaper headline respectfully lamented.[836]

Proper veneration had taken years. Major wars intervened. America became a continental nation, a world power and a more urban society. The old veteran had persisted, finally reaching his objective after so many years. Pittman's war governor had understood: "Great undertakings require time, and it is not by a view of the operations of a single month, or even a year, that results are to be correctly measured."[837]

Conclusion

A More Perfect Union

There never was another day like Antietam. It was sheer concentrated violence...[838]

The Most Stupendous Struggle of Modern Times.[839]

The Confederate invasion of Maryland altered the course of the Civil War. Such was the objective of the Confederate leaders. Davis and Lee sought to expand the ambit of their fledgling nation and undermine the Lincoln administration in the fall 1862 elections. Capitalizing "on McClellan's well-demonstrated caution and excessive deliberation of movement," the Army of Northern Virginia would enjoy September and October and crush the Army of the Potomac north of that river.[840] Instead, defeats at South Mountain and Antietam and the issuance of a proclamation of emancipation transformed the struggle, wrecked Confederate hopes and rendered the campaign "a complete failure."[841] Michiganders had much to do with that result.

Chief among the reasons for that failure was the Lost Order. First came its discovery by men of Alpheus Williams's Division, and then came authentication by Samuel Pittman and rapid affirmation by Williams to the army's commander. It is highly doubtful that McClellan would have joined battle on the South Mountain heights absent the role played by the two Michiganders. The victory on September 14 owed much to the actions of Orlando Willcox and his Michigan regiments, especially the 17th. The vigorous pursuit of Lee's forces to the banks of Antietam Creek by Israel

Richardson and George Custer contributed to bringing on Wednesday's battle. That bloody day saw great and valorous contributions by Williams, Hartsuff, Richardson, Willcox, Hunt and the officers and men in the ranks, most notably those of the 7th Michigan.

The Union victory might have been more complete. Responsibility for that outcome lay not with anyone from Michigan. McClellan's war of moderation, one "respecting Southern constitutional and property rights, the right to own slaves the most important of these," did not accord with the tenor of Michigan's participation. Northern war strategy to preserve the Union became inextricably woven with the destruction of slavery,[842] and liberty-loving Michigan enlisted for the duration.

Confederate leadership sought to sway the new Congress against the war, and inroads were made in some states against the Lincoln administration. Democrats captured a majority of seats in Illinois, Indiana and Ohio and made gains in Minnesota and Wisconsin. The party had denounced and pledged to campaign against the Proclamation,[843] and Michigan Democrats were hopeful of taking power in the campaign "to battle abolitionism."[844] The outcome in the birthplace of the Republican Party, however, proved disappointing.

Michigan's Republicans lauded the Emancipation Proclamation as a heavy "blow against the Slave Power" and paid it "fervent praise."[845] At their convention in Detroit just days after Antietam and Lincoln's action, they passed resolutions in support of the war effort and the Proclamation.[846] In the election on Tuesday, November 4, Union sentiment prevailed. With the 1860 census, the state had gained two more seats in the House of Representatives, for a total of six. Republicans won one of the new seats and held four others; the Democratic-Union candidate took the remaining election. When the 38th Congress convened on March 4, 1863, the two Republican senators, Zachariah Chandler and Jacob Howard, took their seats, while the delegation in the House consisted of Fernando C. Beaman (R), Charles Upson (R), John W. Longyear (R), Francis W. Kellogg (R), John F. Driggs (R) and Augustus C. Baldwin (D/U). Voters statewide had endorsed the Emancipation Proclamation. Lincoln could still count on Michigan.

In the legislature, Republicans maintained their majorities in both houses.[847] Governor Austin Blair was reelected by a popular vote of 68,716 (52.53 percent) to his Democratic opponent (Byron G. Stout) garnering 62,102 (47.47 percent). The margin was smaller than in 1860, when Blair received nearly 57 percent, but given the absence of many voters now in the ranks, total participation was down. The outcome only caused Michigan's political leadership to redouble its efforts to prosecute the war both for

Union and emancipation. When the time came to propose a constitutional prohibition on American slavery—one based on the language of the Northwest Ordinance resembling the ban in Michigan's constitution[848]—all of Michigan's delegation voted "aye." And Michigan ratified the Thirteenth Amendment immediately.

In the 1864 election, George McClellan would run against Abraham Lincoln and lose. The soldier vote went against him, and he would continue to watch the war from the sidelines after being shelved in November 1862. The Michigan delegation continued to be an implacable foe of the Confederacy. Michigan's soldiers may not have joined up to fight for abolition, but they came to regard slavery as a foundation of Southern secession that must be forever eradicated. George Custer exemplified this realization: his friends would testify, he asserted, that "I have insisted that so long as a single slave was held in bondage, I for one, was opposed to peace on any terms."[849] He had well served McClellan, who thought the proclamation inaugurated "servile insurrection" and that emancipating the slaves militarily amounted to "despotism."[850] Custer threw his allegiance to Lincoln, took credit for liberation of many enslaved and called for winning the war rather than negotiating an end to the bloody conflict.[851]

George H. Laird of Colon exemplified the true nature of Michigan sentiment espousing devotion to Union and the end of slavery. Having enlisted as a second lieutenant in Company K, 7th Michigan, at Fort Wayne in Detroit on June 19, 1861, this twenty-one-year-old would see the war through to the bitter end. On June 17, 1862, Laird was commissioned first lieutenant of Company

George H. Laird initially served in the 7th Michigan; at Antietam he was captain of Company H, 17th Michigan Infantry. By war's end, he was lieutenant colonel of the 116th USCT. *Monroe County Historical Museum.*

C, 17th Michigan Infantry, and subsequently as captain of Company H in August 1862. From February to May 1864, Laird served as assistant quartermaster. On July 19, 1864, he resigned and was honorably discharged to receive a commission as lieutenant colonel of the 116th U.S. Colored Troops. Laird and the 116th USCT would see the war to the end in the Appomattox Campaign in April 1865, culminating in the surrender of the Army of Northern Virginia. With the surrender, Sergeant Major William McCeslin of the 29th USCT, another regiment in the brigade with the 116th, wrote, "We, the colored soldiers, have fairly won our rights by loyalty and bravery—shall we obtain them? If we are refused now, we shall demand them." Laird would serve loyally until his discharge on June 7, 1865.[852]

The Civil War settled several constitutional questions, including the status of nonwhites as citizens and whether the American Union was a compact that could be rescinded by individual states. Although much work remained—and still remains—to realize the dream of a democratic society full of equal opportunity to all, the task accomplished imperfectly at South Mountain and Antietam and Shepherdstown sprang open the prison door holding 4 million in chains. During the Civil War centennial, Dr. Martin Luther King Jr. called on America to fulfill the promissory note issued in the Emancipation Proclamation and paid for by the actions and sacrifices at Antietam. During the Civil War sesquicentennial, thousands stood in line at The Henry Ford in Dearborn, Michigan, waiting up to eight hours to glimpse the extraordinary document.

And as an act of solemn commemoration during the sesquicentennial, Michigan is undertaking another unfinished task, to erect on the bloody ground of Antietam a monument to those who fought for the Union and liberty. As a Detroit daily opined long ago about another memorial, in words that still ring true, Michigan "owes it to herself and to her brave dead" to make appropriate, even if belated, recognition and veneration "of their valor and her pride."[853]

Appendix A

Union and Confederate Order of Battle

September 17, 1862

Lt. = Lieutenant
Capt. = Captain
Maj. = Major
Lt.Col. = Lieutenant Colonel
Col. = Colonel
BG = Brigadier General
MG = Major General
Gen. = General

(w) = wounded
(mw) = mortally wounded
(k) = killed
(c) = captured

Unless otherwise noted, casualties occurred on September 17.

Individuals or units in italics are from Michigan.

Appendix A

Army of the Potomac, MG George B. McClellan (commanding)

Escort: Capt. James B. McIntyre
Independent Company Oneida (New York) Cavalry: Capt. Daniel P. Mann
4th United States Cavalry, Company A: Lt. Thomas H. McCormick
4th United States Cavalry, Company E: Capt. James B. McIntyre
Chief of Artillery: BG *Henry J. Hunt*

I Corps

MG Joseph Hooker (w)
BG George G. Meade
Escort: 2nd New York Cavalry (4 companies), Capt. John E. Naylor

1st Division
BG John P. Hatch (w, 9/14)
BG Abner Doubleday

1st Brigade
Col. Walter Phelps Jr.
22nd New York Infantry, Lt.Col. John McKie Jr.
24th New York Infantry, Capt. John D. O'Brian (w)
30th New York Infantry, Col. William M. Searing
90th New York Infantry (14th Militia), Maj. William H. de Bevoise
2nd U.S. Sharpshooters, Col. Henry A.V. Post (w)

2nd Brigade
BG Abner Doubleday
Col. William P. Wainwright (w, 9/14)
Lt.Col. J. William Hofmann
7th Indiana Infantry, Maj. Ira G. Grover
76th New York Infantry, Col. William P. Wainwright, Capt. John W. Young
95th New York Infantry, Maj. Edward Pye
56th Pennsylvania Infantry, Lt.Col. S. William Hofmann, Capt. Frederick Williams

3rd Brigade
BG Marsena R. Patrick
21st New York Infantry, Col. William F. Rogers
23rd New York Infantry, Col. Henry C. Hoffman

35th New York Infantry, Col. Newton B. Lord
89th New York Infantry (20th Militia), Lt.Col. Theodore B. Gates

4TH BRIGADE
BG John Gibbon
19th Indiana Infantry, Col. Solomon Meredith, Lt.Col. Alois O. Bachman (k), Capt. William W. Dudley
2nd Wisconsin Infantry, Col. Lucius Fairchild (w, 9/14), Lt.Col. Thomas S. Allen (w), Capt. George B. Ely
6th Wisconsin Infantry, Lt.Col. Edward S. Bragg (w), Maj. Rufus R. Dawes
7th Wisconsin Infantry, Capt. John B. Callis

ARTILLERY
Capt. J. Albert Monroe
1st New Hampshire, Lt. Frederick M. Edgell D
1st Rhode Island, Capt. J. Albert Monro
L, 1st New York, Capt. John A. Reynolds
B, 4th U.S., Capt. Joseph B. Campbell (w), Lt. James Stewart

2nd Division
BG James B. Ricketts

1ST BRIGADE
BG Abram Duryea
97th New York, Maj. Charles Northrup
104th New York, Maj. Lewis C. Skinner
105th New York, Col. Howard Carroll (mw)
107th Pennsylvania, Capt. James MacThomson

2ND BRIGADE
Col. William A. Christian
Col. Peter Lyle (w)
26th New York, Lt.Col. Richard H. Richardson
94th New York, Lt.Col. Calvin Littlefield
88th Pennsylvania, Lt.Col. George W. Gile (w), Capt. Henry B. Myers
90th Pennsylvania, Col. Peter Lyle, Lt.Col. William A. Leech

3RD BRIGADE
BG *George L. Hartsuff* (w)
Col. Richard Coulter
12th Massachusetts, Maj. Elisha Burbank (mw), Capt. Benjamin F. Cook
13th Massachusetts, Maj. J. Parker Gould

83rd New York (9th Militia), Lt.Col. William Atterbury
11th Pennsylvania, Col. Richard Coulter, Capt. David M. Cook

Artillery
F, 1st Pennsylvania, Capt. Ezra W. Matthews
C, Pennsylvania, Capt. James Thompson

3rd Division
(Pennsylvania Reserves)
BG George G. Meade
BG Truman Seymour

1st Brigade
BG Truman Seymour
Col. R. Biddle Roberts
1st Pennsylvania, Col. R. Biddle Roberts, Capt. William C. Talley
2nd Pennsylvania, Capt. James N. Byrnes
5th Pennsylvania, Col. Joseph W. Fisher
6th Pennsylvania, Col. William Sinclair
13th Pennsylvania (1st Rifles), Col. Hugh W. McNeil (k, 9/16), Capt. Dennis McGee

2nd Brigade
Col. Henry C. Bolinger (w, 9/14)
Col. Albert L. Magilton
3rd Pennsylvania, Lt.Col. John Clark
4th Pennsylvania, Maj. John Nyce
7th Pennsylvania, Col. Henry C. Bolinger (w, 9/14) Maj. Chauncey A. Lyman
8th Pennsylvania, Maj. Silas M. Bailey

3rd Brigade
Col. Thomas F. Gallagher (w)
Lt.Col. Robert Anderson
9th Pennsylvania, Lt.Col. Robert Anderson, Capt. Samuel B. Dick
10th Pennsylvania, Lt.Col. Adoniram J. Warner (w), Capt. Jonathan P. Smith
11th Pennsylvania, Lt.Col. Samuel M. Jackson
12th Pennsylvania, Capt. Richard Gustin

Artillery
A, 1st Pennsylvania, Lt. John G. Simpson
B, 1st Pennsylvania, Capt. James H. Cooper
C, 5th U.S., Capt. Dunbar B. Ransom

II Corps

MG Edwin V. Sumner
Escort: 6th New York Cavalry, Company D, Capt. Henry W. Lyon
6th New York Cavalry, Company K, Capt. Riley Johnson

1st Division
MG *Israel B. Richardson* (mw)
BG John C. Caldwell
BG Winfield S. Hancock

1st Brigade
BG John C. Caldwell
5th New Hampshire, Col. Edward E. Cross (w)
7th New York, Capt. Charles Brestel
61st and 64th New York, Col. Francis C. Barlow (w), Lt.Col. Nelson A. Miles
81st Pennsylvania, Maj. H. Boyd McKeen

2nd Brigade
BG Thomas F. Meagher (w)
Col. John Burke
29th Massachusetts, Lt.Col. Joseph H. Barnes
63rd New York, Col. John Burke, Lt.Col. Henry Fowler (w), Maj. Richard C. Bentley (w), Capt. Joseph O'Neill
69th New York, Lt.Col. James Kelly (w), Maj. James Cavanagh
88th New York, Lt.Col. Patrick Kelly

3rd Brigade
Col. John R. Brooke
2nd Delaware, Capt. David L. Stricker
52nd New York, Col. Paul Frank
57th New York, Lt.Col. Philip S. Parisen (k), Maj. Alford B. Chapman
66th New York, Capt. Julius Wehle, Lt.Col. James H. Bull
53rd Pennsylvania, Lt.Col. Richards McMichael

Artillery

B, 1st New York, Capt. Rufus D. Pettit
A and C, 4th U.S., Lt. Evan Thomas

2nd Division

MG John Sedgwick (w)
BG Oliver O. Howard

1st Brigade

BG Willis A. Gorman

15th Massachusetts, Lt.Col. John W. Kimball
1st Minnesota, Col. Alfred Sully
34th New York, Col. James A. Suitor
82nd New York (2nd Militia), Col. Henry W. Hudson
1st Company Massachusetts Sharpshooters, Capt. John Saunders (k)
3rd Company Minnesota Sharpshooters, Capt. William F. Russell

2nd Brigade

BG Oliver O. Howard
Col. Joshua T. Owen
Col. DeWitt C. Baxter

69th Pennsylvania, Col. Joshua T. Owen
71st Pennsylvania, Col. Isaac J. Wistar (w), Lt. Richard P. Smith, Capt. Enoch E. Lewis
72nd Pennsylvania, Col. DeWitt C. Baxter
106th Pennsylvania, Col. Turner G. Morehead

3rd Brigade

BG Napoleon J. T. Dana (w)
Col. *Norman J. Hall*

19th Massachusetts, Col. Edward W. Hinks (w), Lt.Col. Arthur F. Devereux (w), Capt. H.G. Weymouth
20th Massachusetts, Col. William R. Lee
7th Michigan, Col. Norman J. Hall, Capt. Charles J. Hunt
42nd New York, Lt.Col. George N. Bomford (w), Maj. James E. Mallon
59th New York, Col. William L. Tidball

Artillery

A, 1st Rhode Island, Capt. John A. Tompkins
I, 1st U.S., Lt. *George A. Woodruff*

3rd Division
Gen. William H. French

1st Brigade
BG Nathan Kimball
14th Indiana, Col. William Harrow
8th Ohio, Lt.Col. Franklin Sawyer
132nd Pennsylvania, Col. Richard A. Oakford (k), Lt.Col. Vincent M. Wilcox
7th West Virginia, Col. Joseph Snider

2nd Brigade
Col. Dwight Morris
14th Connecticut, Lt.Col. Sanford H. Perkins
108th New York, Col. Oliver H. Palmer
130th Pennsylvania, Col. Henry I. Zinn

3rd Brigade
BG Max Weber (w)
Col. John W. Andrews
1st Delaware, Col. John W. Andrews, Lt.Col. Oliver Hopkinson (w)
5th Maryland, Maj. Leopold Blumenberg (w), Capt. E.F.M. Faehtz
4th New York, Lt.Col. John D. MacGregor

Unattached Artillery
G, 1st New York, Capt. John D. Frank
B, 1st Rhode Island, Capt. John G. Hazard
G, 1st Rhode Island, Capt. C.D. Owen

V Corps

MG Fitz John Porter
Escort: Detachment, 1st Maine Cavalry, Capt. George J. Summat

1st Division
MG George W. Morell

1st Brigade
Col. James Barnes
2nd Maine, Col. Charles W. Roberts
18th Massachusetts, Lt.Col. Joseph Hayes
22nd Massachusetts, Lt.Col. William S. Tilton

1st Michigan, Capt. Emory W. Belton
13th New York, Col. Elisha G. Marshall
25th New York, Col. Charles A. Johnson
118th Pennsylvania, Col. Charles M. Prevost
2nd Company York Massachusetts Sharpshooters, Capt. Lewis E. Wentworth

2ND BRIGADE
BG Charles Griffin
2nd D.C., Col. Charles M. Alexander
9th Massachusetts, Col. Patrick R. Guiney
32nd Massachusetts, Col. Francis J. Parker
4th Michigan, Col. Jonathan W. Childs
14th New York, Col. James McQuade
62nd Pennsylvania, Col. Jacob B. Sweitzer

3RD BRIGADE
Col. *T.B.W. Stockton*
20th Maine, Col. Adelbert Ames
16th Michigan, Lt.Col. Norval E. Welch
12th New York, Capt. William Huson
17th New York, Lt.Col. Nelson B. Bartram
44th New York, Maj. Freeman Conner
83rd Pennsylvania, Capt. Orpheus S. Woodward
Brady's Company, Michigan Sharpshooters, Lt. Jonas H. Titus Jr.

ARTILLERY
3rd Massachusetts, Capt. Augustus P. Martin
C, 1st Rhode Island, Capt. Richard Waterman
D, 5th U.S., Lt. Charles E. Hazlett

2nd Division
BG George Sykes

1ST BRIGADE
Lt.Col. Robert C. Buchanan
3rd U.S., Capt. John D. Wilkins
4th U.S., Capt. Hiram Dryer
12th U.S. (1st Battalion), Capt. Matthew M. Blunt
12th U.S. (2nd Battalion), Capt. Thomas M. Anderson
14th U.S. (1st Battalion), Capt. W. Harvey Brown
14th U.S. (2nd Battalion), Capt. David B. McKibbin

2nd Brigade
Maj. Charles S. Lovell
1st and 6th U.S., Capt. Levi C. Bootes
2nd and 10th U.S., Capt. John S. Poland
11th U.S., Capt. DeLancey Floyd-Jones
17th U.S., Maj. George L. Andrews

3rd Brigade
Col. Gouverneur K. Warren
5th New York, Capt. Cleveland Winslow
10th New York, Lt.Col. John W. Marshall

Artillery
E and G, 1st U.S., Lt. Alanson M. Randol
I, 5th U.S., Capt. Stephen H. Weed
K, 5th U.S., Lt. William E. Van Reed

3rd Division
(arrived September 18)
BG Andrew A. Humphreys

1st Brigade
BG Erastus B. Tyler
91st Pennsylvania, Col. Edgar M. Gregory
126th Pennsylvania, Col. James G. Elder
129th Pennsylvania, Col. Jacob G. Frick
134th Pennsylvania, Col. Matthew S. Quay

2nd Brigade
Col. Peter H. Allabach
123rd Pennsylvania, Col. John B. Clark
131st Pennsylvania, Lt.Col. William B. Shaut
133rd Pennsylvania, Col. Franklin B. Speakman
155th Pennsylvania, Col. Edward J. Allen

Artillery
C, 1st New York, Capt. Almont Barnes
L, 1st Ohio, Capt. Lucius N. Robinson

Artillery Reserve
Lt.Col. William Hays
A, 1st Battalion New York, Lt. Bernhard Wever
B, 1st Battalion New York, Lt. Alfred von Kleiser

C, 1st Battalion New York, Capt. Robert Langner
D, 1st Battalion New York, Capt. Charles Kusserow
5th New York, Capt. Elijah D. Taft
K, 1st U.S., Capt. William M. Graham
G, 4th U.S., Lt. Marcus P. Miller

VI Corps

MG William B. Franklin
Escort: B and G, 6th Pennsylvania Cavalry, Capt. H.P. Muirheid

1st Division
MG Henry W. Slocum

1ST BRIGADE
Col. Alfred T.A. Torbert
1st New Jersey, Lt.Col. Mark W. Collet
2nd New Jersey, Col. Samuel L. Buck
3rd New Jersey, Col. Henry W. Brown
4th New Jersey, Col. William B. Hatch

2ND BRIGADE
Col. Joseph J. Bartlett
5th Maine, Col. Nathaniel J. Jackson
16th New York, Lt.Col. Joel J. Beaver
27th New York, Lt.Col. Alexander D. Adams
96th Pennsylvania, Col. Henry L. Cake

3RD BRIGADE
BG John Newton
18th New York, Lt.Col. George R. Myers
31st New York, Lt.Col. Francis H. Pinto
32nd New York, Col. Roderick Matheson (mw, 9/14), Maj. George F. Lemon (mw, 9/14)
95th Pennsylvania, Col. Gustavus W. Town

ARTILLERY
Capt. Emory Upton
A, Maryland, Capt. John W. Wolcott
A, 1st Massachusetts, Capt. Josiah Porter
A, 1st New Jersey, Capt. William Hexamer
D, 2nd U.S., Lt. Edward B. Williston

2nd Division
MG William F. Smith

1st Brigade
BG Winfield S. Hancock
Col. Amasa Cobb
6th Maine, Col. Hiram Burnham
43rd New York, Maj. John Wilson
49th Pennsylvania, Lt.Col. William Brisbane
137th Pennsylvania, Col. Henry M. Bossert
5th Wisconsin, Col. Amasa Cobb

2nd Brigade
BG W.T.H. Brooks
2nd Vermont, Maj. James H. Walbridge
3rd Vermont, Col. Breed N. Hyde
4th Vermont, Lt.Col. Charles B. Stoughton
5th Vermont, Col. Lewis A. Grant
6th Vermont, Maj. Oscar L. Tuttle

3rd Brigade
Col. William H. Irwin
7th Maine, Maj. Thomas W. Hyde
20th New York, Col. Ernest von Vegesack
33rd New York, Lt.Col. Joseph W. Corning
49th New York, Lt.Col. William C. Alberger (w), Maj. George W. Johnson
77th New York, Capt. Nathan S. Babcock

Artillery
Capt. Romeyn B. Ayres
B, Maryland, Lt. Theodore J. Vanneman
1st New York, Capt. Andrew Cowan
F, 5th U.S., Lt. Leonard Martin

IX Corps

MG Ambrose E. Burnside
MG Jesse L. Reno (k, 9/14)
BG Jacob D. Cox
Escort: Company G, 1st Maine Cavalry, Capt. Zebulon B. Blethen

1st Division
BG *Orlando B. Willcox*

1ST BRIGADE
Col. Benjamin C. Christ
28th Massachusetts, Capt. Andrew P. Caraher
17th Michigan, Col. William H. Withington
79th New York, Lt.Col. David Morrison
50th Pennsylvania, Maj. Edward Overton (w), Capt. William H. Diehl

2ND BRIGADE
Col. Thomas Welsh
8th Michigan (transferred to 1st Brigade, September 16), Lt.Col. Frank Graves, Maj. Ralph Ely
46th New York, Lt.Col. Joseph Gerhardt
45th Pennsylvania, Lt.Col. John I. Curtin
100th Pennsylvania, Lt.Col. David A. Leckey

ARTILLERY
8th Massachusetts, Capt. Asa M. Cook
E, 2nd U.S., Lt. Samuel N. Benjamin

2nd Division
BG Samuel D. Sturgis

1ST BRIGADE
BG James Nagle
2nd Maryland, Lt.Col. J. Eugene Duryea
6th New Hampshire, Col. Simon G. Griffin
9th New Hampshire, Col. Enoch Q. Fellows
48th Pennsylvania, Lt.Col. Joshua K. Sigfried

2ND BRIGADE
BG Edward Ferrero
21st Massachusetts, Col. William S. Clark
35th Massachusetts, Col. Edward A. Wild (w), Lt.Col. Sumner Carruth (w)
51st New York, Col. Robert B. Potter
51st Pennsylvania, Col. John F. Hartranft

ARTILLERY
D, Pennsylvania, Capt. George W. Durell
E, 4th U.S., Capt. Joseph C. Clark Jr. (w)

3rd Division
BG Isaac P. Rodman (mw)
Col. Edward Harland

1st Brigade
Col. Harrison S. Fairchild
9th New York, Lt.Col. Edgar A. Kimball
89th New York, Maj. Edward Jardine
103rd New York, Maj. Benjamin Ringold

2nd Brigade
Col. Edward Harland
8th Connecticut, Lt.Col. Hiram Appelman (w), Maj. John H. Ward
11th Connecticut, Col. Henry W. Kingsbury (k)
16th Connecticut, Col. Francis Beach
4th Rhode Island, Col. William H.P. Steere (w), Lt.Col. Joseph B. Curtis

Artillery
A, 5th U.S., Lt. Charles P. Muhlenberg

Kanawha Division
Gen. Jacob D. Cox
Col. Eliakim P. Scammon

1st Brigade
Col. Eliakim P. Scammon
Col. Hugh Ewing
12th Ohio, Col. Carr B. White
23rd Ohio, Lt.Col. Rutherford B. Hayes (w, 9/14), Maj. James M. Comly
30th Ohio, Col. Hugh Ewing, Lt.Col. Theodore Jones (w, c), Maj. George H. Hildt
1st Ohio Battery, Capt. James H. McMullin
Gilmore's Company, West Virginia Cavalry, Lt. James Abraham
Harrison's Company, West Virginia Cavalry, Lt. Dennis Delaney

2nd Brigade
Col. Augustus Moor (c)
Col. George Crook
11th Ohio, Lt.Col. Augustus H. Coleman (k), Maj. Lyman J. Jackson
28th Ohio, Lt.Col. Gottfried Becker
36th Ohio, Col. George Crook, Lt.Col. Melvin Clarke (k), Maj. E.B. Andrews

Chicago Illinois Dragoons, Capt. Frederick Schambeck
Kentucky Battery, Capt. Seth J. Simmonds

UNATTACHED TROOPS
6th New York Cavalry (8 companies), Col. Thomas V. Devin
3rd Company Ohio Cavalry, Lt. Jonas Seamen
L and M, 3rd U.S. Artillery, Capt. John Edwards Jr.

XII Corps

MG Joseph K.F. Mansfield (mw)
BG *Alpheus S. Williams*
Escort: *1st Michigan Cavalry, Capt. Melvin Brewer*

1st Division
BG *Alpheus S. Williams*
BG Samuel W. Crawford (w)
BG George H. Gordon

1ST BRIGADE
BG Samuel W. Crawford (w)
Col. Joseph F. Knipe
10th Maine, Col. George L. Beal (w)
28th New York, Capt. William H.H. Mapes
46th Pennsylvania, Col. Joseph F. Knipe, Lt.Col. James L. Selfridge
124th Pennsylvania, Col. Joseph W. Hawley (w), Maj. Isaac L. Haldeman
125th Pennsylvania, Col. Jacob Higgins
128th Pennsylvania, Col. Samuel Croasdale (k), Lt.Col. William W. Hammersly (w), Maj. Joel B. Wanner

3RD BRIGADE
BG George H. Gordon
Col. Thomas H. Ruger (w)
27th Indiana, Col. Silas Colgrove
2nd Massachusetts, Col. George L. Andrews
13th New Jersey, Col. Ezra A. Carman
107th New York, Col. R.B. Van Valkenburgh
Pennsylvania Zouaves d'Afrique
3rd Wisconsin, Col. Thomas H. Ruger (w)

2nd Division
BG George S. Greene

1ST BRIGADE
Lt.Col. Hector Tyndale (w)
Maj. Orrin J. Crane
5th Ohio, Maj. John Collins
7th Ohio, Maj. Orrin J. Crane, Capt. Frederick A. Seymour
66th Ohio, Lt.Col. Eugene Powell (w)
28th Pennsylvania, Maj. Ario Pardee Jr.

2ND BRIGADE
Col. Henry J. Stainrook
3rd Maryland, Lt.Col. Joseph H. Sudsburg
102nd New York, Lt.Col. James C. Lane
111th Pennsylvania, Maj. Thomas M. Walker

3RD BRIGADE
Col. William B. Goodrich (k)
Lt.Col. Jonathan Austin
3rd Delaware, Maj. Arthur Maginnis (w), Capt. William J. McKaig
Purnell (Maryland) Legion, Lt.Col. Benjamin L. Simpson
60th New York, Lt.Col. Charles H. Brundage
78th New York, Lt.Col. Jonathan Austin, Capt. Henry R. Stagg

ARTILLERY
Capt. Clermont L. Best
4th Maine, Capt. O'Neill W. Robinson
6th Maine, Capt. Freeman McGilvery
M, 1st New York, Capt. George W. Cothran
10th New York, Capt. John T. Bruen
E, Pennsylvania, Capt. Joseph H. Knapp
F, Pennsylvania, Capt. Robert B. Hampton
F, 4th U.S., Lt. Edward D. Muhlenberg

Cavalry Corps
BG Alfred Pleasonton

1ST BRIGADE
Maj. Charles J. Whiting
5th U.S., Capt. Joseph H. McArthur
6th U.S., Capt. William P. Sanders

2nd BRIGADE
Col. John F. Farnsworth
8th Illinois, Maj. William H. Medill
3rd Indiana, Maj. George H. Chapman
1st Massachusetts, Capt. Casper Crowninshield
8th Pennsylvania, Capt. Peter Keenan

3rd BRIGADE
Col. Richard H. Rush
4th Pennsylvania, Col. James H. Childs (k), Lt.Col. James K. Kerr
6th Pennsylvania, Lt.Col. C. Ross Smith

4th BRIGADE
Col. Andrew T. McReynolds
1st New York, Maj. Alonzo W. Adams
12th Pennsylvania, Maj. James A. Congdon

5th BRIGADE
Col. Benjamin F. Davis
8th New York, Col. Benjamin F. Davis
3rd Pennsylvania, Lt.Col. Samuel W. Owen

ARTILLERY
A, 2nd U.S., Capt. John C. Tidball
B and L, 2nd U.S., Capt. James M. Robertson
M, 2nd U.S., Lt. Peter C. Hains
C and G, 2nd U.S., Capt. Horatio C. Gibson

UNATTACHED
15th Pennsylvania Cavalry (detachment), Col. William J. Palmer

Appendix A

Army of Northern Virginia, GEN. Robert E. Lee (commanding)

Right Wing (Longstreet's)
MG James Longstreet

McLaws' Division
MG Lafayette McLaws

Kershaw's Brigade
BG Joseph B. Kershaw
2rd South Carolina, Col. John D. Kennedy (w), Maj. Franklin Gaillard
3rd South Carolina, Col. James D. Nance
7th South Carolina, Col. David W. Aiken (w), Capt. John S. Hard
8th South Carolina, Lt.Col. Axalla J. Hoole

Cobb's Brigade
BG Howell Cobb
Lt.Col. Christopher Columbus Sanders
16th Georgia, Lt.Col. Philip Thomas
24th Georgia, Maj. Robert E. McMillan (w)
Cobb's (Georgia) Legion, Lt.Col. Luther Glenn
15th North Carolina, Lt.Col. William MacRae

Semmes' Brigade
BG Paul J. Semmes
10th Georgia, Maj. Willis C. Holt (w), Capt. William Johnston (w), Capt. Philologus H. Loud (w)
53rd Georgia, Lt.Col. Thomas Sloan (mw), Capt. S.W. Marshborne
15th Virginia, Capt. Emmett M. Morrison (w), Capt. Edward J. Willis
32nd Virginia, Col. Edgar B. Montague

Barksdale's Brigade
BG William Barksdale
13th Mississippi, Lt.Col. Kennon McElroy (w, 9/15)
17th Mississippi, Lt.Col. John C. Fiser
18th Mississippi, Maj. James C. Campbell (w), Lt.Col. William H. Luse
21st Mississippi, Capt. John Sims, Col. Benjamin G. Humphreys

Artillery
Maj. Samuel P. Hamilton

Col. Henry C. Cabell
Manly's (A, 1st North Carolina) Battery, Capt. Basil C. Manly
Pulaski (Georgia) Artillery, Capt. John P.W. Read
Richmond (Fayette) Artillery, Capt. Miles C. Macon
Richmond Howitzers (1st Company), Capt. Edward S. McCarthy
Troup (Georgia) Artillery, Capt. Henry H. Carlton

Anderson's Division
MG Richard H. Anderson (w)
BG Roger Pryor

Wilcox's Brigade
Gen. Cadmus Wilcox
Col. Alfred Cumming (w)
Maj. Hilary A. Herbert, Capt. James M. Crow
8th Alabama, Maj. Hilary A. Herbert
9th Alabama, Maj. Jeremiah Henry Johnston (w), Capt. James M. Crow
10th Alabama, Capt. G.C. Whatley (k)
11th Alabama, Maj. J.C. Sanders

Mahone's Brigade
Col. William A. Parham
6th Virginia, Capt. John R. Ludlow
12th Virginia, Capt. John R. Lewellen (w, 9/14)
16th Virginia, Maj. Francis D. Holliday (c, 9/14)
41st Virginia, Col. William A. Parham
61st Virginia, Lt.Col. William F. Neimeyer

Featherston's Brigade
BG Winfield S. Featherston
Col. Carnot Posey
12th Mississippi, Col. William H. Taylor
16th Mississippi, Capt. Abram M. Feltus
19th Mississippi, Col. Nathaniel H. Harris (w)
2nd Mississippi Battalion, Maj. William S. Wilson (mw)

Armistead's Brigade
BG Lewis A. Armistead (w)
Col. James G. Hodges
9th Virginia, Capt. William J. Richardson
14th Virginia, Col. James G. Hodges
38th Virginia, Col. Edward C. Edmonds

53rd Virginia, Capt. W.G. Pollard (k)
57th Virginia, Col. David Dyer

Pryor's Brigade
BG Roger A. Pryor
Col. John C. Hately (w)
14th Alabama, Maj. James A. Broome
2nd Florida, Col. William D. Ballantine (w), Lt. Geiger
5th Florida, Col. John C. Hately (w), Lt.Col. Thomas B. Lamar (w), Maj. Benjamin F. Davis
8th Florida, Lt.Col. George A.C. Coppens (k), Capt. Richard A. Waller (k), Capt. William Baya
3rd Virginia, Col. Joseph Mayo Jr. (w), Lt.Col. Alexander Daniel Callcote

Wright's Brigade
BG Ambrose R. Wright (w)
Col. Robert H. Jones (w)
Col. William Gibson
44th Alabama, Lt.Col. Charles A. Derby (k), Maj. William F. Perry
3rd Georgia, Capt. Reuben B. Nisbit (w), Capt. John T. Jones
22nd Georgia, Col. Robert H. Jones (w), Capt. Lawrence D. Lallerstedt (w)
48th Georgia, Col. William Gibson

Artillery
Maj. John S. Saunders
Dixie (Virginia) Artillery, Capt. William H. Chapman
Donaldsonville (Louisiana) Artillery, Capt. Victor Maurin
Norfolk (Virginia) Huger's Battery, Lt. C.R. Phelps
Moorman's (Virginia) Battery, Capt. Marcellus N. Moorman
Portsmouth (Virginia) Grimes' Battery, Capt. Cary F. Grimes (k)

Jones' Division
BG David R. Jones

Toombs' Brigade
BG Robert A. Toombs
Col. Henry L. Benning
2nd Georgia, Lt.Col. William R. Holmes (k), Maj. Skidmore Harris (w), Capt. Abner M. Lewis
15th Georgia, Col. W.T. Millican (mw), Capt. Thomas H. Jackson
17th Georgia, Capt. J.A. McGregor
20th Georgia, Col. John B. Cumming

DRAYTON'S BRIGADE
BG Thomas F. Drayton
50th Georgia, Lt.Col. Francis Kearse
51st Georgia (unknown)
15th South Carolina, Col. William D. DeSaussure

PICKETT'S BRIGADE
Col. Eppa Hunton
BG Richard B. Garnett
8th Virginia, Col. Eppa Hunton
18th Virginia, Maj. George C. Cabell
19th Virginia, Col. John B. Strange (k, 9/14), Capt. J.L. Cochran, Lt. William N. Wood
28th Virginia, Capt. W.L. Wingfield
56th Virginia, Col. William D. Stuart, Captain John B. McPhail Jr. (w, 9/14)

KEMPER'S BRIGADE
BG James L. Kemper
1st Virginia, Capt. George F. Newton, Maj. William H. Palmer
7th Virginia, Maj. Arthur Herbert
11th Virginia, Maj. Adam Clement (w, 9/14)
17th Virginia, Col. Montgomery D. Corse (w)
24th Virginia, Col. William R. Terry

JENKINS' BRIGADE
Col. Joseph Walker
1st South Carolina (Volunteers), Lt.Col. Daniel Livingston (w)
2nd South Carolina Rifles, Col. Robert A. Thompson
5th South Carolina, Capt. Thomas C. Beckham
6th South Carolina, Capt. E.B. Cantey (w)
4th South Carolina Battalion (5 companies), Lt. W.T. Field
Palmetto (South Carolina) Sharpshooters, Capt. A.H. Foster (w), Capt. F.W. Kirkpatrick

ANDERSON'S BRIGADE
Col. George T. Anderson
1st Georgia (Regulars), Col. William J. Magill (w), Capt. Richard A. Wayne
7th Georgia, Col. George H. Carmical
8th Georgia, Col. John R. Towers
9th Georgia, Lt.Col. John C.L. Mounger (w)
11th Georgia, Maj. Francis H. Little

ARTILLERY

Fauquier (Virginia) Artillery (Stribling's battery) (left at Leesburg, VA)
Loudoun (Virginia) Artillery (Rogers' battery) (left at Leesburg, VA)
Turner (Virginia) Artillery (Leake's battery) (left at Leesburg, VA)
Wise (Virginia) Artillery, Capt. James S. Brown

Walker's Division
Gen. John G. Walker

WALKER'S BRIGADE
Col. Van H. Manning (w),
Col. Edward D. Hall

3rd Arkansas, Capt. John W. Reedy
27th North Carolina, Col. John R. Cooke
46th North Carolina, Col. Edward D. Hall, Lt.Col. William A. Jenkins
48th North Carolina, Col. Robert C. Hill
30th Virginia, Lt.Col. Robert S. Chew (w)
Stafford (Virginia) Battery, Capt. Thomas B. French

RANSOM'S BRIGADE
BG Robert Ransom Jr.

24th North Carolina, Lt.Col. John L. Harris
25th North Carolina, Col. Henry M. Rutledge
35th North Carolina, Col. Matt W. Ransom
49th North Carolina, Lt.Col. Leroy M. McAfee
Branch's (Virginia) Artillery, Capt. James R. Branch

Hood's Division
BG John B. Hood

HOOD'S BRIGADE
Col. William T. Wofford

18th Georgia, Lt.Col. Solon Z. Ruff
Hampton (South Carolina) Legion, Lt.Col. Martin W. Gary
1st Texas, Lt.Col. Philip A. Work
4th Texas, Lt.Col. Benjamin F. Carter
5th Texas, Capt. Ike N.M. Turner

LAW'S BRIGADE
Col. Evander M. Law

4th Alabama, Lt.Col. Owen K. McLemore (mw 9/14), Capt. Lawrence H. Scruggs (w), Capt. William M. Robbins

2nd Mississippi, Col. John M. Stone (w), Lt. Moody
11th Mississippi, Col. Philip F. Liddell (mw 9/16), Lt.Col. Samuel F. Butler (mw), Maj. Taliaferro S. Evans (k)
6th North Carolina, Maj. Robert F. Webb (w)

Artillery
Maj. Bushrod W. Frobel
German (South Carolina) Artillery, Capt. William K. Bachman
Palmetto (South Carolina) Artillery, Capt. Hugh R. Garden
Rowan (North Carolina) Artillery, Capt. James Reilly

Evans' Brigade
BG Nathan G. Evans
Col. Peter F. Stevens (w)
17th South Carolina, Col. Fitz W. McMaster
18th South Carolina, Col. William H. Wallace
22nd South Carolina, Lt.Col. Thomas C. Watkins (mw 9/14), Maj. Miel Hilton
23rd South Carolina, Capt. S.A. Durham (w, 9/14), Lt. E.R. White
Holcombe (South Carolina) Legion, Col. Peter F. Stevens (w)
Macbeth (South Carolina) Artillery, Capt. Robert Boyce

Artillery
Washington (Louisiana) Artillery Col. James B. Walton
1st Company, Capt. Charles W. Squires
2nd Company, Capt. John B. Richardson
3rd Company, Capt. Merritt B. Miller
4th Company, Capt. Benjamin F. Eshleman

Lee's Battalion
Col. S. D. Lee
Ashland (Virginia) Artillery, Capt. Pichegru Woolfolk Jr.
Bedford (Virginia) Artillery, Capt. Tyler C. Jordan
Brooks (South Carolina) Artillery, Lt. William Elliott
Eubank's (Virginia) Battery, Capt. John L. Eubank
Madison (Louisiana) Light Artillery, Capt. George V. Moody
Parker's (Virginia) Battery, Capt. William W. Parker

Left Wing (Jackson's)
MG Thomas J. Jackson
Escort: Company H, 4th Virginia Cavalry, Capt. Robert Randolph
White's Virginia Cavalry (3 companies), Capt. Elijah V. White

Ewell's Division
BG Alexander R. Lawton (w)
BG Jubal A. Early

Lawton's Brigade
Col. Marcellus Douglass (k)
Maj. J.H. Lowe
Col. John H. Lamar
13th Georgia, Capt. D. A. Kidd
26th Georgia, Col. Edmund N. Atkinson
31st Georgia, Lt.Col. John T. Crowder (w), Maj. John H. Lowe
38th Georgia, Capt. W.H. Battey (k), Capt. Peter Brennan
60th Georgia, Maj. Waters B. Jones
61st Georgia, Col. John H. Lamar, Maj. Archibald P. McRae (k)

Early's Brigade
BG Jubal A. Early
Col. William Smith (w)
13th Virginia, Capt. F.V. Winston
25th Virginia, Capt. R.D. Lilley
31st Virginia, Col. John Hoffman
44th Virginia, Capt. David W. Anderson (w)
49th Virginia, Col. William Smith (w), Lt.Col. Jonathan C. Gibson (w)
52nd Virginia, Col. Michael G. Harman
58th Virginia, Col. Edmund Goode

Trimble's Brigade
Col. James A. Walker (w)
15th Alabama, Capt. Isaac B. Feagin
12th Georgia, Capt. James G. Rogers (k), Capt. John T. Carson
21st Georgia, Maj. Thomas C. Glover (w), Capt. James C. Nisbit
21st North Carolina, Capt. F.P. Miller (k)
1st North Carolina Battalion (unknown)
Johnson's (Virginia) Battery, Capt. John R. Johnson

Hays' Brigade
BG Harry T. Hays
5th Louisiana, Col. Henry Forno
6th Louisiana, Col. Henry B. Strong (k)
7th Louisiana (unknown)
8th Louisiana, Lt.Col. Trevanion D. Lewis (w)

14th Louisiana, Col. R.W. Jones
Louisiana Guard Artillery, Capt. Louis E. D'Aquin

ARTILLERY
Maj. Alfred R. Courtney
Charlottesville (Virginia) Artillery, Capt. James M. Carrington
Chesapeake (Maryland) Artillery, Capt. William D. Brown
Courtney (Virginia) Artillery, Capt. Joseph W. Latimer
1st Maryland Battery (Dement's battery), Capt. William F. Dement
Staunton (Virginia) Artillery (Balthis Battery), Lt. Asher W. Garber

Jackson's Division
BG John R. Jones (w)
BG William E. Starke (k)
Col. Andrew J. Grigsby

WINDER'S BRIGADE
Col. Andrew J. Grigsby
Lt.Col. Robert D. Gardner (w)
Maj. Hazael J. Williams
2nd Virginia, Capt. R.T. Colston (detached at Martinsburg, WV)
4th Virginia, Lt.Col. Robert D. Gardner
5th Virginia, Maj. Hazael J. Williams, Capt. E.L. Curtis (w)
27th Virginia, Capt. Frank C. Wilson
33rd Virginia, Capt. Jacob Golladay (w), Lt. David Walton

TALIAFERRO'S BRIGADE
Col. Edward T.H. Warren
Col. James W. Jackson (w)
Col. James L. Sheffield
47th Alabama, Col. James W. Jackson, Maj. James M. Campbell
48th Alabama, Col. James L. Sheffield
10th Virginia, Col. Edward T. Warren
23rd Virginia, Lt.Col. Simeon T. Walton
37th Virginia, Lt.Col. John F. Terry (w)

JONES' BRIGADE
Capt. J.E. Penn (w)
Capt. A.C. Page (w)
Capt. Robert W. Withers
21st Virginia, Capt. A.C. Page
42nd Virginia, Capt. Robert W. Withers, Capt. D.W. Garrett

48th Virginia, Capt. John H. Candler
1st Virginia Battalion, Lt. C.A. Davidson

Starke's Brigade
BG William E. Starke (k)
Col. Jesse M. Williams (w)
Col. Leroy A. Stafford (w)
Col. Edmund Pendleton
1st Louisiana, Lt.Col. Michael Nolan (w), Capt. W.E. Moore
2nd Louisiana, Col. Jesse M. Williams (w)
9th Louisiana, Col. Leroy A. Stafford (w), Lt.Col. William R. Peck
10th Louisiana, Capt. Henry D. Monier
15th Louisiana, Col. Edmund Pendleton
Coppens' (1st Louisiana Zouaves) Battalion, Col. G. Coppens

Artillery
Maj. Lindsay M. Shumaker
Alleghany (Virginia) Battery, Capt. Joseph Carpenter
Baltimore (Maryland) Battery, Capt. John B. Brockenbrough
Danville (Virginia) Battery, Capt. George Wooding
Hampden (Virginia) Battery, Capt. William H. Caskie
Lee Battery (Virginia), Capt. Charles I. Raine
Rockbridge (Virginia) Battery, Capt. William T. Poague

Hill's Light Division
MG Ambrose P. Hill

Branch's Brigade
BG Lawrence O. Branch (k)
Col. James H. Lane
7th North Carolina, Col. Edward G. Haywood
18th North Carolina, Lt.Col. Thomas J. Purdie
28th North Carolina, Col. James H. Lane, Maj. William J. Montgomery
33rd North Carolina, Lt.Col. Robert F. Hoke
37th North Carolina, Capt. William G. Morris

Gregg's Brigade
BG Maxcy Gregg (w)
1st South Carolina (Provisional Army), Col. Daniel H. Hamilton Sr.
1st South Carolina Rifles, Lt.Col. James M. Perrin (w)
12th South Carolina, Col. Dixon Barnes (mw), Maj. William H. McCorkle

13th South Carolina, Col. Oliver E. Edwards
14th South Carolina, Lt.Col. William D. Simpson

FIELD'S BRIGADE
Col. John M. Brockenbrough
40th Virginia, Lt.Col. Fleet W. Cox
47th Virginia, Lt.Col. John W. Lyell
55th Virginia, Maj. Charles N. Lawson
22nd Virginia Battalion, Maj. Edward P. Taylor

ARCHER'S BRIGADE
BG James J. Archer
Col. Peter Turney
5th Alabama Battalion, Capt. Charles M. Hooper
19th Georgia, Maj. James H. Neal, Capt. Tilghman W. Flynt (w), Capt. F.M. Johnston
1st Tennessee (Provisional Army), Col. Peter Turney
7th Tennessee, Maj. Samuel G. Shepard, Lt. G.A. Howard
14th Tennessee, Col. William McComb (w), Lt.Col. James W. Lockert

PENDER'S BRIGADE
BG William D. Pender
16th North Carolina, Lt.Col. William A. Stowe
22nd North Carolina, Maj. Christopher C. Cole
34th North Carolina, Lt.Col. John McDowell
38th North Carolina, Lt.Col. Robert F. Armfield

THOMAS' BRIGADE
Col. Edward L. Thomas
14th Georgia, Col. Robert W. Folsom
35th Georgia, Lt.Col. Bolling H. Holt
45th Georgia, Maj. Washington L. Grace
49th Georgia, Lt.Col. Seaborn M. Manning

ARTILLERY
Lt.Col. Reuben L. Walker
Branch (North Carolina) Artillery (A.C. Latham's battery) (left in Leesburg, VA)
Crenshaw's (Virginia) Battery, Capt. William G. Crenshaw
Fredericksburg (Virginia) Artillery (Braxton's battery), Capt. Carter M. Braxton

Letcher (Virginia) Artillery (Davidson's battery), Capt. Greenlee Davidson
Middlesex (Virginia) Artillery (Fleet's battery) (left in Leesburg, VA)
Pee Dee (South Carolina) Artillery (McIntosh's battery), Capt. David M. McIntosh
Purcell (Virginia) Artillery (Pegram's battery), Capt. William J. Pegram

Hill's Division
MG Daniel Harvey Hill

Ripley's Brigade
BG Roswell S. Ripley (w)
Col. George P. Doles
4th Georgia, Col. George P. Doles, Maj. Robert S. Smith (k), Capt. William H. Willis
44th Georgia, Capt. John C. Key
1st North Carolina, Lt.Col. Hamilton A. Brown
3rd North Carolina, Col. William L. De Rosset (w), Maj. Stephen D. Thruston (w)

Rodes' Brigade
BG Robert E. Rodes (w)
3rd Alabama, Col. Cullen A. Battle
5th Alabama, Maj. Edwin L. Hobson
6th Alabama, Col. John B. Gordon (w), Lt.Col. James.N. Lightfoot (w)
12th Alabama, Col. Bristor B. Gayle (k, 9/14), Lt.Col. Samuel B. Pickens (w, 9/14), Capt. Tucker (k), Capt. Maroney (w), Capt. Adolph Proskauer (w)
26th Alabama, Col. Edward A. O'Neal (w)

Garland's Brigade
BG Samuel Garland Jr. (k, 9/14)
Col. D. K. McRae (w)
5th North Carolina, Col. D. K. McRae (w), Capt. Thomas M. Garrett
12th North Carolina, Capt. S. Snow
13th North Carolina, Lt.Col. Thomas Ruffin Jr. (w), Capt. J.H. Hyman
20th North Carolina, Col. Alfred Iverson
23rd North Carolina, Col. Daniel H. Christie

Anderson's Brigade
BG George B. Anderson (mw)
Col. R.T. Bennett (w)
2nd North Carolina, Col. C.C. Tew (k), Capt. G.M. Roberts
4th North Carolina, Col. Bryan Grimes, Capt. W.T. Marsh (k), Capt. D.P. Latham (k)

14th North Carolina, Col. R.T. Bennett
30th North Carolina, Col. F.M. Parker (w), Maj. W.W. Sillers

Colquitt's Brigade
Col. Alfred H. Colquitt
13th Alabama, Col. Birkett D. Fry (w), Lt.Col. W.H. Betts (w)
6th Georgia, Lt.Col. James M. Newton (k), Maj. Philemon Tracy (mw), Lt. E.P. Bennett
23rd Georgia, Col. W.P. Barclay (k), Lt.Col. Emory F. Best (w), Maj. James H. Huggins (w)
27th Georgia, Col. Levi B. Smith (k), Lt.Col. Charles Thorton Zachry (w), Capt. William H. Rentfro
28th Georgia, Maj. Tully Graybill (w), Capt. N.J. Garrison (w), Capt. George W. Warthen

Artillery
Major Scipio Pierson
Hardaway's (Alabama) Battery, Capt. Robert A. Hardaway
Jefferson Davis (Alabama) Artillery, Capt. James W. Bondurant
Jones' (Virginia) Battery, Capt. William B. Jones
King William (Virginia) Artillery, Capt. Thomas H. Carter

Cavalry
MG James E.B. Stuart

Hampton's Brigade
BG Wade Hampton
1st North Carolina, Col. Lawrence S. Baker
2nd South Carolina, Col. Matthew C. Butler
10th Virginia Cobb's (Georgia) Legion, Lt.Col. Pierce M.B. Young (w), Maj. William G. Delony
Jeff. Davis (Mississippi) Legion, Lt.Col. William T. Martin

Lee's Brigade
BG Fitzhugh Lee
1st Virginia, Lt.Col. Luke Tiernan Brien
3rd Virginia, Lt.Col. John T. Thornton (mw), Capt. Thomas Owens
4th Virginia, Col. Williams C. Wickham
5th Virginia, Col. Thomas L. Rosser
9th Virginia, Col. W.H.F. Lee

Robertson's Brigade
Col. Thomas T. Munford
2nd Virginia, Lt.Col. Richard H. Burks
6th Virginia 7th Virginia, Capt. Samuel B. Myers
12th Virginia, Col. Asher W. Harman
17th Virginia Battalion, Maj. Thomas B. Massie

Horse Artillery
Capt. John Pelham
Chew's (Virginia) Battery, Capt. Roger P. Chew
Hart's (South Carolina) Battery, Capt. James F. Hart
Pelham's (Virginia) Battery, Capt. John Pelham

Artillery Reserve
BG William N. Pendleton

Brown's Battalion
Col. J. Thompson Brown
Powhatan (Virginia) Artillery, Capt. Willis J. Dance
Richmond (Virginia) Howitzers, 2nd Company, Capt. David Watson
Richmond (Virginia) Howitzers, 3rd Company, Capt. Benjamin H. Smith Jr.
Salem (Virginia) Artillery, Capt. Abraham Hupp
Williamsburg (Virginia) Artillery, Capt. John A. Coke

Cutts' Battalion
Lt.Col. Allen S. Cutts
Blackshears' (Georgia) Battery, Capt. James A. Blackshear
Irwin (Georgia) Artillery, Capt. John Lane
Lloyd's (North Carolina) Battery, Capt. Whitmel P. Lloyd
Patterson's (Georgia) Battery, Capt. George M. Patterson
Ross' (Georgia) Battery, Capt. Hugh M. Ross

Jones' Battalion
Maj. Hillary P. Jones
Morris (Virginia) Artillery, Richard C.M. Page's Battery
Orange (Virginia) Artillery, Capt. Jefferson Peyton
Turner's (Virginia) Battery, Capt. William H. Turner
Long Island (Virginia) Battery, Capt. Abram Wimbish

Nelson's Battalion

Maj. William Nelson

Amherst (Virginia) Artillery, Capt. Thomas J. Kirkpatrick's
Fluvanna (Virginia) Artillery, Capt. John J. Ancell
Huckstep's (Virginia) Battery, Capt. Charles T. Huckstep
Johnson's (Virginia) Battery, Capt. Marmaduke Johnson
Milledge (Georgia) Artillery, Capt. John Milledge

Miscellaneous Batteries

Cutshaw's (Virginia) Battery, Capt. W.E. Cutshaw
Magruder (Virginia) Artillery (T.J. Page Jr.'s Battery)
Rice's (Virginia) Battery, Capt. W.H. Rice
Thomas (Virginia) Artillery (E.J. Anderson's Battery) (left in Leesburg)

Appendix B

Michigan at Antietam Day Proclamation

STATE OF MICHIGAN

CERTIFICATE OF PROCLAMATION

ON BEHALF OF THE PEOPLE OF MICHIGAN
I, Rick Snyder, governor of Michigan, do hereby proclaim
August 26, 2012 as

MICHIGAN AT ANTIETAM DAY

WHEREAS, during the American Civil War, the state of Michigan sent more than 90,000 soldiers, nearly one-quarter of the state's male population, to serve as members of the Union army; nearly 15,000 of those brave and loyal citizen soldiers paid the ultimate sacrifice; and,

WHEREAS, on September 17, 1862, several thousand Michigan soldiers defended their nation during the Antietam Campaign of the American Civil War, with the 7th and 17th Michigan Volunteer Infantry suffering severe casualties; and,

WHEREAS, the Union victory at Antietam enabled President Abraham Lincoln to issue the Emancipation Proclamation in fulfillment of a more perfect Union in which all persons are created equal and possess certain inalienable rights; and,

WHEREAS, on this day, we join with the Michigan Historical Commission, Michigan Historical Center and the Civil War Sesquicentennial History Partners as they host a Michigan Tribute Ceremony at Antietam National Cemetery; we encourage citizens of the Great Lakes State to honor and remember the sacrifice and outstanding leadership of those Michigan service members and the women who provided soldier aid relief efforts on the single bloodiest day in U.S. military history;

NOW, THEREFORE, I, Rick Snyder, governor of Michigan, do hereby proclaim Sunday, August 26, 2012 as Michigan at Antietam Day.

Rick Snyder
Governor

Governor Rick Snyder's proclamation for "Michigan at Antietam Day," August 26, 2012. *State of Michigan.*

Appendix C

John A. Clark Story

1st Lieutenant Company D, 7th Michigan Infantry

Within a few short days after the Battle of Antietam, a two-photographer team from Mathew Brady's New York Photographic Studio—Alexander Gardner and James Gibson—arrived at Sharpsburg, Maryland, to record scenes from what was to become known as "America's Bloodiest Day." Taking about seventy images of death, carnage and destruction found on the battlefield, Gardner and Gibson provided the material for Brady's latest exhibition, "The Dead of Antietam," to open in October 1862.[854] Never before had the horrors of war been covered by the relatively new process of photography. As television brought scenes from the Vietnam War into the living rooms of Americans in the 1960s and early '70s, photography brought the Civil War to millions on the homefront. An article appearing in the *New York Times* by a reporter who had witnessed the exhibit speaks directly to closing the gap between the horrors of war and the homefront:

> *Brady has done something to bring home to us the terrible reality and earnestness of war. If he has not brought bodies and laid them in our dooryards and along the streets, he has done something very like it. There is one side of the picture that the sun did not catch, one phase that has escaped photographic skill. It is the background of widows and orphans, torn from the bosom of their natural protectors by the red remorseless hand of Battle, and thrown upon the fatherhood of God. Homes have been made desolate, and the light of life in thousands of hearts has been quenched forever. All of this desolation imagination must paint—broken hearts cannot be photographed.*[855]

Grave of Lieutenant John A. Clark, 7th Michigan Infantry, where he fell at the "epicenter" of the Antietam battlefield, photo by Alexander Gardner. *Library of Congress.*

Among the series of images taken during those days in September, none is more poignant than Gardner's stereo no. 551 taken of a hastily constructed grave on the D.R. Miller property. Captioned, "A Contrast: A Federal buried, Confederate unburied, where they fell, on Battle-field [*sic*] of Antietam," this image encapsulated the sentiments expressed by the *New York Times* article. The priority of burial tells us the Federal army held the field as its soldiers were buried first. History may never tell us if the family of the fallen Confederate soldier, very easily identifiable to those who knew him, ever saw this image.

In 1978, William A. Frassanito published the seminal and groundbreaking work on the photographs of Antietam titled *Antietam: A Photographic Legacy of America's Bloodiest Day*. An exceptional historian and masterful scholar with an investigative eye for historical evidence, Frassanito sought to discover every last detail of each image, the story behind the subject matter and the original location where each was taken on the field. Having access to the originals located in the Library of Congress, he examined and scrutinized each image, garnering every last bit of information possible. Examining stereo view no. 551, he was able to decipher the writing on the temporary wooden headboard in the image as "J.A. Clark, 7th Mich." Further research would prove that this was the grave of Lieutenant John A. Clark, Company D, 7th Michigan Infantry, of Monroe. Upon further investigation, a carte de visite photograph of Lieutenant Clark in uniform was housed in the Monroe Country Historical Museum collection. With the publication of his book, Frassanito introduced to the world the soldier who had been previously anonymous for the past 110 years and "secured from the clutches of obscurity, a soldier who died long ago."[856]

In 1989, I received a copy of Frassanito's book, and as a college student majoring in history, I set out to consume its contents promptly. Having read his previously published work on the photographs of Gettysburg, I neglected all required coursework readings until I had finished *Antietam*. To my great surprise, I read the story of Lieutenant John A. Clark, and thus a peculiar "friendship" with an 1860s Monroe resident began. Having been born and raised in Monroe and at the time the same age of John when he enlisted, I was moved by his tragic story—a story so emblematic of the hundreds of thousands like him who perished during the Civil War. As a lifelong

Lieutenant John A. Clark of Monroe, 7th Michigan Infantry, killed in action at Antietam. *Monroe County Historical Museum.*

student of history, with a deep and profound interest in Civil War subject matter, I was inspired to learn more about this young soldier from my hometown who, like me at the time, had joyous visions of the future with a whole life full of possibilities ahead of him. As I peered at his image in the book and knowing that he was buried in the freshly constructed grave, it had a profound and very relevant effect on me. He paid the ultimate sacrifice, forfeiting those joyous and innocent visions of the future, in order to secure the freedom we all enjoy today.

Captivated by the story and appreciative of what Frassanito revealed, I wrote to the author explaining how I enjoyed his work, was going to school for history and that I was from John Clark's hometown. Concluding the letter, I offered my assistance with any future research needs he might have with regards to John Clark. To my delight, I received a letter back shortly thereafter acknowledging receipt of mine and, to my great excitement, a request for more information on the Clark family. In it Frassanito wrote, "I have never been to Monroe…I would like to have slides of the graves and the farmhouse, if it still exists today." Eager at this opportunity to conduct research for Mr. Frassanito, I quickly set out to learn more and fulfill my mission to provide the requested items. Over the course of the subsequent nine months, I gathered what amounted to a master's thesis of information exploring the life and death of John and the Clark family of Monroe, Michigan.

Twenty-year-old John A. Clark enlisted as a sergeant in Company D of the 7th Michigan Infantry on June 19, 1861, for three years. John's conduct and record as a noncommissioned officer earned him an officer's commission as second lieutenant by March 18, 1862, and as first lieutenant a little over a month later. Having survived the battles of the Peninsula Campaign in the spring and early summer of 1862, John contracted illness in the swamp of the Chickahominy and suffered greatly in the retreat from Richmond to Fort Monroe. He applied for a leave of absence for health reasons on July 1 and was soon sent to a hospital in Washington, D.C. On July 8, surgeon K. Barnes reported, "I certify that I have carefully examined this officer and find that he has been sick…with an attack of remittent fever." Upon recovery at home, Lieutenant Clark returned to the 7th Michigan around the first part of September. On September 17, 1862, while trying to rally the men of Company D, John A. Clark was "shot through the head and instantly killed."[857] (See Chapter 6.)

John was buried near the location where he fell on the David R. Miller farm, aptly named the "epicenter" of the Battle of Antietam. It may be assumed that surviving members of the 7th Michigan or at least those of Dana's Brigade could have buried Lieutenant Clark and fashioned a crude headboard marking the grave. It has long been thought that John's father, Thomas, and brother, Edward, traveled to Sharpsburg, Maryland, from Monroe to retrieve the body. However, it was boyhood friend and neighbor Frederick Nims who brought Lieutenant Clark's body back to Monroe. An interview by Marion Childs with Frederick's daughter, Katherine, regarding Monroe's early history brought this to light. In the interview, Katherine recalled "Dr. Robert Clark, the pioneer who lived on West Elm Ave. and whose [grand]son John was Katherine's [my] father's boyhood chum. John and Frederick Nims enlisted together for the Civil War. John was killed early in its history and his body brought home to Monroe accompanied by Frederick."

A bit later in the recollection, the bond between John and Frederick was reiterated: "Katherine's father's boyhood playmates were the [grand]sons of Dr. Robert Clark (and especially John Clark, who went to war with him). Another playmate was Libby Bacon, who was to marry General Custer." Although not listed directly by name, a few of those playmates (grandsons of Dr. Clark) would be John's brother, Edward, and another teenager named John C. Anderson. Upon Frederick's return to Monroe with the body in the fall of 1862, Lieutenant Clark was buried in the family's plot in Monroe's Woodland Cemetery.[858]

Lieutenant Frederick Nims brought the body of his boyhood friend John A. Clark home to Monroe after the battle. *Monroe County Historical Museum.*

Twenty-one-year-old Frederick Nims, the same age as Clark, enlisted in Company C, 5th Michigan Cavalry, as a first sergeant on August 22, 1862. He was commissioned a second lieutenant of Company F on January 12, 1864. Looking for able-minded, trustworthy and reliable men, now Major General George Custer appointed Nims as an aide-de-camp from July to September 30, 1864. He was commissioned first lieutenant of Company B in March 1865, being honorably discharged at Detroit on August 22, 1865.[859] In 1907, Michigan governor Fred M. Warner appointed Frederick Nims to the Custer Equestrian Monument Commission. The monument was dedicated in Monroe on June 4, 1910, by President William H. Taft and Elizabeth Bacon Custer. Nims, one of Custer's last staff members, died on October 2, 1921, and is buried next to the Custer Family Plot less than one hundred yards from John Clark in Woodland Cemetery.[860]

John's parents, Thomas and Lavonia, married in October 1833, and to them three children were born: Edward, Helen and John. The Clark family lived in the city's Third Ward, north of the River Raisin on Water (now Elm) Street. This section of the city, near where Camp Monroe was established, had large tracts of lands extending in long narrow strips away from the river known as ribbon farms. Brothers John and Edward assisted their father, who listed his occupation in the 1860 census and subsequent city directories as a farmer. The Nims property was to the north and adjacent to the Clark farm. As kids growing up together on adjacent property, undoubtedly a deep friendship developed, as expressed by Katherine. By 1872, with his only surviving son, Edward, in Chicago, Thomas sold the farm to Ilgenfritz and Sons, which promptly turned the once-owned Clark property into a nursery and orchard.[861]

With deep roots to the founding fathers of Monroe, Thomas Clark was a well-respected and active community citizen. He served as an elder in the local Presbyterian church along with other several prominent Monroe citizens, including the father-in-law of George Armstrong Custer, Judge Daniel Bacon. When he died at the age of seventy-four, Clark's obituary praised him and his role in the Monroe community as a long-standing political figure, church elder, husband, father and respected citizen of the city. The Clark family home survives today and is occupied. Although changes over time have altered its 1860s appearance as John would have known it, the core of the structure still exists.[862]

The Clark family section in Monroe's historic Woodland Cemetery is a typical mid- to late nineteenth-century middle-class cemetery plot. The center stone obelisk lists the names of the family members with a meek epitaph stating that John was killed at the Battle of Antietam, although it is barely legible due to the weathering and patina of the inscription. John's individual headstone simply reads, "John A." Disturbed by the fact that the grave of this soldier, who paid so dearly for his country, was not properly identified with a military headstone, I applied to the Veterans Administration for one. Having secured donations to include the additional inscription, "Killed at the Battle of Antietam—Sept 17 1862," I secured a stone military marker for Lieutenant Clark.

A dedication ceremony was planned for May 16, 1992, where presentations were made, rifle and cannon salutes fired, taps played and all the other elements of a proper military funeral conducted—one that appears to have never been originally afforded him. Historians, including David D. Finney Jr., who wrote the foreword to this book, presented a history of the 7th Michigan, Monroe's role in the Civil War and a biography of John's military service. Period music was played and sung by the some two hundred citizens gathered. At the designated time, an enlarged photograph of John, the one Frassanito published in 1978, was unveiled. Shortly thereafter, Monroe mayor pro tem Mark Worrell unveiled Clark's new headstone, where a wreath and flowers were immediately placed by the ladies of Monroe. At last, this young soldier had the proper thank-you for the sacrifice he made to his country.

The evening before the dedication ceremony, my father, Barry Egen, assisted me in installing Lieutenant Clark's new headstone. My grandfather Norman Egen owned a local tombstone business in Monroe, and both my father and I spent a great deal of time in cemeteries, especially Woodland, in the process of installing and repairing gravestones. With permission from the cemetery board, my father and I removed the small and barely legible "John A." footstone to be replaced by the new 230-pound military tombstone. On my knees, I dug a deeper hole to receive the new gravestone, and at one point the earth in that vicinity caved in slightly, creating a small, dark void in the ground above the grave. My father and I paused. After a moment, I looked up to him and said, "I want to shake his hand and thank him for his service." My father replied, "I know, son." We continued our effort, and as the sun set among the mature trees of the cemetery, John A. Clark finally had the proper military headstone marking his final resting place. We covered the stone in preparation for the ceremony the following day.

Shortly after the dedication ceremony in May 1992, Jim Ryland and Christine Kull at the Monroe County Historical Museum reexamined a 1860s carte de visite photo album held in its collection. The album was assembled by George A. Custer on one of his final military leaves spent in Monroe as a birthday gift to his former Sunday school teacher, Samuel M. Sacket. It was filled with pictures of the businessmen of Monroe, including Thomas Clark, as well as officers from the city. Contained within was another photograph of John A. Clark, without the inked inscription on the face as published previously and noted here. With hesitation, the staff showed me the page where the image was inserted, and along the upper edge in pencil was written "John Anderson." Looking in the service records, my heart sank as I learned that a John C. Anderson of Monroe, the same age as Clark, enlisted in the same company and regiment, eventually rising to the rank of lieutenant. Did someone years after the war, in an attempt to identify the photos in the album, inadvertently mix up the two cousins' names? Was the name "Clark" accidentally not written following the "John Anderson?" The only way to determine if the lieutenant in the image was John A. Clark or John C. Anderson was to find another image of one of them and conduct further research.

John C. Anderson enlisted in Company D, 7th Michigan Infantry, at Monroe for three years on October 21, 1861. He was severely wounded in the shoulder blade at Antietam on September 17 and was sent to Fort Schuyler, New York, to recover. Having recovered from his wounding, he returned to the regiment and participated in the Battles of Fredericksburg, Chancellorsville and Gettysburg. He reenlisted in December 1863 and became second lieutenant on December 18, 1864. Lieutenant Anderson would survive the war, being mustered out in July 1865.[863]

Research into this story would reveal that John A. Clark and John C. Anderson were first cousins. Sources indicate that the initial "C" in the latter's name was from his mother's maiden name, Jane Stewart (Clark). Although I have not been able to substantiate that the "A" in John A. Clark stood for Anderson, it can be deduced that these first two cousins, born within a year of each other, shared the other family's last name, thus John Clark Anderson and John Anderson Clark. John Clark and John Anderson's lineage can be traced back to the original settlement of Monroe (initially called Frenchtown). Although generations removed, each of these young soldiers can claim direct lineage to Colonel John Anderson, one of Monroe's earliest and more colorful citizens. John Anderson was appointed by Michigan's first territorial governor, William Hull, as colonel of the 2nd Regiment Michigan Militia. With the commencement of the War of 1812 and the surrender of Detroit on August 16, 1812, Colonel Anderson became a marked man by the British and their Indian allies. Having survived the war, he became a local businessman and prominent citizen of the community. Colonel John Anderson, dying on July 3, 1840, would never know his two namesake descendants who would enlist in the 7th Michigan and fight during the Civil War.[864]

Multiple copies of the CDV images were common, so the fact that there existed two images of John A. Clark is not uncommon. However, the fact that one was labeled as "John A. Clark" and one as "John Anderson" begged the question as to which John was in the photo. Not soon after, through the help of friend and Civil War historian Dale Niesen, I tracked down an image of a "John Anderson" from the 7th Michigan. Although in civilian clothes and not a uniform, this image was positively identified as John Anderson. Collector of Michigan Civil War images Mike Waskul owned the image and shared it with me. With great anticipation, I sincerely hoped that the man in this image was different than the John Clark we all had come to know. To my relief and satisfaction, the image, although strikingly similar to the John Clark established and previously published, was a different person. Furthermore, the Waskul image showed this individual wearing a trefoil badge on his lapel.

The trefoil was the II Corps symbol, to which the 7th Michigan belonged. These symbol badges identified the army corps to which a unit belonged and were affixed to uniforms for identification. Formalized, these corps badges were often a source of pride, and such devices often found their way onto civilian clothing in the form of lapel pins. The creation and issuance of corps badges did not occur until adopted by Major General Joseph Hooker after he took command of the Army of the Potomac on January 26, 1863. John A. Clark would have never worn a corps badge, having died nearly four months prior to it being used by the army. The soldier whom Frassanito had identified as the man in John A. Clark's grave at Antietam was indeed correct.

John Clark Anderson, having survived wounding and four years of the war, would finally succumb to illnesses contracted during his service. On Thanksgiving Day 1866, while "partaking of a family dinner he was seized with a pain in the back, and had to be carried home….When his recovery became doubtful, his mother informed him of it." Upon recognition of this somber news, he provided a message to his absent brother and sister: "Tell them I love them and I want them to meet me in heaven." On Wednesday, December 26, 1866, John C. Anderson died. He was buried at Woodland Cemetery not more than seventy-five yards from his cousin, John A. Clark. He was twenty-four years old.[865]

Over the past twenty-six years, I have studied the life and death of John A. Clark and his family. Having attended high school just a block away from his boyhood home and having played baseball on a field that once was the farm on which he helped his father work, I have walked in his footsteps. The house that I, my wife and daughter currently live in, built in 1858, is situated directly across the River Raisin from the Clark family house and property. I have often pondered that John Clark undoubtedly saw the

Wounded in action at Antietam, John Clark Anderson of Monroe was Lieutenant John A. Clark's first cousin, both in Company D, 7th Michigan Infantry. *Mike Waskul.*

brick house I live in being constructed across the river. I frequently walk down to the river's edge behind our home and gaze upon the other shore, where I can envision a young John Clark, Frederick Nims, John Anderson and maybe even Libby Custer fishing innocently, completely unaware that the impending storm of war would devastate, like so many other communities, the tranquil and peaceful environs of their life forever. We must continue to remember their sacrifice and keep relevant their actions so unselfishly delivered for us and future generations. As one veteran so aptly stated, "May life cease to exist if these memories be not cherished in our hearts as things 'sacred forever.'" Let John A. Clark represent all veterans who have paid the ultimate sacrifice for the freedoms we enjoy today. To them, we owe a debt of gratitude that no words can ever adequately convey. Although I never met John Clark, I know him well.

Brian James Egen

Appendix D

Woodruff's Battery

At 10:00 a.m. on September 17, Lieutenant George Augustus Woodruff brought his Light Battery I, 1st U.S. Artillery, consisting of six twelve-pounder Napoleon cannons,[866] onto the "epicenter" of the Antietam battlefield.

Woodruff was born in Marshall, Michigan, on May 27, 1840. He entered West Point in 1857 with an appointment from Michigan, graduating sixteenth of thirty-four in the second class of 1861 with the rank of lieutenant. He served in the defenses of Washington, D.C., at the Battle of Ball's Bluff and during the Peninsula Campaign, including the Seven Days Battles, where his skills as a fine artillery officer were evident. He was on sick leave from July 21 until September 1862.[867]

Woodruff crossed his battery over Antietam Creek late on September 16 and parked near the Hoffman farm. Responding to an urgent order from the II Corps' chief of artillery, he moved to the aid of Sedgwick's Division. The battery "went thru the East Woods at a gallop and over the fields straight for the Hagerstown Road through a stream of fugitives." Finding a position south of the Miller Cornfield, the battery unlimbered 150 yards from the road and 350 yards northeast of the Dunker Church.[868] Woodruff immediately opened with canister on Kershaw's brigade, which was moving up the slope opposite the church. The Confederates fell back and sought cover, as "Woodruff's canister was too much for them." The battery continued to fire, without the presence of supporting infantry, for some time. Its task accomplished, it was ordered to retire and resupply.

Captain James Robertson (left) and Lieutenant George Augustus Woodruff (right), West Pointer from Michigan, who commanded a battery at the Antietam "epicenter." *Library of Congress.*

At about 5:00 p.m., Woodruff was ordered by one of McClellan's staff to assist either on the right of the Union line or in the center, where Hancock had assumed command after Richardson's wounding. Ending up at the latter location, the battery was ordered not to fire except in reply or in case of a Confederate attack. It remained in position until being relieved at 2:00 p.m. on the eighteenth. While in action on September 17, the battery expended 168 rounds of canister, 75 rounds of spherical case and 27 rounds of solid shot. The only casualties were several horses.[869]

Woodruff's battery received mention by McClellan for "doing good service" and pouring on such powerful salvos that the enemy was "unable to withstand this deadly fire."[870]

Woodruff had three brothers, two of whom died while fighting for the Union. On July 4, 1863, Lieutenant Woodruff died of wounds incurred during "Pickett's Charge" at the Battle of Gettysburg.[871] He was twenty-three.

Appendix E

Michigan Losses by Regiment

Maryland Campaign

Battle of South Mountain[872]

17th Michigan Infantry

26 enlisted men killed
4 officers wounded
102 enlisted men wounded
Lt. George R. Galligan (mw)

8th Michigan Infantry

8 enlisted men wounded

Battle of Antietam[873]

7th Michigan Infantry

3 officers killed
36 enlisted men killed
12 officers wounded
166 enlisted men wounded
4 enlisted men captured/missing
Capt. J. Henry Turrill (k)
Lt. John A. Clark (k)
Lt. John P. Eberhard (k)
Capt. Allen H. Zacharias (mw)

17th Michigan Infantry

18 enlisted men killed

9 officers wounded

80 enlisted men wounded

Lt. William M. Duffield (mw)

8th Michigan Infantry

4 officers wounded

25 enlisted men wounded

2 enlisted men captured/missing

Skirmishes on September 19 and 20[874]

1st Michigan Infantry

1 enlisted man killed

1 enlisted man wounded

2 enlisted men captured/missing

4th Michigan Infantry

1 enlisted man killed

1 officer wounded

5 enlisted men wounded

Note: Does not include subsequent losses.

NOTES

PREFACE

1. Stephen W. Sears, "High Stakes at Antietam," *American Heritage* (Summer 2012): 40.
2. Rufus R. Dawes, *Service with the Sixth Wisconsin Volunteers* (Marietta, GA: E.R. Alderman & Sons, 1890), 90.
3. Edward G. Morton, ed., "Terrible Accident at Pittsburg," *Monroe (MI) Monitor*, September 24, 1862. Original copies in the Monroe County Historical Museum (hereafter MCHM).
4. Harold Holzer, *Dear Mr. Lincoln: Letters to the President* (Carbondale: Southern Illinois University Press, 2006), 161.
5. Archive of American Innovation, "Letter from Abraham Lincoln to Nathan Sargent," 1859, Dearborn, Michigan, Object ID: 53.45.1. This three-page handwritten letter resides in the Archive of American Innovation at The Henry Ford.

CHAPTER 1

6. Date is likely the tenth, given climatological data and troop movements. Joseph L. Harsh, *Sounding the Shallows: A Confederate Companion for the Maryland Campaign of 1862* (Kent, OH: Kent State University Press, 2000), 12.
7. John Miller, "Civil War Diary: The Confederate Soldier during the 1862 Maryland Campaign," article on the Emmitsburg Area Historical Society website, http://www.emmitsburg.net/history, accessed on January 27, 2015.

8. Besides those in 1861 at First Bull Run and Balls' Bluff under a different designation.
9. Francis W. Palfrey, *The Antietam and Fredericksburg* (New York: Charles Scribner's Sons, 1893), 12.
10. James Longstreet, "The Invasion of Maryland," in *Hearts Touched by Fire: The Best of Battles and Leaders of the Civil War*, ed. Harold Holzer (New York: Modern Library, 2011), 417.
11. Gary W. Gallagher, ed., *Fighting for the Confederacy: The Personal Recollections of General Edward Porter Alexander* (Chapel Hill: University of North Carolina Press, 1989), 139. Lee's confidence in his men, "& theirs in him, were so equal that no man can yet say which was greatest," id.
12. Four of five infantrymen had been in two or more major battles; all had been in at least one. Harsh, *Sounding the Shallows*, 103.
13. Lynda L. Crist, ed., *The Papers of Jefferson Davis*, vol. VIII, *1862* (Baton Rouge: Louisiana State University Press, 1995), 373–75.
14. McClellan wrote that Lincoln "regarded Washington as lost." George B. McClellan, "From the Peninsula to Antietam," in *Battles & Leaders of the Civil War*, eds. Robert U. Johnson and Clarence C. Buel (New York: Century Company, 1887), vol. II, 549.
15. *The War of the Rebellion: A Compilation of the Official Records of the Union and Confederate Armies* (Washington, D.C.: Government Printing Office, 1880–1901), series I, vol. XIX, part I, 37 (hereafter *OR*, and all series I references are implicit).
16. Stephen W. Sears, *Landscape Turned Red: The Battle of Antietam* (New Haven, CT: Ticknor & Fields, 1983), 79–80.
17. D. Scott Hartwig, *To Antietam Creek: The Maryland Campaign of September 1862* (Baltimore, MD: Johns Hopkins University Press, 2012), 1.
18. Palfrey, *Antietam and Fredericksburg*, 17.
19. James G. Randall, *Lincoln the President: Springfield to Gettysburg*, vol. II (New York: Dodd, Mead & Company, 1945), 154. "I remember as we were marching…the gloom that overshadowed us and the thought that only the heroic efforts and sacrifice of brave men could save our national capital and possibly our government." Nelson A. Miles, "My Recollections of Antietam," *Cosmopolitan* 53, no. 5 (October 1912), 581.
20. Edward J. Stackpole, *From Cedar Mountain to Antietam* (Harrisburg, PA: Stackpole Books, 1993), 290.
21. *OR*, vol. XIX, part II, 590–91, 593–94.
22. Elizabeth R. Varon, *Appomattox: Victory, Defeat, and Freedom at the End of the Civil War* (New York: Oxford University Press, 2014), 26.
23. Ibid., 54. A native Marylander would play a role in one of the final fatalities of the war at Ford's Theatre on April 14, 1865.

24. Alabama, Florida, Georgia, Louisiana, Mississippi and South Carolina adopted provisional constitutions in February 1861 favoring expansion: "Congress shall have power to admit other States" (Art. I, Sec. 6(18)). With the March 1861 constitution (Art. IV, Sec. 3(1)), Arkansas, North Carolina, Tennessee, Texas and Virginia joined, and the seat of government moved to Richmond.
25. Charles B. Dew, *Apostles of Disunion: Southern Secession Commissioners and the Causes of the Civil War* (Charlottesville: University Press of Virginia, 2010), 56–57.
26. *OR*, series IV, vol. I, 281–82.
27. Ibid., 805–6.
28. See the Papers of Jefferson Davis, Rice University, http://jeffersondavis.rice.edu/Content.aspx?id=107, accessed on November 5, 2014.
29. It was not a new military idea. In September 1861, the Confederate commander in Northern Virginia was writing of a potential "advance into Maryland." *OR*, vol. V, 881–82. An invasion across the Potomac was also advocated in April and May 1862. *OR*, vol. II, 477, 485. Also see *Lee the Soldier*, ed. Gary Gallagher (Lincoln: University of Nebraska Press, 1996), 15 (Jackson to Lee "proposing to go to Md." during the Valley Campaign of 1862).
30. Clifford Dowdey, ed., *The Wartime Papers of R.E. Lee* (Boston: Little Brown, 1961), 183–84.
31. Roy P. Basler, ed., *The Collected Works of Abraham Lincoln*, vol. V (New Brunswick, NJ: Rutgers University Press, 1953–55), 317–19.
32. Joseph L. Harsh, *Taken at the Flood: Robert E. Lee and Confederate Strategy in the Maryland Campaign of 1862* (Kent, OH: Kent State University Press, 1999), 27.
33. *OR*, vol. XI, part II, 497.
34. Ibid., vol. XIX, part I, 144.
35. Ibid., part II, 591–92.
36. Joseph Pierro, ed., *The Maryland Campaign of September 1862: Ezra A. Carman's Definitive Study of the Union and Confederate Armies at Antietam* (New York: Routledge Taylor & Francis Group, 2008), 45–47. Concluded by the close of September 7. *OR*, vol. XIX, part I, 144–45. Based on the tune "O Tannenbaum," as was the 1862 "Michigan, My Michigan."
37. Lewis Henry Steiner, *Report of Lewis H. Steiner: Inspector of the Sanitary Commission, Containing a Diary Kept During the Rebel Occupation of Frederick, Md., and an Account of the Operations of the U.S. Sanitary Commission during the Campaign in Maryland, September, 1862* (New York: A.D.F. Randolph, 1862), 7. Steiner addressed the report and diary to Frederick L. Olmsted, secretary of the U.S. Sanitary Commission.
38. *OR*, vol. XIX, part II, 596.

39. Douglas S. Freeman, *R.E. Lee: A Biography*, vol. II (New York: Charles Scribner's Sons, 1962), 356–57.
40. *OR*, vol. XIX, part II, 598–99. For a discussion on this proclamation, see James V. Murfin, *The Gleam of Bayonets: The Battle of Antietam and the Maryland Campaign of 1862* (Baton Rouge: Louisiana State University Press, 1965), Appendix B. Harsh, *Taken at the Flood*, also notes that the proclamation was aimed not at the people of a border state (217). Davis had intended to join Lee's army at Leesburg and, it appears, "from the head of his victorious army call for recognition." Crist, *Papers of Jefferson Davis*, vol. VIII, *1862*, 389, n.1.
41. Steiner, *Report of Lewis H. Steiner*, 18.
42. Johnson had served as Maryland State's attorney, chairman of the Maryland State Democratic Committee and delegate to both Democratic Party national conventions in 1860.
43. Steiner, *Report of Lewis H. Steiner*, 14–15.
44. Ibid., 16.
45. *OR*, vol. XIX, part II, 600.
46. Milo M. Quaife, ed., *From the Cannon's Mouth: The Civil War Letters of General Alpheus S. Williams* (Lincoln: University of Nebraska Press, 1995), 33.
47. Hicks moved the General Assembly to Frederick knowing its anti-secession sentiment. He felt that the Union was paramount, as noted in his address to the Assembly on April 25, 1861: "The only safety of Maryland lies in preserving a neutral position between our brethren of the North and of the South." Maryland State Archives, "Straddling Secession: Thomas Holliday Hicks and the Beginning of the Civil War in Maryland," April 1861, http://msa.maryland.gov/mas/educ/exhibits/hicks/html/case1.html, accessed on February 6, 2014.
48. See Western Maryland Historical Library, http://whilbr.org/HeraldofFreedom/index.aspx, accessed on October 4, 2014.
49. No unit was from Michigan.
50. *OR*, vol. XIX, part I, 25.
51. One historian opined that morale was low but not at its nadir and that McClellan's restoration to command alleviated much of the gloom pervading the army. Ethan S. Rafuse, *McClellan's War: The Failure of Moderation in the Struggle for the Union* (Bloomington: Indiana University Press, 2005), 274.
52. *OR*, vol. XIX, part I, 38.
53. Ibid., 118, 127.
54. Ibid., 119.
55. J. Willard Brown, *The Signal Corps, U.S.A. in the War of the Rebellion* (Boston: U.S. Veteran Signal Corps Association, 1896), 241–42.
56. *OR*, vol. XIX, part I, 38.

57. Ibid., part II, 192.
58. Ibid., 192, 195; Pierro, *Maryland Campaign of September 1862*, 82.
59. *OR*, vol. XIX, part II, 601, 602.
60. Ibid., 603.
61. Harsh, *Taken at the Flood*, 47.
62. John Conline, *Recollections of the Battle of Antietam and the Maryland Campaign, in War Papers Read Before the Michigan Commandery of the Military Order of the Loyal Legion of the United States*, vol. II (Detroit: James H. Stone & Company, 1898), 113.
63. *OR*, vol. XIX, part I, 39.
64. Ibid., 43.
65. Ibid., 40.
66. McClellan, "From the Peninsula to Antietam," 554.
67. *OR*, vol. XIX, part I, 41.
68. *Collected Works of Abraham Lincoln*, vol. V, 414.
69. Pierro, *Maryland Campaign of September 1862*, 53, quoting Bradley T. Johnson in the *Montgomery County Sentinel*, September 12, 1862.
70. Harsh, *Taken at the Flood*, 47.

CHAPTER 2

71. *OR*, vol. XIX, part II, 603–4.
72. *OR*, vol. LI, part I, 824.
73. Ibid., 824–25.
74. Steiner, *Report of Lewis H. Steiner*, 24; Harsh, *Taken at the Flood*, 237. U.S. Sanitary Commission volunteer Lewis H. Steiner owned the farm (it included "Schifferstadt," today a Frederick museum) abutting the National Pike. See Frederick County Landmarks Foundation, "Schifferstadt General Info," http://www.frederickcountylandmarksfoundation.org/fclf_schiffgen.html, accessed on November 10, 2014. Alpheus Williams wrote from there in June 1863. Quaife, *From the Cannon's Mouth*, 220.
75. *OR*, vol. LI, part I, 821, 823; Wilbur D. Jones Jr., *Giants in the Cornfield: The 27th Indiana Infantry* (Shippensburg, PA: White Mane Publishing Company, 1997), 229. Crum's Ford today is called Reich's Ford; the Crum-Reich House is a State Historic Site. See Joseph V. Collins, *Battle of West Frederick, July 7, 1864: Prelude to Battle of Monocacy* (N.p.: Xlibris Corporation, 2011), 248. Williams "forded the Monocacy and encamped about a mile east" of Frederick. Quaife, *From the Cannon's Mouth*, 122.
76. Henry K. Douglas, *I Rode with Stonewall* (Chapel Hill: University of North Carolina Press, 1940), 148.

77. This treatment relies heavily on expertise of Park Service ranger Tracy Evans, Monocacy National Battlefield Park. "It is not known exactly where the lost copy of Special Orders 191 was found." *The Lost Orders: Confederate General Robert E. Lee's Special Orders 191 and the 1862 Campaign* (n.p.: National Park Service, n.d.), 17 (with map showing discovery north of Best farm); see also Special Orders 191, "The Lost Orders," 2012 reproduction, Monocacy NBP; Harsh, *Taken at the Flood*, 153, names the site as "Best's Grove," with the find two miles away on the Myers Farm; Murfin, *Gleam of Bayonets*, 102, also uses Best's Grove; Jones, *Giants in the Cornfield*, 229, puts the location "in a clover field two miles south of Frederick" several hundred yards above the river and one hundred years east of the pike (see note 75).

78. Samuel E. Pittman, Story of the "Famous Lost Dispatch," Ladies Evening, Michigan Commandery, Military Order of the Loyal Legion of the United States, March 5, 1903, Samuel Pittman Papers, Williams College, 3.

79. Silas Colgrove, "The Finding of Lee's Lost Order," in *Battles & Leaders of the Civil War*, 603; Jones, *Giants in the Cornfield*, 229–31.

80. The corps was officially denominated on September 12, re-designated from Pope's army. *OR*, vol. XIX, part II, 279.

81. Quaife, *From the Cannon's Mouth*, 4–7; Detroit would be home until his death in 1878, id., 5. Also see Albert Castel, "'Old Pap': Michigan's Top Civil War General," *Michigan History* 82, no. 4 (July/August 1998): 19.

82. Jeffrey Charnley, "Michigan's General A.S. Williams and Civil War Historians: A Century of Neglect," *Michigan Historical Review* 12, no. 1 (Spring 1986): 2. This piece demonstrates that Williams was key to the early readiness of Michigan troops; the 1st Michigan Infantry was the first "Western" (Midwest) regiment to arrive in Washington, D.C., after war erupted.

83. Albert E. Castel, *Articles of War: Winners, Losers, and Some Who Were Both in the Civil War* (Mechanicsburg, PA: Stackpole Books, 2001), 70. One historian terms him "a political general," apparently because of his lack of a West Point education. Rafuse, *McClellan's War*, 282.

84. Charnley, "Michigan's General A.S. Williams," 2.

85. Samuel E. Pittman Papers, Burton Historical Collection, Detroit Public Library.

86. Charnley, "Michigan's General A.S. Williams," 3.

87. Joseph Greusel, *General Alpheus S. Williams* (Detroit: Seidel Printing Company, 1911), 14.

88. Charnley, "Michigan's General A.S. Williams," 3.

89. The same seniority as Ulysses S. Grant and William T. Sherman. Castel, *Articles of War*, 71.

90. Charnley, "Michigan's General A.S. Williams," 4. On several occasions, Williams was recommended for promotion to major general, with support

from William T. Sherman, George H. Thomas and Joseph Hooker, as well as the officers of the 1st Division of the XII Corps. Samuel E. Pittman Papers, Burton Historical Collection, Detroit Public Library.

91. Jeffrey G. Charnley, "'Neglected Honor': The Life of General A.S. Williams of Michigan (1810–1878)," PhD diss., Michigan State University, 1983, i.

92. Castel, *Articles of War*, 71.

93. Charnley, "Michigan's General A.S. Williams," 25.

94. Pierro, *Maryland Campaign of September 1862*, 78; Thomas G. Clemens, ed., *The Maryland Campaign of 1862, vol. 1, South Mountain, by Ezra Carman* (New York: Savas Beatie, 2010), 161.

95. *Detroit Sunday News-Tribune*, February 11, 1894.

96. The same as George H. Thomas.

97. Charnley, "Michigan's General A.S. Williams," 1.

98. Quaife, *From the Cannon's Mouth*, 111.

99. Some histories use "headquarters" in referring to the location where Williams and Pittman received the document. More accurately, it was at the head of a resting column while on the march: "At the time the paper came to us the entire command was drawn up as usual ready for marching in such direction as might be given by the commanding general, and General Williams, myself and escort, with some general or field officers present, as was often the case, at the head of the Division that was to be the leading one." Pittman letter to E.A. Carman, May 24, 1897, Pittman Papers, Williams College.

100. John Robertson, *Michigan in the War* (Lansing, MI: W.S. Grove & Company, 1882), 907.

101. Samuel E. Pittman Papers, Burton Historical Collection, Detroit Public Library. Two other Detroiters served Williams as aides. William D. Wilkins had been taken prisoner at the Battle of Cedar Mountain (and would again at Chancellorsville). Henry M. Whittlesey served as quartermaster of the 1st Division of XII Corps. Afterward, Whittlesey served in the Freedmen's Bureau. Robertson, *Michigan in the War*, 965–66; *New York Times*, August 16, 1873.

102. R. Steven Jones, *The Right Hand of Command: Use and Disuse of Personal Staffs in the American Civil War* (Mechanicsburg, PA: Stackpole Books, 2000), 38–40, 43. He graduated from West Point in the class with two division commanders of the Army of the Potomac, John Sedgwick and Joseph Hooker.

103. Colgrove, "Finding of Lee's Lost Order," 603.

104. Charles B. Dew, "How Samuel E. Pittman Validated Lee's 'Lost Orders' Prior to Antietam: A Historical Note," *Journal of Southern History* 70, no. 4 (November 2004): 865–70. Pittman wrote this account in a letter of May 28, 1897. Secretary of War Davis had appointed Chilton to the position of army paymaster. Jones, *Right Hand of Command*, 39.

105. Pittman, Story of the "Famous Lost Dispatch," 4. Some histories mistakenly report that the two men shared prewar military service.
106. Greusel, *General Alpheus S. Williams*, 16.
107. Pittman, Story of the "Famous Lost Dispatch," 4.
108. Quaife, *From the Cannon's Mouth*, 36. His older brother, James E. Pittman, had joined the Brady Guards and in December 1847 enlisted in the Michigan regiment to serve in Mexico, through which he likely came to know Williams. His Civil War service included posts as state paymaster, member of the State Military Board and inspector general. Silas Farmer, *The History of Detroit and Michigan*, vol. II (Detroit: S. Farmer & Company, 1884), 1,166; LeRoy Barnett and Roger Rosentreter, *Michigan's Early Military Forces* (Detroit: Wayne State University Press, 2003), 462–63.
109. Charnley, "Michigan's General A.S. Williams," 8–9.
110. Quaife, *From the Cannon's Mouth*, 342.
111. Pittman, Story of the "Famous Lost Dispatch," 4.
112. Ibid. Some histories—such as Stephen W. Sears, *Controversies & Commanders: Dispatches from the Army of the Potomac* (Boston: Houghton Mifflin, 1999)—report that Pittman went to McClellan's headquarters, but Pittman's own words are best evidence: "I did not take the order myself as we were momentarily expecting orders to move forward, which expectation was heightened by the importance of the paper so opportunely falling into our possession." He started to make a copy, envisioning "such an important paper was likely to become a fact of history," but Williams "objected to even that much delay." Before Pittman "could get two lines copied," Williams peremptorily directed it to be dispatched without "the delay of even a few moments." Pittman letter to Silas Colgrove, June 9, 1886, Pittman Papers, Williams University; Dew, "How Samuel E. Pittman Validated Lee's 'Lost Orders,'" 867–68.
113. Dew, "How Samuel E. Pittman Validated Lee's 'Lost Orders,'" 870.
114. Longstreet, "Invasion of Maryland," 418–19. *Ruse de guerre* is French for a "ruse of war," the most famous being the Trojan Horse.
115. Hartwig, *To Antietam Creek*, 283.
116. David L. Thompson, "In the Ranks to the Antietam," in *Battles & Leaders of the Civil War*, 556.
117. *OR*, vol. LI, part I, 829. McClellan averred, "I was satisfied in regard to the genuineness of the order and made no further inquiries." Murfin, *Gleam of Bayonets*, 332. Pleasonton was to verify its continued operability.
118. Ibid., vol. XIX, part I, 432; vol. LI, part I, 827–28.
119. *OR*, vol. XIX, part I, 432.
120. Jack D. Welsh, *Medical Histories of Union Generals* (Kent, OH: Kent State University Press, 2005), 369. In January 1862, the Michigan legislature and Blair called for an exchange of prisoners, singling out Willcox, "who

is now held in close confinement as a hostage in a southern dungeon." Congressman Rowland E. Trowbridge presented the resolution. *Congressional Globe*, 37th Congress, 2nd Session, January 27, 1862, 487.

121. *Collected Works of Abraham Lincoln*, vol. V, 380–81.

122. The 17th Michigan, under command of his friend William Withington, was invited by organizer James Romeyn to participate in the event on its way to Washington, D.C., to accompany Marshall of the Day James E. Pittman. William Withington Papers, Bentley Historical Library, University of Michigan, Ann Arbor.

123. Robert G. Scott, *Forgotten Valor: The Memoirs, Journals & Civil War Letters of Orlando B. Willcox* (Kent, OH: Kent State University Press, 1999), 346–50.

124. Eighth of thirty-eight, ahead of Ayres, Burnside, Gibbon, Griffin, Heth and A.P. Hill.

125. Frank B. Woodford, *Father Abraham's Children: Michigan Episodes in the Civil War* (Detroit: Wayne State University Press, 2014), 37, 41; Robert B. Ross, *The Early Bench and Bar of Detroit from 1805 to the End of 1850* (Detroit: Joy and Burton, 1907), 224. Willcox was one of Michigan's earliest published authors.

126. Wells B. Fox, *What I Remember of the Great Rebellion* (Lansing, MI: Darius D. Thorp, 1892), 174.

127. See, generally, Scott, *Forgotten Valor*.

128. Charnley, "Michigan's General A.S. Williams," 9.

129. Hartwig, *To Antietam Creek*, 287.

130. *OR*, vol. LI, part I, 826.

131. Ibid., vol. XIX, part I, 45.

132. Ibid., vol. LI, part I, 826.

133. George B. McClellan, "From the Peninsula to Antietam," 553–55.

134. John Gibbon, *Personal Recollections of the Civil War* (New York: G.P. Putnam's Sons, 1928), 73.

135. *OR*, vol. XIX, part I, 281. The reference to "this evening" was incorrect. The dispatch also reports on intelligence of Lee's intentions to invade Pennsylvania.

136. Ibid. Some histories mistakenly give the time as noon.

Chapter 3

137. *OR*, vol. XIX, part I, 145.

138. Ibid., part II, 605.

139. Palfrey, *Antietam and Fredericksburg*, 17.

140. *OR*, vol. XIX, part. II, 606.

141. Ibid., part I, 140; Gallagher, *Lee the Soldier*, 8, 26; Freeman, *R.E. Lee*, 367–69.

142. *OR*, vol. XIX, part II, 607.
143. Ibid., 608.
144. Jacob D. Cox, "Forcing Fox's Gap and Turner's Gap," in *Battles & Leaders of the Civil War*, 585.
145. Palfrey, *Antietam and Fredericksburg*, 34.
146. Quaife, *From the Cannon's Mouth*, 120–21.
147. Harsh, *Sounding the Shallows*, 15. McClellan described it a "bright, sunny Sunday." George B. McClellan, *McClellan's Own Story: The War for the Union, the Soldiers Who Fought It, the Civilians Who Directed It and His Relations to It and to Them*, ed. William C. Prime (New York: Charles L. Webster & Company, 1887), 571.
148. John W. Schildt, *The Twelfth Corps at Antietam* (Sharpsburg, PA: self-published, 2012), 64.
149. Hartwig, *To Antietam Creek*, 303–4.
150. Richard Slotkin, *The Long Road to Antietam: How the Civil War Became a Revolution* (New York: W.W. Norton & Company, 2012), 195–98.
151. *OR*, vol. XIX, part I, 427; Pierro, *Maryland Campaign of September 1862*, 150; Clemens, *Maryland Campaign of 1862*, 333.
152. Hartwig, *To Antietam Creek*, 331.
153. Pierro, *Maryland Campaign of September 1862*, 150; Clemens, *Maryland Campaign of 1862*, 333.
154. Pierro, *Maryland Campaign of September 1862*, 150; Clemens, *Maryland Campaign of 1862*, 333.
155. *OR*, vol. XIX, part I, 428; Pierro, *Maryland Campaign of September 1862*, 150–51; Clemens, *Maryland Campaign of 1862*, 334.
156. Robertson, *Michigan in the War*, 281.
157. Ibid., 282–86.
158. William Ward, *List of Cadets Admitted into the United States Military Academy, West Point, N.Y., from Its Origin Till September 1, 1886* (Washington, D.C.: Government Printing Office, 1887), 30. Absence of mention in Cullum's *Register* (the nineteenth-century listing of all West Point graduates) indicates that he did not finish. Robert E. Lee was then commandant. George W. Cullum, *Biographical Register of the Officers and Graduates of the U.S. Military Academy from 1802 to 1867* (New York: D. Van Nostrand, 1868–79).
159. Robertson, *Michigan in the War*, 838.
160. From Find-a-Grave website entry, accessed on November 17, 2014.
161. Fox, *What I Remember of the Great Rebellion*, 55.
162. *OR*, vol. XIX, part I, 428.
163. Pierro, *Maryland Campaign of September 1862*, 151; Clemens, *Maryland Campaign of 1862*, 334.
164. Ted Becker, "The Stonewall Regiment: 'Seldom Equaled & Never Surpassed,'" *Michigan History* 95, no. 5 (September/October 2011): 48.

An excellent overview of the regiment's service including a sidebar on Michigan collegians and the war.

165. Duty station of Ulysses Grant after the Mexican-American War.

166. Charles Lanman, *The Red Book of Michigan: A Civil, Military and Biographical History* (Detroit: E.B. Smith & Company, 1871), 365.

167. David Lane, *A Soldier's Diary: The Story of a Volunteer, 1862–1865* (Jackson, MI, 1905), 5.

168. Robertson, *Michigan in the War*, 374–75; Lane, *Soldier's Diary*, 8–9.

169. Palfrey, *Antietam and Fredericksburg*, 39.

170. Elon Mills Diary, Bentley Historical Library, University of Michigan, Ann Arbor, 13.

171. Lane, *Soldier's Diary*, 11.

172. Harsh, *Sounding the Shallows*, 177.

173. Hartwig, *To Antietam Creek*, 342. On August 20, 1862, Willcox invited Withington to be his division adjutant. Despite their friendship, Withington declined in order to command his own regiment. William Withington Papers, Bentley Historical Library.

174. Robertson, *Michigan in the War*, 375.

175. A regimental officer put the unit's strength at between seven hundred and eight hundred. Hartwig, *To Antietam Creek*, 729, n.34.

176. Pierro, *Maryland Campaign of September 1862*, 151; Clemens, *Maryland Campaign of 1862*, 335 (Carman's text is somewhat different in this version).

177. Lanman, *Red Book of Michigan*, 365.

178. Scott, *Forgotten Valor*, 354.

179. Pierro, *Maryland Campaign of September 1862*, 151; Clemens, *Maryland Campaign of 1862*, 334. When the 24th Michigan visited the scene in early October, "Mr. Wise was present to give us particulars of the fighting. His log house was pitted with bullets like small pox scars." O.B. Curtis, *History of the Twenty-fourth Michigan of the Iron Brigade: Known as the Detroit and Wayne County Regiment* (Detroit: Winn & Hammond, 1891), 64.

180. Lanman, *Red Book of Michigan*, 366.

181. *OR*, vol. XIX, part I, 428.

182. William Withington Papers, Bentley Historical Library; Robertson, *Michigan in the War*, 375.

183. *OR*, vol. XIX, part I, 428.

184. Brian M. Jordan, *Unholy Sabbath: The Battle of South Mountain in History and Memory* (New York: Savas Beatie, 2012), 165, quoting the 1952 book by Bell I. Wiley, *The Life of Billy Yank*. Jordan's work, along with John D. Hoptak's *The Battle of South Mountain* (Charleston, SC: The History Press, 2011), form modern studies of the battle.

185. Elon G. Mills Diary, Bentley Library, 8 (likely the Lorenz model).

186. Swift, thirty-one-year-old captain of Company F, had joined the regiment in Detroit after being commissioned on June 17, 1862.
187. Lanman, *Red Book of Michigan*, 366. The map in Hartwig, *To Antietam Creek*, 346, portrays the 17th attacking the position along the Old Sharpsburg Road; Pierro, *Maryland Campaign of September 1862*, 151, and Clemens, *Maryland Campaign of 1862*, 335–36, relate that Drayton had posted his men "behind these stone fences, running north and south from the Sharpsburg road."
188. John M. Priest, *Before Antietam: The Battle for South Mountain* (New York: Oxford University Press, 1992), 212.
189. Pierro, *Maryland Campaign of September 1862*, 152; Clemens, *Maryland Campaign of 1862*, 336.
190. *OR*, vol. XIX, part I, 428–29.
191. Ibid., 437.
192. Priest, *Before Antietam*, 175.
193. Hartwig, *To Antietam Creek*, 341, 352, quoting Campbell letter.
194. *OR*, vol. XIX, part I, 461.
195. David A. Welker, *Tempest at Ox Hill: The Battle of Chantilly* (Cambridge, MA: Da Capo Press, 2007), 149.
196. George M. Blackburn, ed., *The Diary of Captain Ralph Ely of the Eighth Michigan Infantry* (Mount Pleasant: Central Michigan University Press, 1965), 42.
197. *OR*, vol. XIX, part I, 429.
198. Ibid., 215.
199. David D. Finney Jr. and Judith Stermer McIntosh, *Remembering Michigan's Civil War Soldiers* (Charleston, SC: Arcadia Publishing, 2015), 14.
200. *OR*, vol. XII, part II, 345, 383.
201. He had also contracted yellow fever while on duty in Texas in 1853. *New York Herald*, May 7, 1863; Welsh, *Medical Histories of Union Generals*, 155.
202. Cullum, *Biographical Register*. Hartsuff arguably was one of the four most prominent of that class—George Crook, Alexander D. McCook and Henry W. Slocum being the others.
203. On September 8, 1860, he was a passenger on the steamer *Lady Elgin* when it collided with another ship between Chicago and Milwaukee; nearly 400 passengers died and some 150 survived. Welsh, *Medical Histories of Union Generals*, 155–56.
204. Robertson, *Michigan in the War*, 979.
205. *OR*, vol. XIX, part I, 215.
206. He also mentioned having "had many narrow escapes personally," including a horse killed. Scott, *Forgotten Valor*, 365–66.
207. *OR*, vol. XIX, part I, 429.
208. Ibid., 437.

209. Becker, "Stonewall Regiment," 47.
210. Robertson, *Michigan in the War*, 374, 915.
211. Ibid., 951.
212. Becker, "Stonewall Regiment," 47.
213. William Withington Papers, Bentley Historical Library. Future U.S. president Rutherford B. Hayes was also among the wounded. Withington received a brevet for his actions.
214. David L. Poremba, ed., *If I Am Found Dead: Michigan Voices from the Civil War* (Ann Arbor, MI: Ann Arbor Media Group, 2006), 54.
215. Harsh, *Sounding the Shallows*, 222.
216. Lanman, *Red Book of Michigan*, 366; Robertson, *Michigan in the War*, 375. *OR*, vol. XIX, part I, 186, shows fewer wounded.
217. Robertson, *Michigan in the War*, 832; *OR*, vol. XIX, part I, 188.
218. Lane, *Soldier's Diary*, 12.
219. Robertson, *Michigan in the War*, 835, 896, 943, 945. All four resigned for disability: Goldsmith on January 24, 1863; Summers on March 14, 1863; Thayer on his second tour after a first lieutenancy in the 6th Infantry, on May 15, 1863; and Newman on June 30, 1864. Comparable information on Newman and Thayer has not been discovered.
220. Item in *Detroit Advertiser and Tribune*, Withington Papers. He had been the subject of a previous item in the *Detroit Free Press* accusing him of being absent; this letter to the editor sought to refute the charge. The letter indicated that Thomas had been appointed "Acting Aid-de-Camp" to the commander of the 1st Brigade of Willcox's Division.
221. *OR*, vol. XIX, part I, 438, 461.
222. Ibid., 186.
223. Freeman, *R.E. Lee*, 373.
224. *OR*, vol. XIX, part I, 140.
225. Ibid., vol. LI, part II, 618–19.
226. *Collected Works of Abraham Lincoln*, vol. V, 425–26.

Chapter 4

227. *OR*, vol. XI, part I, 61.
228. Ibid., series 3, vol. II, 180.
229. Ibid., 187.
230. Ibid., 187–88.
231. Ibid., 208.
232. Robertson, *Michigan in the War*, 384.
233. *OR*, series 3, vol. II, 283–84.
234. Robertson, *Michigan in the War*, 384.

235. Ibid., 429.
236. *New York Times* Opinionator, "Birth of the 'Battle Cry,'" http://opinionator.blogs.nytimes.com/2012/07/27/birth-of-the-battle-hymn/?_r=0, accessed on November 22, 2014.
237. Robertson, *Michigan in the War*, 438.
238. Ibid., 439; Curtis, *History of the Twenty-fourth Michigan*, 49–54.
239. Quaife, *From the Cannon's Mouth*, 111.
240. Curtis, *History of the Twenty-fourth Michigan*, 55–56.
241. *OR*, vol. XIX, part I, 951.
242. Helen Ashe Hays, *The Antietam and Its Bridges: The Annals of an Historic Stream* (New York: G.P. Putnam Son's, 1910), 4.
243. *OR*, vol. XIX, part I, 5 (Henry Halleck).
244. Harsh, *Taken at the Flood*, 301–2.
245. Palfrey, *Antietam and Fredericksburg*, 72.
246. Pierro, *Maryland Campaign of September 1862*, 173; Clemens, *Maryland Campaign of 1862*, 392.
247. Harsh, *Taken at the Flood*, 302; Pierro, *Maryland Campaign of September 1862*, 173, 175; Clemens, *Maryland Campaign of 1862*, 392, 398.
248. Robertson, *Michigan in the War*, 915.
249. Jack C. Mason, *Until Antietam: The Life and Letters of Major General Israel B. Richardson, U.S. Army* (Carbondale: Southern Illinois University Press, 2009), 129.
250. Ibid., 123.
251. Ibid., 121, 132, 137, 148.
252. Biographical Directory of the United States Congress, "Norvell, John (1789–1850)," http://bioguide.congress.gov/scripts/biodisplay.pl?index=N000158, accessed on November 25, 2014.
253. Robertson, *Michigan in the War*, 898.
254. Thomas M. O'Brien and Oliver Diefendorf, *General Orders of the War Department: Embracing the Years 1861, 1862 & 1863*, vol. I (New York: Derby & Miller, 1864), 437.
255. Hartwig, *To Antietam Creek*, 494.
256. McClellan, *McClellan's Own Story*, 584, 587.
257. Marion V. Armstrong Jr., *Unfurl Those Colors! McClellan, Sumner, and the Second Army Corps in the Antietam Campaign* (Tuscaloosa: University of Alabama Press, 2008), 134.
258. Palfrey, *Antietam and Fredericksburg*, 48.
259. Hartwig, *To Antietam Creek*, 504; Pierro, *Maryland Campaign of September 1862*, 176–77; Clemens, *Maryland Campaign of 1862*, 401.
260. *OR*, vol. XIX, part I, 300. Richardson appeared at this advance position on the morning of the sixteenth to order the unit back to the rest of the division.
261. Armstrong, *Unfurl Those Colors!*, 134–39.

262. Pierro, *Maryland Campaign of September 1862*, 177; Clemens, *Maryland Campaign of 1862*, 402; Hartwig, *To Antietam Creek*, 512.
263. Jay Monaghan, *Custer: The Life of General George Armstrong Custer* (Lincoln: University of Nebraska Press, 1971), 96–97; Paul A. Hutton, *The Custer Reader* (Lincoln: University of Nebraska Press, 1971), 11, 27, n.20; Hartwig, *To Antietam Creek*, 494.
264. *OR*, vol. XIX, part I, 210; Hartwig, *To Antietam Creek*, 148.
265. He was born in New Rumley, Ohio.
266. *OR*, vol. XI, part I, 153, 526, 536, 543, 651.
267. Ibid., 653.
268. Ibid., 651.
269. Jeffry D. Wert, *Custer: The Controversial Life of George Armstrong Custer* (New York: Simon & Schuster, 1996), 53.
270. McClellan, *McClellan's Own Story*, 123.
271. Duane Schultz, *Custer: Lessons in Leadership* (New York: Palgrave Macmillan, 2010), 23.
272. Monaghan, *Custer*, 94–96.
273. *OR*, vol. XIX, part I, 210.
274. Custer to Colonel Colburn, McClellan Papers, Library of Congress. The message appears to say, "and they are leaving everything as we wish." The heading is, "Sept 17 ? 1862, 10 o'clock, M."—not in Custer's hand; the correct date and time is September 15, ten o'clock. Colburn was a headquarters aide-de-camp and Tidball an artillery battery commander.
275. Ezra J. Warner, *Generals in Blue: Lives of the Union Commanders* (Baton Rouge: Louisiana State University Press, 2006), 148–49.
276. Gilder-Lehman Collection, http://www.gilderlehrman.org/collections/501782e3-0de5-4a5e-977a-265100309749, accessed on May 9, 2015, gives the date of the message as the seventeenth or eighteenth. Only on the fifteenth was Custer free to be in the van. Jones, *Right Hand of Command*, 31. Since Pleasanton roamed the countryside, taking CSA pieces on this road rings true on the fifteenth. It was also the occasion of his commendation of Custer's actions. *OR*, vol. XIX, part I, 210.
277. American Heritage, "What Did General George Custer Write at the Battle of Antietam," http://blog.americanheritage1.com/blog/bid/56496/WHAT-DID-GENERAL-GE*OR*GE-CUSTER-WRITE-AT-THE-BATTLE-OF-ANTIETAM, accessed on May 9, 2015.
278. Hartwig, *To Antietam Creek*, 494, 507.
279. *OR*, vol. XIX, part II, 294.
280. Ibid., part I, 53.
281. Pierro, *Maryland Campaign of September 1862*, 180; Clemens, *Maryland Campaign of 1862*, 409.
282. Hartwig, *To Antietam Creek*, 506, 513.

283. Pierro, *Maryland Campaign of September 1862*, 180; Clemens, *Maryland Campaign of 1862*, 409.
284. *OR*, vol. XIX, part II, 294; Hartwig, *To Antietam Creek*, 505–6.
285. *OR*, vol. XIX, part II, 295.
286. Pierro, *Maryland Campaign of September 1862*, 202.
287. *OR*, vol. XIX, part I, 951.
288. Ibid., 141.
289. Harsh, *Taken at the Flood*, 302–4, 361.
290. Ibid., 308; Harsh, *Sounding the Shallows*, 182; Pierro, *Maryland Campaign of September 1862*, 187; Clemens, *Maryland Campaign of 1862*, 426–28.
291. *OR*, vol. XIX, part II, 296.
292. Ibid., 297.
293. Ibid., part I, 307.
294. Harsh, *Taken at the Flood*, 314.
295. *OR*, vol. LI, part I, 839.
296. Ibid., vol. XIX, part I, 54–55; McClellan, *McClellan's Own Story*, 588; Hartwig, *To Antietam Creek*, 589.
297. Nineteenth of thirty-one, behind Henry Halleck.
298. *OR*, vol. LI, part I, 423.
299. Edward G. Longacre, *The Man Behind the Guns: A Military Biography of General Henry J. Hunt* (Cambridge, MA: Da Capo Press, 2003), 24–30, 36, 87–93, 114–16; Robertson, *Michigan in the War*, 980.
300. Jeffry D. Wert, *The Sword of Lincoln: The Army of the Potomac* (New York: Simon & Schuster, 2005), 40.
301. Longacre, *Man Behind the Guns*, 36; Wert, *Sword of Lincoln*, 40, 118.
302. *OR*, vol. LI, part I, 528.
303. Ibid., vol. XIX, part II, 188.
304. McClellan, *McClellan's Own Story*, 117.
305. L. VanLoan Naisawald, *Grape & Canister: The Story of the Field Artillery of the Army of the Potomac, 1861–1865* (Mechanicsburg, PA: Stackpole Books, 1999), 141–43.
306. Ibid., 588.
307. Harsh, *Taken at the Flood*, 306.
308. Ibid., 294, 306.
309. Hartwig, *To Antietam Creek*, 151, 158–59. This study describes the effort as having "accomplished miracles."
310. Pierro, *Maryland Campaign of September 1862*, 203.
311. Naisawald, *Grape & Canister*, 146; *OR*, vol. XIX, part I, 206.
312. *OR*, vol. XIX, part I, 30, 55.
313. Ibid., 55.
314. Harsh, *Taken at the Flood*, 347.
315. Armstrong, *Unfurl Those Colors!*, 160.

316. Harsh, *Taken at the Flood*, 349. McClellan may also have had Porter's V Corps in mind for the blow.
317. *OR*, vol. XIX, part I, 141.
318. As is evident from McClellan's 3:45 p.m. dispatch to Pleasanton to collect all his cavalry to be ready at a moment's notice "to make pursuit of the enemy." *OR*, vol. LI, part I, 840.
319. Martin N. Bertera and Kim Crawford, *The 4th Michigan Infantry in the Civil War* (East Lansing: Michigan State University Press, 2010), 104.
320. Hartwig, *To Antietam Creek*, 641.
321. Likely the Nicodemus Mill Complex east of Keedysville.
322. Quaife, *From the Cannon's Mouth*, 122–25.
323. Samuel Pittman to Mollie Pittman, September 21, 1862, Pittman Papers, Williams College. Pittman's use of "long s" is revised.
324. Quaife, *From the Cannon's Mouth*, 125; *OR*, vol. XIX, part I, 55.
325. Quaife, *From the Cannon's Mouth*, 125.

CHAPTER 5

326. Pierro, *Maryland Campaign of September 1862*, 195–97.
327. McClellan, *McClellan's Own Story*, 591; Hartwig, *To Antietam Creek*, 608.
328. Hartwig, *To Antietam Creek*, 608.
329. John W. Schildt, *Roads to Antietam* (Shippensburg, PA: Burd Street Press, 1997), 133; Schildt, *Twelfth Corps at Antietam*, 71.
330. Kathleen A. Ernst, *Too Afraid to Cry: Maryland Civilians in the Antietam Campaign* (Mechanicsburg, PA: Stackpole Books, 1999), 121.
331. Phone conversation with John W. Schildt, February 17, 2015, at 4:16 p.m.
332. Jack Dempsey, *Michigan and the Civil War: A Great and Bloody Sacrifice* (Charleston, SC: The History Press, 2011), 55, 95, 133.
333. Pierro, *Maryland Campaign of September 1862*, 215.
334. Harsh, *Sounding the Shallows*, 1–31
335. Quaife, *From the Cannon's Mouth*, 125.
336. *OR*, vol. XIX, part I, 956.
337. Ibid., 218.
338. Ibid., 259.
339. Both this and the Seminole War projectile remained in Hartsuff's body. Welsh, *Medical Histories of Union Generals*, 156–57.
340. *OR*, vol. XIX, part I, 56.
341. Armstrong, *Unfurl Those Colors!*, 167.
342. Sears, *Landscape Turned Red*, 300. Added to nearly one thousand from South Mountain. Jay Luvaas and Harold W. Nelson, eds., *Guide to the Battle of Antietam: The Maryland Campaign of 1862* (Lawrence: University Press of Kansas, 1987), 301.

343. Luvaas and Nelson, *Guide to the Battle of Antietam*, 302.
344. Palfrey, *Antietam and Fredericksburg*, 73.
345. Edward J. Stackpole, *From Cedar Mountain to Antietam* (Harrisburg, PA: Stackpole Books, 1993), 379.
346. Pierro, *Maryland Campaign of September 1862*, 235.
347. Quaife, *From the Cannon's Mouth*, 125; see Armstrong, *Unfurl Those Colors!*, 35. Mansfield was "the weakest link in McClellan's chain of command." Ted Alexander, *The Battle of Antietam: The Bloodiest Day* (Charleston, SC: The History Press, 2011), 31.
348. Pierro, *Maryland Campaign of September 1862*, 235.
349. Ibid., 235–36.
350. Quaife, *From the Cannon's Mouth*, 125.
351. John M. Priest, *Antietam: The Soldiers' Battle* (New York: Oxford University Press, 1989), 74.
352. Pierro, *Maryland Campaign of September 1862*, 236–38.
353. Contrasted with the I Corps situation. Compare *OR*, vol. XIX, part I, 475, with part II, 315.
354. Schildt, *Twelfth Corps at Antietam*, 99; Jim Murphy, *A Savage Thunder: Antietam and the Bloody Road to Freedom* (New York: Simon & Schuster, 2009), 45.
355. Perry D. Jamieson, *Death in September: The Antietam Campaign* (Abilene, TX: McWhiney Foundation Press, 1999), 60.
356. Quaife, *From the Cannon's Mouth*, 126.
357. Pierro, *Maryland Campaign of September 1862*, 239.
358. *OR*, vol. XIX, part I, 485.
359. Bruce Catton, *Mr. Lincoln's Army* (Garden City, NY: Doubleday & Company, 1951, 1962), 273.
360. Sears, *Landscape Turned Red*, 181.
361. Ibid., 209.
362. Pierro, *Maryland Campaign of September 1862*, 241.
363. Ibid. Carman was a XII Corps regimental officer.
364. *OR*, vol. XIX, part I, 218.
365. Ibid., 244.
366. Quaife, *From the Cannon's Mouth*, 126.
367. Ibid., 127.
368. Sears, *Landscape Turned Red*, 213.
369. Quaife, *From the Cannon's Mouth*, 127.
370. Palfrey, *Antietam and Fredericksburg*, 62.
371. *OR*, vol. XIX, part I, 476.
372. Palfrey, *Antietam and Fredericksburg*, 78.
373. Ibid., 78–79.
374. Charnley, "Michigan's General A.S. Williams," 10, n.27.

375. The exception refers to XII Corps at Antietam as "Williams's Corps." As one example, Benjamin F. Cooling, *Counter-Thrust: From the Peninsula to the Antietam* (Lincoln: University of Nebraska Press, 2007), 187.
376. Charnley, "Neglected Honor," 143.
377. *OR*, vol. XIX, part I, 476.
378. Rafuse, *McClellan's War*, 315.
379. Charnley, "Michigan's General A.S. Williams," 10. He also sized up key strategic points and directed artillery to where most needed, id.
380. Quaife, *From the Cannon's Mouth*, 127–28.
381. *OR*, vol. XIX, part I, 476.
382. Catton, *Mr. Lincoln's Army*, 282.
383. Palfrey, *Antietam and Fredericksburg*, 80.
384. Pierro, *Maryland Campaign of September 1862*, 252.
385. *OR*, vol. XIX, part I, 476.
386. Ibid., vol. LI, part I, 842.
387. Quaife, *From the Cannon's Mouth*, 127.

CHAPTER 6

388. Robertson, *Michigan in the War*, 751.
389. Talcott E. Wing, *History of Monroe County Michigan* (New York: Munsell & Company, 1890), 527.
390. *Monroe Commercial*, April 18, 1861. The *Commercial* was one of two wartime newspapers in Monroe. Original bound volumes are located at the MCHM.
391. Joan E. Cashin, *First Lady of the Confederacy: Varina Davis's Civil War* (Cambridge, MA: Harvard University Press, 2006), 102–3.
392. *Prescott Transcript*, April 20, 1861. See the Civil War and Northwest Wisconsin, "1861 April 15: Lincoln's Call for Troops," https://thecivilwarandnorthwestwisconsin.wordpress.com/2011/04/15/1861-april-15-lincolns-call-for-troops; Robertson, *Michigan in the War*, 17.
393. Robertson, *Michigan in the War*, 24; see U.S. Census Bureau, "Resident Population and Apportionment of the U.S. House of Representatives," https://www.census.gov/dmd/www/resapport/states/michigan.pdf. Various sources list the strength of the U.S. Regular Army at 16,000. The U.S. Army Center of Military History lists the number as 1,080 officers and 14,926 enlisted men on June 30, 1860; see Chapter 9 in *American Military History*, vol. I, *The Civil War, 1861*, United States Army Center of Military History, http://www.history.army.mil/books/amh-v1/ch09.htm.
394. Robertson, *Michigan in the War*, 17, 165.
395. Monroe County Historic Marker, located in the 400 block of St. Mary's Avenue and south of West Lorain Street in Monroe, Michigan, dedicated

on Friday, July 4, 2014. See *Monroe News*, "Civil War's Camp Monroe Dedicated," http://www.monroenews.com/news/2014/jul/06/civil-wars-camp-monroe-dedicated; *Monroe Commercial*, August 8, 1861.

396. James R. Johnson, "A Community Caught in the Cross-fire: The Citizens of Sharpsburg, Maryland Before, During, and After the Battle of Antietam," master's thesis, Wayne State University, 2007, 36–38; George H. Brown, *Record of Service of Michigan Volunteers in the Civil War, 1861–1865*, vol. VII (Kalamazoo, MI: Ihling Brothers & Everard, 1900), 120.

397. *Monroe Commercial*, August 8, 1861; Wing, *History of Monroe County Michigan*, 448–53. Brown, *Record of Service*, 47. Although only four regiments were officially mustered into Federal service, the "skeletons" of the 5th, 6th and 7th Regiments, the commissioned and noncommissioned officers, were designated and in a camp of instruction at Fort Wayne in Detroit. Examination of commission and enlistment dates of officers and noncommissioned officers of these units often predate the August 3, 1861 call for 500,000 additional troops by President Lincoln. After First Bull Run and the presidential call-up of troops, Governor Blair ordered these three regiments filled up for service, and within fifty days they were making preparations to join the armies in the field. Governor Blair anticipated the need for the state to furnish more troops and made preparations accordingly, thus resulting in the expeditious delivery of three additional infantry regiments.

398. Brown, *Record of Service*, 115.

399. See *From Regiment to President: The Structure and Command of Civil War Armies*, National Park Service, http://www.nps.gov/resources/story.htm?id=299; Robertson, *Michigan in the War*, 17.

400. Hillary J. Everson, "Monroe and the Civil War Years," master's thesis, Wayne State University, Detroit, 1950, 45–46. The *Monroe Commercial* also commented about fifty recruits arriving from the Upper Peninsula appearing "fine, athletic and vigorous looking." The men were issued army rations but had to do their own cooking; Wing, *History of Monroe County Michigan*, 566.

401. Robertson, *Michigan in the War*, 270; Brown, *Record of Service*, 1. Companies were typically commanded by a captain and designated with the letters A through K (the letter *J* was not used because it looked too much like *I*).

402. Everson, "Monroe and the Civil War Years," 46. At the company level, soldiers were trained by the "School of the Soldier" and "School of the Company" wherein they learned the manual of arms and basic marching, facings and company-level maneuvering. The "School of the Battalion" was instruction of how the companies within the regiment maneuvered collectively as a whole.

403. Lanman, *Red Book of Michigan*, 337; Brown, *Record of Service*, 119.

404. Brown, *Record of Service*, 119; *Monroe Commercial*, September 12 and 19, 1861; Everson, "Monroe and the Civil War Years," 47; *Monroe Commercial*, September 21, 1861.

405. Robertson, *Michigan in the War*, 271; Brown, *Record of Service*, 120. This information is nearly identical in both books: Frederick W. Oesterle, "Incidents Connected with the Civil War Years as Recorded by One of the Veterans, Fifty Years After," F.W.O., 1911, Pontiac, Michigan, typed copy at the Monroe Country Historical Museum in Monroe, Michigan. There is some confusion regarding Oesterle's comment that they carried the flag "for four long years." The 7th received a new flag of heavy silk, trimmed with gold fringe, with the names of several battles inscribed along with an embroidered state arms and "Tuebor." This flag, displayed at the MCHM, was presented by the ladies of Monroe. According to the museum label, this flag was delivered by Captain Williams on May 26, 1864. A June 19, 1864 article in the *Monroe Commercial* reports that the flag was received on May 28. Robertson, *Michigan in the War*, indicates that it was July 1864 and that Corporal Williams brought the flag to the regiment.

406. Jody L. Egen (Chansuolme), "The Michigan Soldiers' Aid Society during the American Civil War: Its Purpose, Contributions, and Activities, 1861–1865," unpublished manuscript/term paper, Wayne State University, Detroit, 2001, 1–3.

407. *Monroe Commercial*, August 29, 1861.

408. Ibid. A "housewife" as mentioned in this article was a small "emergency" sewing kit that was often sent to the soldiers at the front lines. Typically made of oilcloth and/or scrap fabrics and trims, these small sewing kits typically contained a few needles, thread, pins, buttons and possibly a small pair of scissors that the soldier would carry with him for small repairs and alterations of uniforms. Sewing, whether attending to replacing buttons or the fabrication of a complete garment (typically shirts), was one of the many activities soldiers employed to pass the time. In decades to come, the U.S. government issued housewives to military personnel, as the necessity of such a small but practical and indispensable item was obvious.

409. Brown, *Record of Service*, 31; Robertson, *Michigan in the War*, 809. In these two sources, Darrah is also spelled "Darragh." An article in the May 8, 1862 *Monroe Commercial* reads, "At a meeting of Monroe Lodge, on Wednesday evening, May 7, 1862, the death of Capt. Darrah was announced when the following resolution was adopted. Resolved that we have heard with deep regret of the death of Brother James Darrah, a Past Master of this lodge, while in the service of the country as a Captain in the 7th Michigan Regiment of Volunteers, near Yorktown, Virginia, on the 11th ultimate."

Then again in October, presumably after Captain Darrah's body returned home, another article appeared on the twenty-third of that month: "The funeral service of Capt. James Darrah of the 7th Regiment were attended last Saturday, under the direction of Monroe Lodge of F and A Masons." He is buried in an unmarked grave at Woodland Cemetery in Monroe, where many other soldiers of the 7th Michigan have their final resting place. See "Capt. James C. Darrah," Find-a-Grave, http://www.findagrave.com/cgi-bin/fg.cgi?page=gr&GRid=92411424.

410. *Monroe Commercial*, December 5, 1861.

411. William F. Fox, *Regimental Losses in the American Civil War, 1861–1865* (Albany, NY: Albany Publishing Company, 1889), 385.

412. Robertson, *Michigan in the War*, 271.

413. David G. Townshend, *The Seventh Michigan Volunteer Infantry* (Fort Lauderdale, FL: Southeast Publications, 1993), 38–48.

414. Wing, *History of Monroe County Michigan*, 453; Brown, *Record of Service*, 47; Robertson, *Michigan in the War*, 841. Halleck was made general-in-chief as of July 23, thirteen days after Grosvenor's resignation. On July 24, the *Monroe Commercial* printed an article stating that the possible explanation of the refused furlough was on account of a "difference of opinion with Gen. McClellan." The article claims this to be in error, as the paper was "credibly informed Col. G. has always warmly approved of Gen. McClellan's plans and policy."

415. *Monroe Commercial*, July 24, 1862.

416. Oesterle, "Incidents Connected," 2–3.

417. Ibid., 4; Robertson, *Michigan in the War*, 271; see Civil War in the East, "7th Michigan Infantry Regiment," http://www.civilwarintheeast.com/USA/MI/7MI.php.

418. Norman J. Hall, "Field and Staff Muster Roll" for July and August 1862, National Archives Record Administration, Washington, D.C.

419. Townshend, *Seventh Michigan Volunteer Infantry*, 50.

420. A copy of Hall's commission is on exhibit at the MCHM, with the original in the collection of David Finney. As was commonly done, commissions were often backdated to the actual date when the officer began acting and serving in the capacity of the rank. See also Brown, *Record of Service*, 48; Robertson, *Michigan in the War*, 843; Wing, *History of Monroe County Michigan*, 567; Cullum, *Biographical Register*, 488–89.

421. Dempsey, *Michigan and the Civil War*, 12–13; exhibit labels with the Norman Hall exhibit at the MCHM; Cullum, *Biographical Register*, 488. The museum has many Hall-related artifacts, including his West Point commission, as well as uniforms, swords, medals and other items.

422. Frank J. Welcher, *The Union Army, 1861–1865, Organization and Operations*, vol. I, *The Eastern Theater* (Bloomington: Indiana University Press, 1989),

699; Frances H. Kennedy, *The Civil War Battlefield Guide*, 2nd ed. (Boston: Houghton Mifflin Company, 1998), 1; Cullum, *Biographical Register*, 488; Charles M. Hubbard, *The Burden of Confederate Diplomacy* (Knoxville: University of Tennessee Press, 1988), 12; Abner Doubleday, *Reminiscences of Forts Sumter and Moultrie in 1860–'61* (New York: Harper & Brothers, 1876), 49–54. See also Sons of the South, "The Battle of Fort Sumter," http://www.sonofthesouth.net/leefoundation/battle-fort-sumter.htm; Dempsey, *Michigan and the Civil War*, 15. Various sources have Hall rescuing the flag and "nailing it back up," others mention only Sergeant Peter Hart and others still cite a combination of both. Although Doubleday does not list Hall as having nailed the flag to a new spar and goes into great detail of Hart doing so, it is likely that Hart did the nailing and hoisting of the flag. In postwar years there appeared an illustration captioned, "Sergeant Hart nailing the colors to the flag-staff at Fort Sumter." Several secondary sources state that Hall "burned off his eyebrows permanently" or the like. A photograph of Hall as colonel, taken after July 7, 1862, shows him with a full pair of eyebrows.

423. Bradley M. Gottfried, *The Maps of Antietam* (El Dorado Hills, CA: Savas Beatie LLC, 2012), 4; *OR*, vol. XIX, part I, 173.

424. McClellan, *McClellan's Own Story*, 587; Hartwig, *To Antietam Creek*, 515; Johnson, "Caught in the Cross-fire," 55; John Billings, *Hardtack and Coffee: Or, The Unwritten Story of Army Life* (Boston: George M. Smith & Company, 1888), 129. Accounts speak of the soldiers' comfort and rejuvenating nature of drinking coffee, especially after a long day's march. Billings wrote, "One of the most interesting scenes presented in army life took place at night when the army was on the point of bivouacking. As soon as this became known along the column…little camp-fires…would shoot up along the hills and plains…soon surrounded by soldiers, who made it an almost invariably rule to cook their coffee first."

425. McClellan, *McClellan's Own Story*, 591; Johnson, "Caught in the Cross-fire," 48; Clemens, *Maryland Campaign of 1862*, 54.

426. Oesterle, "Incidents Connected," 4–5.

427. Hartwig, *To Antietam Creek*, 646.

428. Video interview of D. Scott Hartwig, September 1996, for the National Park Service project *Antietam: A Documentary Film* (1997); Hartwig, *To Antietam Creek*, 645–52. This section of the chapter is entitled "A Deathlike Stillness" and provides a most excellent description of what the soldiers on the battlefield experienced only hours before the battle.

429. Oesterle, "Incidents Connected," 5.

430. Hodgman enlisted in Company I as a first sergeant in June 1861 for three years. He was discharged on September 1, 1862, to accept a promotion and was commissioned second lieutenant the following

day. Brown, *Record of Service*, 54 (this entry has his name spelled "Hodgeman").

431. Roger L. Rosentreter, "Samuel Hodgman's Civil War," *Michigan History* 64 (November/December 1980): 34–36.

432. See Antietam on the Web, "Diary of Private Basil Deshetler," http://antietam.aotw.org/index.php. This website is a great resource for the study of Antietam. New information and updates are made frequently; Armstrong, *Disaster in the West Woods*, 2; see U.S. Naval Observatory Astronomical Applications Department, "Sun and Moon Data for One Day ~ Sharpsburg, Washington County, MD," http://aa.usno.navy.mil/rstt/onedaytable?form=1&ID=AA&year=1862&month=9&day=17&state=MD&place=Sharpsburg. Begin civil twilight at 5:27 a.m., sunrise at 5:45 a.m., sunset at 6:17 p.m. and end civil twilight at 6:43 p.m.; McClellan, *McClellan's Own Story*, 591.

433. Clemens, *Maryland Campaign of 1862*, 178.

434. Armstrong, *Disaster in the West Woods*, 3; Johnson, "Caught in the Cross-fire," 36–38, 63, 73; McClellan, *McClellan's Own Story*, 592; *OR*, vol. XIX, part I, 275.

435. McClellan, *McClellan's Own Story*, 592; Bradley Graham, *The Antietam Effect* (Gettysburg, PA: Media Magic, 2012), 210.

436. Gibbon, *Personal Recollections*, 88.

437. *OR*, vol. XIX, part I, 310–11; McClellan, *McClellan's Own Story*, 593; Gottfried, *Maps of Antietam*, 172–73.

438. *OR*, vol. XIX, part I, 319–20.

439. Although parts of the East Woods no longer exist, it is impossible to see portions of the Miller Farm west of the Smoketown Road from the valley leading down to Antietam Creek.

440. Gibbon, *Personal Recollections*, 89; Lawrence A. Kreiser Jr., *Defeating Lee: A History of the Second Corps, Army of the Potomac* (Indianapolis: Indiana University Press, 2011), 51. Although evidence suggests that Sumner was indeed impatient to get into the fight, there does not seem to exist overt suggestions by him to McClellan in throwing the entire army at Lee. However, Sumner may have assumed that McClellan would have been apt to do so and been less inclined to press an issue he deemed obvious. Hindsight is the clearest lens to view any past event and appears to be the filter in which Sumner regarded his role in the battle.

441. Johnson, "Caught in the Cross-fire," 36, 38; Graham, *Antietam Effect*, 210.

442. Oesterle, "Incidents Connected," 5. The portion of the field the 7th traversed was farther south of the Miller Cornfield area where the exchange of ground occurred several more times than the point where Oesterle refers to as being fought over twice.

443. Western Michigan University, Civil War Collection (electronic edition accessed), "Letters of Samuel Chase Hodgman." See also U.S. Civil War

Collection, Samuel Hodgman letter, November 17, 1862, http://quod.lib.umich.edu/c/civilwar1/USCW0023.0001.001?rgn=main;view=fulltext, 12–13. This amazing and very detailed thirty-two-page letter was written to his father while a patient at the U.S. General Hospital in west Philadelphia.

444. *OR*, vol. XIX, part I, 320; McClellan, *McClellan's Own Story*, 593; Gottfried, *Maps of Antietam*, 172–73.

445. *OR*, vol. XIX, part I, 305, 320, 883; Gottfried, *Maps of Antietam*, 172–73; McClellan, *McClellan's Own Story*, 593.

446. *OR*, vol. XIX, part I, 320; Western Michigan University, Civil War Collection, "Letters of Samuel Chase Hodgman," 10–12.

447. *OR*, vol. XIX, part I, 320, 883.

448. Henry Woodhead, ed., *Antietam: Voices of the Civil War* (Alexandria, VA: Time-Life Books, 1996), 95–96.

449. Gottfried, *Maps of Antietam*, 174–75; Kreiser, *Defeating Lee*, 51; Gregory A. Coco, ed., *From Ball's Bluff to Gettysburg…and Beyond: The Civil War Letters of Private Roland E. Bowen, 15th Massachusetts Infantry 1861–1864* (Gettysburg, PA: Thomas Publications, 1994), 135. The average top speed of a horse is approximately twenty-five to thirty miles per hour and probably his frame of reference, especially using the word "gait." Major Rufus Dawes of the 6th Wisconsin Infantry wrote in his memoirs, "[A]s we appeared at the edge of corn, a long line of men in butternut and gray rose up out of the ground." Men of Sedgwick's Division described very similar situations of overwhelming numbers of Confederates appearing on three sides.

450. *OR*, vol. XIX, part I, 307, 321.

451. Oesterle, "Incidents Connected," 5; *Monroe Monitor*, October 1, 1862. The *Free Press* article was picked up and run in the Monroe paper.

452. *OR*, vol. XIX, part I, 321, 307.

453. McClellan, *McClellan's Own Story*, 593. See Civil War Trust, "Major General John Sedgwick," http://www.civilwar.org/education/history/biographies/john-sedgwick-1.html.

454. *OR*, vol. XIX, part I, 306.

455. Western Michigan University, Civil War Collection, "Letters of Samuel Chase Hodgman," 13; Oesterle, "Incidents Connected," 5.

456. Brown, *Record of Service*, 117, 121.

457. *Monroe Monitor*, October 1, 1862.

458. Ibid.

459. *Monroe Commercial*, September 25, 1862.

460. Cullum, *Biographical Register*, 488–89; *OR*, vol. XIX, part I, 307. For subsequent actions at Fredericksburg and Gettysburg, Hall would ultimately receive a brevet lieutenant colonel ranking.

461. Kreiser, *Defeating Lee*, 51; *OR*, vol. XIX, part I, 275–77; McClellan, *McClellan's Own Story*, 601.

462. Kreiser, *Defeating Lee*, 264–65; Fox, *Regimental Losses*, 385, 432; *OR*, vol. XIX, part I, 308; Oesterle, "Incidents Connected," 5; *OR*, vol. XIX, part I, 193–203. As with all casualty numbers during the Civil War, there are variances on the reporting, due to those who died later or were captured or missing who rejoined their units later, as well as the overall challenge of tracking during that time. New information and research is continually updating and adjusting the accepted numbers to provide a more accurate understanding of the losses sustained during the war.
463. Johnson, "Caught in the Cross-fire," 36–38; Brown, *Record of Service*, 120; Fox, *Regimental Losses*, 385. The next greatest loss was at Gettysburg in July 1863, where the regiment lost twenty-seven killed and mortally wounded.
464. *OR*, vol. XIX, part I, 308.

CHAPTER 7

465. Pierro, *Maryland Campaign of September 1862*, 297.
466. Armstrong, *Unfurl Those Colors!*, 220.
467. Ibid., 201.
468. Palfrey, *Antietam and Fredericksburg*, 82; Pierro, *Maryland Campaign of September 1862*, 284.
469. Armstrong, *Unfurl Those Colors!*, 220.
470. Ibid., 221.
471. Pierro, *Maryland Campaign of September 1862*, 284; Palfrey, *Antietam and Fredericksburg*, 99.
472. Mason, *Until Antietam*, 121, 178.
473. Armstrong, *Unfurl Those Colors!*, 221.
474. Pierro, *Maryland Campaign of September 1862*, 284. This may understate the case, as the stream at Pry's Ford was waist-deep; Armstrong, *Unfurl Those Colors!*, 167.
475. Armstrong, *Unfurl Those Colors!*, 221.
476. McClellan used passive tense and indirection to describe Richardson's movement. Sumner was absent; he did not direct Richardson. *OR*, vol. XIX, part I, 56, 58–59, 275–76.
477. Pierro, *Maryland Campaign of September 1862*, 284.
478. Sears, *Landscape Turned Red*, 236; *OR*, vol. XIX, part I, 1,022.
479. *OR*, vol. XIX, part I, 293.
480. Mason, *Until Antietam*, 136.
481. Jacob H. Cole, *Under Five Commanders, or A Boy's Experience with the Army of the Potomac* (Paterson, NJ: News Printing Company, 1906), 19; Armstrong, *Unfurl Those Colors!*, 221.

482. Quoting Peter Mayo, soldier in the 2nd Michigan. Mason, *Until Antietam*, 121.
483. Rafuse, *McClellan's War*, 316–18.
484. Sears, *Landscape Turned Red*, 240.
485. Armstrong, *Unfurl Those Colors!*, 222. Richardson was 450 yards east of the Roulette farm and 700 yards northeast of the Sunken Road. Pierro, *Maryland Campaign of September 1862*, 284.
486. Armstrong, *Unfurl Those Colors!*, 222.
487. Ibid., 222–28; Davis, *Until Antietam*, 178–79.
488. Armstrong, *Unfurl Those Colors!*, 226–28; Mason, *Until Antietam*, 180.
489. Pierro, *Maryland Campaign of September 1862*, 291.
490. *OR*, vol. XIX, part I, 285.
491. Pierro, *Maryland Campaign of September 1862*, 291.
492. Mason, *Until Antietam*, 181, quoting Carman Papers, ANB.
493. Armstrong, *Unfurl Those Colors!*, 235.
494. Sears, *Landscape Turned Red*, 242–43, 247; Mason, *Until Antietam*, 181.
495. *OR*, vol. XIX, part I, 1,023; Sears, *Landscape Turned Red*, 241.
496. *OR*, vol. XIX, part I, 1,051.
497. Gottfried, *Maps of Antietam*, 190–91.
498. *OR*, vol. XIX, part I, 289.
499. Pierro, *Maryland Campaign of September 1862*, 291.
500. *OR*, vol. XIX, part I, 289.
501. Sears, *Landscape Turned Red*, 245.
502. *OR*, vol. XIX, part I, 1,037.
503. Ibid., 1,048.
504. Sears, *Landscape Turned Red*, 245.
505. *OR*, vol. XIX, part I, 285.
506. Ibid., 300.
507. Ibid., 286.
508. Ibid., 59, 289–90; Miles, "My Recollections of Antietam," 588; Richard F. Welch, *The Boy General: The Life and Careers of Francis Channing Barlow* (Kent, OH: Kent State University Press, 2003), 69–71.
509. *OR*, vol. XIX, part I, 302.
510. Catton, *Mr. Lincoln's Army*, 300.
511. *OR*, vol. XIX, part I, 301.
512. Mason, *Until Antietam*, 187; Douglas S. Freeman, *Lee's Lieutenants: A Study in Command*, vol. II (New York: Charles Scribner's Sons, 1943), 213.
513. E. Porter Alexander, quoted in Freeman, *Lee's Lieutenants*, 213.
514. *OR*, vol. LI, part I, 843.
515. Rafuse, *McClellan's War*, 320.
516. *OR*, vol. XIX, part II, 312.

517. Stephen W. Sears, *The Civil War Papers of George B. McClellan: Selected Correspondence, 1860–1865* (New York: Ticknor & Fields, 1989), 467.
518. *OR*, vol. XIX, part I, 67.
519. Ibid., vol. LI, part I, 843.
520. Ibid., vol. XIX, part I, 338, 349.
521. Harsh, *Taken at the Flood*, 397; see *OR*, vol. XIX, part I, 277–305.
522. *Contradictions and Divided Loyalties: Slavery on the Antietam Battleground*, National Park Service brochure. Henry Piper owned six slaves in 1860, five of them children.
523. *OR*, vol. XIX, part I, 285.
524. Ibid.
525. Ibid., 285–86, 290, 291, 292.
526. Richardson had sought rifled artillery, but Hunt had none to send. Pierro, *Maryland Campaign of September 1862*, 296.
527. Perry D. Jamieson, *Death in September: The Antietam Campaign* (Abilene, TX: McWhiney Foundation Press, 1999), 81.
528. Thomas L. Livermore, *Days and Events, 1860–1866* (Boston: Houghton Mifflin Company, 1920), 137–38; also quoted in Sam Abell and Brian Pohanka, *The Civil War: An Aerial Portrait* (Charlottesville, VA: Thomasson-Grant, 1990), 57. Livermore indicates that Caldwell was the field officer being sought.
529. *OR*, vol. XIX, part I, 302.
530. Mason, *Until Antietam*, 189; *OR*, vol. XIX, part I, 343.
531. Pierro, *Maryland Campaign of September 1862*, 297.
532. *OR*, vol. XIX, part I, 299; Pierro, *Maryland Campaign of September 1862*, 297; Livermore, *Days and Events*, 143–44; Mason, *Until Antietam*, 189, 191; Priest, *Antietam*, 207.
533. Mason, *Until Antietam*, 189.
534. Livermore, *Days and Events*, 138.
535. Pierro, *Maryland Campaign of September 1862*, 298. Although grievous, it was the lowest of the three II Corps divisions. *OR*, vol. XIX, part I, 191–93.
536. *The Most Fearful Ordeal: Original Coverage of the Civil War by Writers and Reporters of the New York Times*, with introduction and notes by James M. McPherson (New York: St. Martin's Press, 2004), 198.
537. Armstrong, *Unfurl Those Colors!*, 247.

CHAPTER 8

538. *OR*, vol. XIX, part I, 429–30.
539. Ibid., vol. LI, part I, 844.
540. Hays, *Antietam and Its Bridges*, 78.

541. Pierro, *Maryland Campaign of September 1862*, 340.
542. Lane, *Soldier's Diary*, 13; Palfrey, *Antietam and Fredericksburg*, 112.
543. Pierro, *Maryland Campaign of September 1862*, 340, 342.
544. *OR*, vol. XIX, part I, 430. Carman's account incorporates this portion of Willcox's after-action report almost verbatim (without attribution). Pierro, *Maryland Campaign of September 1862*, 340.
545. *OR*, vol. XIX, part I, 430.
546. Rafuse, *McClellan's War*, 325.
547. *OR*, vol. XIX, part I, 430.
548. Elon G. Mills Diary, Bentley Historical Library, University of Michigan, Ann Arbor, 7–18.
549. *OR*, vol. XIX, part I, 430.
550. Pierro, *Maryland Campaign of September 1862*, 342.
551. Except where noted, the remainder of this description derives from Willcox's report, *OR*, vol. XIX, part I, 429–32.
552. Jacob D. Cox, "Battle of Antietam," in *Hearts Touched by Fire*, 457.
553. Pierro, *Maryland Campaign of September 1862*, 342.
554. Ibid.
555. Ibid.
556. Ibid.
557. Ibid. Sometimes referred to as "Cemetery Hill."
558. Ibid., 343.
559. Ibid.
560. *OR*, vol. XIX, part I, 438–39.
561. Pierro, *Maryland Campaign of September 1862*, 343.
562. Ibid.
563. *OR*, vol. XIX, part I, 440.
564. Ibid., 440–41.
565. Ibid., 431.
566. Cox, *Battle of Antietam*, 457–58.
567. Pierro, *Maryland Campaign of September 1862*, 343.
568. Rafuse, *McClellan's War*, 325; Cox, *Battle of Antietam*, 458. This interval compares very favorably to that required for the corps to cross the Antietam.
569. *OR*, vol. XIX, part I, 441.
570. Ibid., 440.
571. Scott, *Forgotten Valor*, 361.
572. Ibid., 372. A Signal Corps station (not William Roe's) had sent Burnside a 3:00 p.m. message reporting that a strong enemy force was moving toward his left. *OR*, vol. XIX, part I, 138.
573. Rafuse, *McClellan's War*, 325.
574. Diary entries for September 16 and 17, George Lockley Collection, Bentley Library.

575. *OR*, vol. LI, part I, 845.
576. Cox, *Battle of Antietam*, 458–59.
577. Martin F. Schmitt, ed., *General George Crook: His Autobiography* (Norman: University of Oklahoma Press, 1986), 100.
578. Scott, *Forgotten Valor*, 366–67.
579. Ibid., 367. The general missed home and was also anticipating cooler weather with the request of these woolen garments.
580. Richards left to recuperate at home (Ann Arbor) on the eighteenth. William Withington Papers, Bentley Historical Library.
581. Gallagher, *Fighting for the Confederacy*, 153.
582. A. Wilson Greene, "'I Fought the Battle Splendidly': George B. McClellan and the Maryland Campaign," in Gary W. Gallagher, ed., *Antietam: Essays on the 1862 Maryland Campaign* (Kent, OH: Kent State University Press, 1989), 78.
583. *OR*, vol. XIX, part I, 2.
584. Cox, *Battle of Antietam*, 457.
585. *OR*, vol. XIX, part I, 431.
586. According to Robertson, *Michigan in the War*, 984, his commission dated from September 8, 1862.
587. Cox, *Battle of Antietam*, 459.
588. See *McClellan's Own Story*, 608.
589. Scott, *Forgotten Valor*, 363.
590. Ibid., 366. Willcox's wife, Marie, complained that "it is a great shame that he was not permitted to drive the enemy as he wanted to." Id., 371.
591. Blackburn, *Diary of Captain Ralph Ely*, 43.
592. *OR*, vol. XIX, part II, 322. Lincoln telegraphed on the eighth, tenth and twelfth (4:00 a.m.), identically: "How does it look now?" McClellan reported on the Lost Order and South Mountain; he did not immediately report here. *OR*, vol. XIX, part II, 210, 232, 270.
593. *OR*, vol. XIX, part II, 330.
594. Ibid., vol. LI, part I, 842.
595. Allen C. Guelzo, *Lincoln's Emancipation Proclamation: The End of Slavery in America* (New York: Simon & Schuster, 2004), 168, 170; Randall, *Lincoln the President*, 159; Francis B. Carpenter, *Six Months at the White House: The Story of a Picture* (New York: Hurd and Houghton, 1866), 22–23.

CHAPTER 9

596. Harsh, *Sounding the Shallows*, 21; entry for September 18, George Lockley Collection, Bentley Library.
597. *OR*, vol. XIX, part I, 141; Crist, *Papers of Jefferson Davis*, vol. VIII, *1862*, 393–94.

598. Sears, *Civil War Papers of George B. McClellan*, 469.
599. Ibid.
600. *OR*, vol. XIX, part II, 322.
601. Ibid., vol. LI, part I, 847.
602. Ibid., 848–49.
603. Ibid., vol. XIX, part I, 65.
604. Ibid., 66.
605. Ibid., 280.
606. William Withington Papers, Bentley Historical Library.
607. *OR*, vol. LI, part I, 847–48.
608. Harsh, *Sounding the Shallows*, 22.
609. *OR*, vol. LI, part I, 850.
610. Ibid., vol. XIX, part II, 331; vol. LI, part I, 850.
611. Sears, *Civil War Papers of George B. McClellan*, 469.
612. *OR*, vol. XIX, part II, 330. The *New York Times* omitted "complete"; *Most Fearful Ordeal*, 187.
613. *OR*, vol. XIX, part II, 330.
614. Sears, *Civil War Papers of George B. McClellan*, 470.
615. Ibid., 473.
616. *Most Fearful Ordeal*, 188.
617. Ibid., 191.
618. *OR*, vol. XIX, part II, 331.
619. Ibid., part I, 378–79.
620. Ibid., 479–80. On the eighteenth, Williams "assumed" official command of the corps. Id., 158.
621. *OR*, vol. LI, part I, 849. Headquarters was moved to a non-hospital near Keedysville. Id., 850.
622. *OR*, vol. XIX, part I, 339.
623. Also known as Blackford's Ford.
624. *OR*, vol. XII, part II, 472.
625. Brown, *Record of Service*, 4th Michigan Volunteers, 25.
626. Ibid., 16th Michigan Volunteers, 162.
627. Ibid., 159.
628. Graduating sixteenth of thirty-eight. Cullum, *Biographical Register*, vol. I, 394; Brown, *Record of Service*, 16th Michigan Volunteers, 154.
629. Entry for September 19, John Milton Bancroft Diary/Scrapbook, Auburn University Libraries, 118.
630. *OR*, vol. XIX, part I, 349.
631. Thomas A. McGrath, *Shepherdstown: Last Clash of the Antietam Campaign, September 19–20, 1862* (Lynchburg, VA: Schroeder Publications, 2008), 60.
632. Ibid., 66.

633. Entry for September 18, George Lockley Collection, Bentley Library.
634. *OR*, vol. XIX, part I, 339.
635. John Milton Bancroft Diary/Scrapbook, 118.
636. *OR*, vol. XIX, part I, 339.
637. Harsh, *Taken at the Flood*, 454. Porter singled out Hunt "for services rendered voluntarily"; *OR*, vol. XIX, part I, 341.
638. McGrath, *Shepherdstown*, 70–72; Harsh, *Taken at the Flood*, 455; J.B. Moore, "Sharpsburg," *Southern Historical Society Papers* 27 (1899).
639. *OR*, vol. XIX, part I, 349.
640. McGrath, *Shepherdstown*, 72.
641. *OR*, vol. XIX, part I, 345.
642. McGrath, *Shepherdstown*, 72–73.
643. *OR*, vol. XIX, part I, 350; Bertera and Crawford, *4th Michigan Infantry in the Civil War*, 107; McGrath, *Shepherdstown*, 76–78.
644. From 4th Michigan Volunteer Infantry Regiment, "Roster of the 4th Michigan Volunteer Infantry 1861–1866," http://www.4thmichigan.com/4th_michigan_roster.htm, accessed on March 17, 2015.
645. *OR*, vol. LI, part I, 853.
646. McGraft, *Shepherdstown*, 82.
647. Ibid., 83.
648. *OR*, vol. LI, part I, 853.
649. Ibid., vol. XIX, part I, 331.
650. Ibid., 334.
651. Harsh, *Taken at the Flood*, 23.
652. Entry for September 20, John Milton Bancroft Diary/Scrapbook, 121.
653. *OR*, vol. XIX, part I, 350.
654. Ibid., 334.
655. Ibid., 346; McGrath, *Shepherdstown*, 99–103.
656. Entry for September 20, George Lockley Collection, Bentley Library.
657. *OR*, vol. XIX, part I, 346–47.
658. McGrath, *Shepherdstown*, 122.
659. Porter did not cross with the 4th Michigan as promised. *OR*, vol. XIX, part II, 331.
660. *OR*, vol. XIX, part I, 346.
661. Ibid., 352.
662. Harsh, *Taken at the Flood*, 456; *OR*, vol. XIX, part I, 347.
663. Gottfried, *Maps of Antietam*, 248–49.
664. Entry for September 20, George Lockley Collection, Bentley Library.
665. *OR*, vol. XIX, part I, 340.
666. Ibid., 348.
667. McGraft, *Shepherdstown*, 132.
668. Ibid., 162.

669. *OR*, vol. XIX, part I, 68; vol. LI, part I, 853.
670. *OR*, vol. XIX, part I, 340.
671. Ibid., 68.
672. See, for example, *OR*, vol. LI, part II, 620.
673. Ibid., vol. XIX, part I, 820.
674. Harsh, *Taken at the Flood*, 444; Harsh, *Sounding the Shallows*, Chapter 10, Sections E and F.
675. *OR*, vol. XIX, part I, 830.
676. Ibid., 820–21.
677. Brown, *Record of Service*, 1st Michigan Volunteers, 14; McGraft, *Shepherdstown*, 160, 162.
678. *OR*, vol. XIX, part I, 830–34; Harsh, *Taken at the Flood*, 461.
679. *OR*, vol. XIX, part I, 142; *Papers of Jefferson Davis*, vol. VIII, 396.
680. *OR*, vol. XIX, part I, 142.
681. Ibid., 821, 824.
682. Harsh, *Taken at the Flood*, 448.
683. *OR*, vol. XIX, part I, 142–43.
684. Ibid., part II, 622–23.
685. Letter from George W.C. Lee, *Papers of Jefferson Davis*, vol. VIII, 405–6, from "Camp near Martinsburg."
686. *OR*, vol. XIX, part II, 626.
687. Ibid., 628–29.
688. Ibid., 633.
689. Ibid., part I, 152; Harsh, *Taken at the Flood*, 466.
690. *OR*, vol. XIX, part I, 143.
691. Entry for September 21, John Milton Bancroft Diary/Scrapbook, 121.
692. Harsh, *Taken at the Flood*, 453.
693. *OR*, vol. XIX, part I, 479–80. The 2nd Division was on the road all night of the nineteenth.
694. Ibid., 69.
695. Ibid., 70–72.
696. Entries for September 22 and 26, George Lockley Collection, Bentley Library.
697. Perseus Digital Library, http://www.perseus.tufts.edu/hopper/text?doc=Perseus%3Atext%3A2006.05.0574, accessed on November 6, 2014.
698. Letter dated September 17, 1862, from Detroit. William Withington Papers, Bentley Historical Library.
699. William Withington Papers, Bentley Historical Library.
700. Ibid.
701. McGraft, *Shepherdstown*, 190.
702. *Detroit Free Press*, September 24, 1862, 2.
703. *OR*, vol. XIX, part I, 139.

CHAPTER 10

704. Marguerite Merington, ed., *The Custer Story: The Life and Letters of General George A. Custer and His Wife Elizabeth* (New York: Barnes & Noble Books, 1994), 35.

705. *OR*, vol. XIX, part I, 275.

706. Quaife, *From the Cannon's Mouth*, 136.

707. *OR*, vol. XIX, part I, 181–82.

708. Newspaper item, William Withington Papers, Bentley Historical Library.

709. Robert K. Krick, "It Appeared as Though Mutual Extermination Would Put a Stop to the Awful Carnage: Confederates in Sharpsburg's Bloody Lane," in *The Antietam Campaign*, ed. Gary Gallagher (Chapel Hill: University of North Carolina Press, 1999), 223.

710. The first, enacted on August 6, 1861, employed judicial means for certain takings and extended to persons held to labor or service under state law employed in arms or in military capacities against the United States "during the present insurrection." *U.S. Statutes at Large*, vol. XII, 319, at http://memory.loc.gov/ammem/amlaw/lwsl.html. See James Oakes, *Freedom National: The Destruction of Slavery in the United States, 1861–1865* (New York: W.W. Norton & Company, 2013), 137–38.

711. *U.S. Statutes at Large*, vol. XII, 589–92; Oakes, *Freedom National*, 224–36.

712. *Congressional Globe*, 2nd Session, April 18, 1862, 1,714.

713. Oakes, *Freedom National*, 225.

714. Ibid., 234.

715. *Congressional Globe*, 2nd Session, July 16, 1862, 3,383.

716. Ibid., 3,400; Oakes, *Freedom National*, 239.

717. *Congressional Globe*, 2nd Session, Appendix, 203–5.

718. Oakes, *Freedom National*, 303 and n.4.

719. Diary of Salmon P. Chase, in *Annual Report of the American Historical Association for the Year 1902*, vol. II (Washington, D.C.: Government Printing Office, 1903), 87–88. Early that year, the Lincolns lost their middle son, Willie. "He was too good for this earth," the president had said tearfully, "but then we loved him so." Joshua Zeitz, *Lincoln's Boys: John Hay, John Nicolay, and the War for Lincoln's Image* (New York: Penguin Books, 2014), 111. The president's faith, in the face of grievous loss, deserves more from historians. The Emancipation Proclamation concluded by invoking "the gracious favor of Almighty God."

720. The January 1 proclamation also authorized the military employment of African Americans in uniform, not only in supporting efforts. Keeping pace with national emancipation progress, in October 1864, two years after the Battle of Antietam, Maryland voters approved a state constitutional amendment to outlaw slavery.

721. William Withington Papers, Bentley Historical Library.
722. Brown, *Record of Service*, 17th Michigan Volunteers, 77; Robertson, *Michigan in the War*, 896; William Withington Papers, Bentley Historical Library. He would resign and be honorably discharged for disability on June 30, 1864, "on account of wounds received in action."
723. William Withington Papers, Bentley Historical Library.
724. *OR*, series III, vol. II, 582–84. Not all Northern states were so aligned. The Illinois legislature passed a resolution opposing the proclamation as "unwarrantable." Henry Steele Commager, ed., *The Civil War Archive: The History of the Civil War in Documents* (New York: Tess Press, 2000), 613–14.
725. Lane, *Soldier's Diary*, 17.
726. Letter of September 23, 1862, Eugene Deverney Young Collection, Bentley Historical Library.
727. J. Benton Kennedy letter to father, October 10, 1862, Kennedy Family Papers, Collection 68, Michigan State University Archives and Historical Collections, East Lansing, Michigan. Midwestern soldiers "were capable and resourceful and tended to assume that they could handle anything the war brought their way." Steven E. Woodworth and Charles D. Grear, eds., *The Chattanooga Campaign* (Carbondale: Southern Illinois University Press, 2012), 53–54.
728. They were supported by civilians in towns all across Michigan. See, for example, Rick Liblong, *Answering the Call to Duty: Saving Custer, Heroism at Gettysburg, POWs and Other Stories of Michigan Small Town Soldiers in the Civil War* (Traverse City, MI: Arbutus Press, 2011), 20.
729. John W. Schildt, *Antietam Hospitals* (Chewsville, MD: Antietam Publications, 1987), 20–21.
730. Mason, *Until Antietam*, 192.
731. Schildt, *Antietam Hospitals*, 44. His nephew was Elon J. Farnsworth. See Chapter 4.
732. Abner Hard, MD, *History of the Eighth Cavalry Volunteers Illinois Volunteers, during the Great Rebellion* (Aurora, IL: self-published, 1868), 186. Barton is memorialized by a battlefield monument.
733. Elon Mills Diary, Bentley Historical Library, 24.
734. Benjamin F. Marsh letter to Augustus, October 2, 1862, Marsh Family Papers, Collection 47, Michigan State University Archives and Historical Collections, East Lansing, Michigan.
735. Scott, *Forgotten Valor*, 370.
736. *OR*, vol. XIX, part I, 433; Scott, *Forgotten Valor*, 374, n.47. He held it until January 16, 1863, and eight subsequent times.
737. William Withington Papers, Bentley Historical Library.
738. Curtis, *History of the Twenty-fourth Michigan*, 62–65. The name honored Wayne County's prosecuting attorney. The regiment would move on to

Camp Penniman near Bakersville, Maryland, named for a leading citizen of Plymouth. Id., 69–70.

739. Ibid., 65.

740. *History of Branch County, Michigan* (Philadelphia: Everts & Abbott, 1879), 156; Robertson, *Michigan in the War*, 772; Curtis, *History of the Twenty-fourth Michigan*, 42, 270, 359.

741. Robertson, *Michigan in the War*, 932; Curtis, *History of the Twenty-fourth Michigan*, 42.

742. Curtis, *History of the Twenty-fourth Michigan*, 35.

743. Robertson, *Michigan in the War*, 800.

744. Newspaper item, William Withington Papers, Bentley Historical Library.

745. Abel Peck letter to "Dear Child," October 12, 1862, Abel Peck Papers, Collection 107, Michigan State University Archives and Historical Collections, East Lansing, Michigan.

746. Curtis, *History of the Twenty-fourth Michigan*, 62.

747. Quaife, *From the Cannon's Mouth*, 136.

748. Lane, *Soldier's Diary*, 14.

749. Jacob D. Cox, *Military Reminiscences of the Civil War* (New York: Charles Scribner's Sons, 1900), 364.

750. Ward H. Lamon, *Recollections of Abraham Lincoln, 1847–1865*, ed. Dorothy Lamon (Chicago: A.C. McClurg & Company, 1896), 145.

751. Lamon, *Recollections of Abraham Lincoln*, 145.

752. Mason, *Until Antietam*, 194–95, 218, n.48; Lamon, *Recollections of Abraham Lincoln*, 148.

753. "Trophies of the Field of Antietam," in *The Rebellion Record: A Diary of American Events, with Documents, Narratives, Illustrative Incidents, Poetry, Etc.*, vol. VI, ed. Frank Moore (New York: G.P. Putnam, 1863), 30 ("Poetry, Rumors and Incidents" section). This emblem was the first one shown to the delegation.

754. Ibid. Another, not described, was from the "Seventeenth regiment New-york volunteers, Caldwell's brigade, Richardson's division." The reporter was mistaken here, as the 17th New York Infantry was a 5th Corps unit not involved in the action on September 17. Another was from North Carolina, its provenance unrecorded.

755. The 11th Alabama flag matches the descriptions made of it by participants in that photographed meeting of Lincoln and McClellan. See Civil War Trust, "Flags of Antietam," http://www.civilwar.org/battlefields/antietam/history/antietam-flags.

756. Lamon, *Recollections of Abraham Lincoln*, 148; *Washington Star*, October 6, 1862.

757. *New York Tribune*, October 6, 1862; *Collected Works of Abraham Lincoln*, vol. V, 450.

758. See Preservation Petersburg, "Centre Hill Mansion," http://www.preservationpetersburg.org/explore_centre_hill.html, accessed on March 30, 2015.
759. *Bay City Tribune*, February 7, 1923. The record of service gives his age as seventeen.
760. Charles Moore, *History of Michigan*, vol. II (Chicago: Lewis Publishing Company, 1915), 726 (incorrectly giving the regiment as the 7th).
761. *Bay City Tribune*, October 7, 1894.
762. Newspaper item, William Withington Papers, Bentley Historical Library.
763. His name is alternately given as "George B." and "George D."
764. *History of Jackson County Michigan* (Chicago: Inter-State Publishing Company, 1881), 959. The cemetery is half a mile south of the village on M-50/Brooklyn Road. George S. May, comp., *"Let Their Memories Be Cherished": Michigan Civil War Monuments* (Lansing: Michigan Civil War Centennial Observance Commission, 1965), 38.
765. *Catalogue of the Officers and Students of the University of Michigan 1858* (Ann Arbor: Davis & Cole/University of Michigan, 1858). He is also reported as graduating with honors from the Medical College of Washington, D.C.
766. A relative and the colonel commanding the 6th Michigan Infantry, Edward Bacon of Niles, would write one of the earliest Civil War books, *Among the Cotton Thieves*, released in 1867.
767. Diary of Cyrus Bacon, Archives of Michigan, Lansing, Michigan. The succeeding description derives from this source, available online at http://seekingmichigan.org.
768. In his diary, he wrote, "O God, be thou with me. If thou, O Lord, blessest me then am I blessed indeed, but if thou dost withhold thy blessings I shall not prosper. Lord, go thou with me for Christ's sake. Do good and God will bless thee."
769. *Walt Whitman's Civil War*, ed. Walter Lowenfels (Boston: Da Capo Press, 1989), 86.
770. Julia S. Wheelock Freeman, *The Boys in White: The Experience of a Hospital Agent In and Around Washington* (New York: Lange and Hillman, 1870), 10 (the title refers to the apparel in which the deceased were clothed); Weldon Petz, "Michigan's Florence Nightingale," *Michigan History* 82, no. 4 (July/August 1998): 66.
771. Freeman, *Boys in White*, 11–23, 29–31, 51.
772. Ibid., 31–32.
773. Julia Pferdehirt, *More than Petticoats: Remarkable Michigan Women* (Guilford, CT: Morris Book Publishing, 2007), 34. This equates to twenty dollars per month, which exceeded the thirteen dollars per month the soldier received until an increase to sixteen dollars per month in June 1864.
774. Michigan Civil War Centennial Observance Commission, *Michigan Women in the Civil War* (Lansing, MI, 1963), 18–19, 68–69.

775. Quaife, *From the Cannon's Mouth*, 163.

776. Curtis, *History of the Twenty-fourth Michigan*, 60. On July 1, 1863, the regiment would experience its own tragedy, losing, among many, Second Lieutenant Gilbert A. Dickey of the first graduating class of Michigan Agricultural College (now Michigan State University).

777. *Jackson Weekly Citizen*, October 15, 1862.

778. Wheelock, *Boys in White*, 5, 37–38.

779. Michigander Sarah Emma Edmonds reported being at Antietam, disguising herself as Private Franklin Thompson, 2nd Michigan Infantry. Deanne Blanton and Lauren M. Cook, *They Fought Like Demons: Women Soldiers in the American Civil War* (Baton Rouge: Louisiana State University Press, 2002), 14. This work reports that seven women fought at Antietam in Union uniforms. The regiment was not in the Maryland Campaign. Robertson, *Michigan in the War*, 194. See Patricia Majher, *Great Girls in Michigan History* (Detroit: Wayne State University Press, 2015), 33–42.

780. 1 Mich. L. J. 331 (1892).

781. Mason, *Until Antietam*, 196.

782. William Withington Papers, Bentley Historical Library.

783. Ibid.

784. Exact cause of Richardson's death is not clear. For conditions in the medical corps, see Jonathan Letterman, *Medical Recollections of the Army of the Potomac* (New York: D. Appleton and Company, 1866), 32–51; Joseph K. Barnes, *The Medical and Surgical History of the War of the Rebellion (1861–65)* (Washington, D.C.: Government Printing Office, 1870), 96–99; George W. Adams, *Doctors in Blue: The Medical History of the Union Army in the Civil War* (New York: Henry Schuman, 1952), 76–77.

785. Death notice, *Jackson Weekly Citizen*, October 15, 1862.

786. The Tuttles lost an adopted son, George W., on August 15, 1865.

787. *OR*, vol. XIX, part I, 431. Slocum commanded a division in VI Corps that saw little action. McClellan also telegraphed Halleck at 8:15 p.m. on September 19 to urge, as "an act of justice," that Hooker be promoted in the U.S. Army to replace Mansfield. *OR*, vol. XIX, part I, 182. His own congratulatory message commended the "brilliant conduct of Reno's and Hooker's Corps, under Burnside, at Turner's Gap" and at Antietam the troops under "Hooker, Mansfield, and Sumner"; those of Franklin; and those composing the "vigorous support of Porter and Pleasanton." *OR*, vol. XIX, part I, 182–83. Rarely did McClellan refer to "Williams' corps" on September 14. *OR*, vol. LI, part I, 831, 858, and see 855 for the Marcy communiqué using "Williams' [Banks's] corps." Hooker would replace Porter when Lincoln relieved McClellan of command. *OR*, vol. XIX, part II, 545.

788. *OR*, vol. XIX, part I, 24 ff. McClellan's account of how Mansfield was succeeded appears to rely on the law of gravity: he wrote that "the

command of the Twelfth Corps fell upon General Williams." Williams received a total of three mentions in McClellan's three official reports (initial, September 29 and October 15; voluminous final, August 5, 1863).

789. *New York Times* Opinionator, "The Lieber Codes," http://opinionator.blogs.nytimes.com/2013/04/24/the-lieber-codes/?_r=0.

790. *OR*, vol. XIX, part I, 550.

791. Robertson, *Michigan in the War*, 974; Warner, *Generals in Blue*, 12; Edwin P. Augur, comp., "Family History and Genealogy of the Descendants of Robert Augur," New Haven Colony, Middletown, Connecticut, 1904.

792. *OR*, vol. XIX, part I, 794–800.

793. *Governor's Message to the Legislature of the State of Michigan, in Session, January 7, 1863* (Lansing, MI: John A. Kerr & Company, 1863), 30.

794. Ibid., 16, 20.

Chapter 11

795. Charles W. Snell and Sharon A. Brown, *Antietam National Battlefield and National Cemetery, Sharpsburg, Maryland: An Administrative History* (Washington, D.C.: National Park Service, 1986), 1–5. Major influence on this chapter derives from Susan W. Trail, "Remembering Antietam: Commemoration and Preservation of a Civil War Battlefield," PhD diss. (College Park: University of Maryland, 2005).

796. Snell and Brown, *Antietam National Battlefield*, 12.

797. Ibid., 8–9; *History of Antietam National Cemetery* (Baltimore, MD: John W. Woods, 1869), 9–16. Proportions were based on Congressional representation.

798. John R. Neff, *Honoring the Civil War Dead: Commemoration and the Problem of Reconciliation* (Lawrence: University Press of Kansas, 2005), 116–17.

799. Neff, *Honoring the Civil War Dead*, 122.

800. Bagley was member of the Detroit Board of Police Commissioners from 1865 to 1872 and chairman of the Republican State Committee from 1868 to 1870. He won election as Michigan's sixteenth governor in 1872 and reelection in 1874.

801. William W. Williams, ed., *Magazine of Western History* 4 (May 1886–October 1886): 520.

802. George H. Hopkins, *Memorial Address on the Life and Character of John Judson Bagley* (Detroit: Wm. Graham, 1882), 21.

803. Ibid.

804. *New York Times*, June 13, 1867. In the session of 1867, the state appropriated its "proportion," $3,334.88; Lanman, *Red Book of Michigan*, 221.

805. Neff, *Honoring the Civil War Dead*, 117–20. J. Thomas Scharf, *History of Western Maryland: Being a History of Frederick, Montgomery, Carroll, Washington, Allegany, and Garrett Counties from the Earliest Period to the Present Day*, vol. I (Philadelphia, PA: L.H. Everts, 1882), 1,215.

806. Snell and Brown, *Antietam National Battlefield*, 14–15, 26. The U.S. government sought consent from each of the states to transfer their interest in title to the property. Michigan gave its consent by March 3, 1879. Id., 31.

807. Trail, *Remembering Antietam*, 421, 423.

808. Snell and Brown, *Antietam National Battlefield*, 539–40.

809. Lanman, *Red Book of Michigan*, 221. In 1887, Michigan appropriated funds for Gettysburg monuments, dedicated in 1889, then Chickamauga/Chattanooga in 1895, Andersonville in 1903–4, Vicksburg in 1903–16 and Shiloh in 1917–19. May, "*Let Their Memories Be Cherished*," 6–8. Michigan was the first state to declare May 30 as "Decoration Day," an official holiday. Patricia Charter, "Memorial Day: How It All Began," in *Michigan History* 99, no. 3 (May/June 2015): 38.

810. Douglas S. Freeman, *Lee's Lieutenants*, vol. II, 716–17.

811. Gallagher, *Lee the Soldier*, 13; Freeman, *Lee's Lieutenants*, 717.

812. Charles Marshall to D.H. Hill, November 11, 1867, Daniel Harvey Hill Papers, Virginia State Archives.

813. Gallagher, *Fighting for the Confederacy*, 141.

814. Longstreet, "Invasion of Maryland," 422, 430.

815. Scott, *Forgotten Valor*, 250.

816. Mason, *Until Antietam*, 190.

817. Ibid., 190, 217.

818. History Net, "Battle of South Mountain: Battlefield and Beyond," www.historynet.com/battle-of-south-mountain.htm, accessed on April 9, 2015; Society of the Army of the Potomac, *Report of the Nineteenth Annual Re-Union at Gettysburg, Pennsylvania, July 1st, 2d and 3d, 1888* (New York: Macgowan & Slipper, 1888), 81.

819. Newspaper item, William Withington Papers, Bentley Historical Library. The city named an athletic stadium for him. Jackson County funded a memorial tablet at Michigan State College in 1927.

820. George R. Large and Joe A. Swisher, *Battle of Antietam: The Official History by the Antietam Battlefield Board* (Shippensburg, PA: Burd Street Press, 1998), viii. Not included was Fox's Gap.

821. Snell and Brown, *Antietam National Battlefield*, 83.

822. Pittman, Story of the "Famous Lost Dispatch," 6. He made the same observation in a letter to Ezra Carman of May 7, 1897: "We were all impressed by the apparent inattention to so valuable information." Pittman Papers, Williams College.

823. Pittman, Story of the "Famous Lost Dispatch," 7.
824. George Lockley Collection, Bentley Historical Library.
825. Trail, *Remembering Antietam*, 370.
826. Harsh, *Taken at the Flood*, 3, 4
827. Bruce Catton, *This Hallowed Ground: The Story of the Union Side of the Civil War* (Garden City, NY: Doubleday & Company, 1956), 145, 161, 169.
828. Trail, *Remembering Antietam*, 395.
829. Jordan, *Unholy Sabbath*, 326.
830. May, "Let Their Memories Be Cherished," 38.
831. Ibid., 44; said to be the first in the nation to honor women's efforts in the war. See Sons of Union Veterans of the Civil War, "Loyal Legion Vignettes," http://www.suvcw.org/mollus/art031.htm, accessed on February 6, 2015.
832. See Appendix B.
833. See note 856 herein, 154, 178–85.
834. Samuel E. Pittman Papers, Burton Historical Library.
835. Edition of May 28, 1909.
836. *Detroit News*, April 1, 1922. An excellent description of the monument and its history is found at www.historicdetroit.org.
837. *Governor's Message to the Legislature*, 28.

Conclusion

838. Catton, *This Hallowed Ground*, 166.
839. *Most Fearful Ordeal*, 191.
840. Herman Hattaway and Archer Jones, *How the North Won: A Military History of the Civil War* (Urbana: University of Illinois Press, 1983), 240.
841. Catton, *This Hallowed Ground*, 115.
842. Rafuse, *McClellan's War*, 2, 387.
843. James M. McPherson, *Crossroads of Freedom: Antietam* (New York: Oxford University Press, 2002), 140.
844. Martin J. Hershock, *The Paradox of Progress: Economic Change, Individual Enterprise, and Political Culture in Michigan, 1837–1878* (Athens: Ohio University Press, 2003), 170–76.
845. Ibid., 171.
846. Ibid., 172.
847. Ibid., 273, n.50.
848. Oakes, *Freedom National*, 440. America annually observes September 17 as Constitution Day, coincident with the anniversary of the bloodiest day in its history.
849. Wert, *Custer*, 133.

850. Sears, *Civil War Papers of George B. McClellan*, 481–82.
851. Wert, *Custer*, 133.
852. Per Special Order 285. Brown, *Record of Service*, 59; "Field and Staff Muster Roll," George H. Laird for July and August 1865, National Archives and Record Administration, Washington, D.C.; see Appomattox Court House National Historic Site, "Black Soldiers on the Appomattox Campaign," http://www.nps.gov/apco/black-soldiers.htm, accessed on May 29, 2015.
853. *Detroit News*, February 1910, regarding the A.S. Williams monument on Belle Isle.

APPENDIX C

854. William A. Frassanito, *Antietam: The Photographic Legacy of America's Bloodiest Day* (New York: Charles Scribner's Sons, 1978), 14–15.
855. *New York Times*, "Brady's Photographs: Pictures of the Dead at Antietam," October 20, 1862.
856. Frassanito, *Antietam*, 178–85; speech authored by William A. Frassanito and delivered (via proxy by then Monroe Museum director Matthew C. Switlik) on May 16, 1992, during the dedication ceremony of Lieutenant Clark's military headstone in Woodland Cemetery, Monroe, Michigan.
857. Jason King Jr., *Notes on Civil War Veterans of Monroe County* (Monroe, MI: Monroe County Historical Commission, 1979), 41; Brown, *Record of Service*, vol. VII, 24; Wing, *History of Monroe County Michigan*, 147; "Field and Staff Muster Roll," John A. Clark for July and August 1862, National Archives and Record Administration, Washington, D.C.; *Monroe Commercial*, September 25, 1862; *Monroe Monitor*, October 1, 1862.
858. Johnson, "Caught in the Cross-fire," 36–38; Frassanito, *Antietam*, 185; Marion W. Childs, "Recollections of Life in Monroe County," unpublished collection of oral interviews of Monroe's eldest citizens by Marion W. Childs, 1956–62, Monroe County Historical Museum, 398.
859. Brown, *Record of Service*, vol. XXXV, 105.
860. Shirley A. Leckie, *Elizabeth Bacon Custer and the Making of a Myth* (Norman: University of Oklahoma Press, 1993), 278–79. See "Frederick Augustus Nims," Find-a-Grave, http://www.findagrave.com/cgi-bin/fg.cgi?page=gr&GRid=92702480.
861. Wing, *History of Monroe County Michigan*, 195–96; 1859 Wall Map, MCHM; 1876 Beers Atlas, MCHM; Shirley Keehn and Frieda Kellie, "Woodland Cemetery Index," unpublished index in Monroe County Historical Museum, 1979, 88; United States Federal Census 1860, Third Ward, Dwelling 708, Family 708, Roll #554, Monroe, Michigan; Wing,

History of Monroe County Michigan, 259; *Monroe City Directory 1874*, Monroe, Michigan, 5.

862. "Presbyterian Church Elders Monroe, Michigan" (photograph), circa 1865, MCHM; *Monroe Commercial*, August 19 and September 5, 1879; *Register of Deeds*, Monroe, Michigan, 1872, Liber 78, 441–42, and 1882, Book #104, 207–8; *Monroe Democrat*, April 9, 1909; *Assessment Role*, Fourth Ward, City of Monroe, 1904–8, Monroe, Michigan.

863. King, *Notes on Civil War Veterans*, 38; Brown, *Record of Service*, vol. VII, 5.

864. Wing, *History of Monroe County Michigan*, 146–47; Robert B. Ross, *History of the Knaggs Family of Ohio and Michigan* (Detroit: Clarence M. Burton, 1907), 29–30.

865. *Monroe Commercial*, January 3, 1867.

APPENDIX D

866. "Twelve-pounder" refers to the approximate weight of the projectile the artillery piece fired. The vast majority of Civil War ordnance was referred to by the weight of the projectile, especially for the smoothbore guns. The Model 1841 6-Pounder was simply referred to as "6-Pounder." Even the rifled guns, such as the Parrott, were designated ten-, twenty-, one-hundred- or two-hundred-pounder.

867. Cullum, *Biographical Register*, vol. II, 823.

868. See MAP 5.

869. *OR*, vol. XIX, part I, 306, 309–10; Johnson, "Caught in the Cross-fire," 38; Pierro, *Maryland Campaign of September 1862*, 268, 272, 299; Priest, *Antietam*, 120, 127, 150–51, 164; Naisawald, *Grape & Canister*, 160–61.

870. *McClellan's Own Story*, 593.

871. Robertson, *Michigan in the War*, 987.

APPENDIX E

872. *OR*, vol. XIX, part I, 186–88.

873. Ibid., 193–203.

874. Ibid., 204.

Bibliographical Note

A complete bibliography for this work can be found at http://micwc.typepad.com/blog.

Index

K

L

M

N

O

P

R

About the Authors

Photo by Todd McInturle and courtesy the Detroit News.

Jack Dempsey is author of the award-winning *Michigan and the Civil War: A Great and Bloody Sacrifice* and articles on Michigan involvement in the Civil War. His fascination with the Civil War dates to the third grade; his first visit to Antietam came in 1973. He co-authored (with Dave Dempsey) the Michigan Notable Book *Ink Trails: Michigan's Famous and Forgotten Authors* and a forthcoming sequel, and he is author of *Capitol Park: Historic Heart of Detroit.* A Super Lawyer® in the Ann Arbor office of Dickinson Wright PLLC, he has served on the Michigan Historical Commission since 2007; he was elected its president in 2012. Born in Detroit, he lives in Plymouth, Michigan, with his wife of forty-one years, Suzzanne.

http://jackdempseybooks.com

Brian James Egen is an award-winning film director and co-producer, Civil War living history and material culture historian and lifelong student of the Civil War. He is executive producer at The Henry Ford in Dearborn, where for many years he was responsible for the implementation of the "Civil War Remembrance" program on Memorial Day weekend devoted to study and commemoration of the Civil War. He is a coordinator for the Emmy Award-winning CBS program *The Henry Ford Innovation Nation*. He has served on the Michigan Historical Commission since 2011 and is chairman of its Civil War Sesquicentennial Committee. He served as assistant director and historical consultant for *Antietam: A Documentary Film* for the U.S. Department of the Interior on the Battle of Antietam, and his fascination with the Antietam story dates to the early 1980s. Born in Monroe, Michigan, he lives there in a historic home with his wife, Jody, and daughter, Scarlett.